AVIA

Selected other publications by Nathaniel Tarn

Old Savage/Young City (1964)
Where Babylon Ends (1969)
The Beautiful Contradictions (1969)
October (1969)
The Silence (1969)
A Nowhere for Vallejo (1971)
Section: The Artemision (1973)
The Persephones (1974; revised edition, 2008)
Lyrics for the Bride of God (1975)
The House of Leaves (1976)
The Microcosm (1977)
The Ground of Our Great Admiration of Nature (with Janet Rodney, 1977)
The Forest: from Alashka (with Janet Rodney, 1978)
Atitlán/Alashka (Alashka with Janet Rodney) (1979)
Weekends in Mexico (1982)
The Desert Mothers (1984)
At the Western Gates (1985)
Seeing America First (1989)
Home One (1990)
The Army has Announced that Body Bags . . . (1992)
Caja del Río (1993)
Flying the Body (1993)
The Architextures (2000)
Three Letters from the City: the St. Petersburg Poems (2001)
Selected Poems: 1950-2000 (2002)
Recollections of Being (2004)
Ins & Outs of the Forest Rivers (2008)

Translations
The Heights of Macchu Picchu (Pablo Neruda) (1966)
Con Cuba (1969)
Stelae (Segalen) (1969)
Selected Poems (Pablo Neruda) (1970)
The Rabinal Achi, Act 4 (1973)
The Penguin Neruda (1975)

Prose
Views from the Weaving Mountain: Selected Essays (1991)
Scandals in the House of Birds: Shamans & Priests on Lake Atitlán (1998)
The Embattled Lyric; Essays & Conversations in Poetics & Anthropology (2007)

AVIA

Nathaniel Tarn

Shearsman Books
Exeter

Published in the United Kingdom in 2008 by
Shearsman Books Ltd
58 Velwell Road
Exeter EX4 4LD

ISBN 978-1-84861-002-6

Copyright © Nathaniel Tarn, 2008.

The right of Nathaniel Tarn to be identified as the author of this work has been asserted by him in accordance with the Copyrights, Designs and Patents Act of 1988. All rights reserved.

Contents

1. CAL'S DREAM

I	The Purpose	12
II	*A distillation, from St. Exupéry, for France*	17
III	After the Flight, to sleep . . .	19
IV	The Dream Continues; out to Herm	24
V	The Departure	27
VI	Ultima Thule	29
VII	The Voices	31

2. THE PHONY WAR

I	A Voice comes forward, acts as Prologue	34
II	Fighters	38
III	Whatever Pilot's View: the Lady of the Spheres	41
IV	Rules of the Game, or "Bible"	49
V	Time Interlude: Survivor	55

3. BRITAIN

I	Build up to *Adlertag*	58
II	Just before Eagle Day	62
III	Time Interlude: Personal. Geoffrey Page: the Burn	66
IV	The Eagle Day itself	69
V	Göring's Black Thursday	75
VI	Time Interlude: Personal. Brian Lane	80
VII	Thursday still black	81
VIII	August 16	85
IX	A rest, then all Hell loose	91
X	Near Triumph, after which the Switch	95
XI	September 7, London blitzed	103
XII	Time Interlude: Personal. Thomas Gleave in the Golden Cage	109
XIII	September 9	111
XIV	September 15: "Battle of Britain Day"	115

	XV	Time interlude (n.d.): Personal.	
		Roger Hall, the *Heinkel*	122
	XVI	Shelving Invasion	125
	XVII	In the form of Coda	129

4. MALTA

	I	Malta: the View	134
	II	Malta: the Program	140
	III	Time Interlude: the "King of the Mediterranean"	144
	IV	*Intercalation from: Sweet towns I have not known*	148
	V	*Luftwaffe* steps up pace	149
	VI	Time-interlude: Personal. Rod Smith:	
		Too High Too Fast	157
	VII	To make an End of it	160

5. RUSSIA

	I	Upon this Rock; Leningrad, 1941–44	169
	II	*Taran* and such	179
	III	The White Red Rose of Stalingrad, 1941–3	182
	IV	The Kuban: Feb.–Jun., 1943	189
	V	*Zitadelle*: Kursk, Jul. 1943	200
	VI	*Luftwaffe: Ostfront*	209
	VII	South Kursk: Eighth Soviet Fighter Division	213
	VIII	An Interlude: Personal: Vorozheikin, Andrei	216
	IX	Coda	224

6. RETURN TO EUROPE: BOMBERS & FRIENDS — 227

7. PACIFIC: SETTING SUN

	I	Lindbergh, Pacific	242
	II	Wind of the Gods	251

8. SPACE LAIR, GERMANY — 261

9. POSTMORTEM DEBRIEF — 267

10 APPENDICES

    1   Abbreviations   276
    2   Glossary   282
    3   Principal Individuals   289

AFTERWORD   296

To my boyhood and its hopes

"When I'm ready to leave Europe, I can step into the cockpit again and fly on round the world, through Egypt, and India, and China, until I reach the West by flying East. There's no place on earth I can't go."

"As a matter of fact, how *will* I return home? *Why not* fly on around the world?"

. . . .

"Flying on around the world would show again what modern airplanes can accomplish. Besides, it's beneath the dignity of the *Spirit of St. Louis* to return to the United States on board a boat. Rather than that, I'll make the westward flight back over the route I've just followed."

Charles Lindbergh "The 32nd hour."
The Spirit of St. Louis, pp.482–3

"I had hoped to visit Sweden and Germany, to spend several weeks in Europe and then to return to the United States either by crossing the Atlantic Ocean westward or by flying on around the world. But while I was in London, the American Ambassador informed me that President Coolidge had ordered a warship to carry me back home."

Charles Lindbergh:
Autobiography of Values, p.13

1: CAL'S DREAM

With intrusions by Antoine de Saint-Exupéry

I: THE PURPOSE

Set keel to breakers, forth on the godly sea
Y bajamos a la nave, enfilamos quilla a los cachones
Mais quand nous étions descendus—la nef, la mer:

Before it is too late:
    before:
        will fails, as it nearly did,
        day I set out, came here to another side,
        the other side, as I suppose, of all temptation,
        bank of the greatest river,
        river so big it had devoured the sea,
        become entirely the sea—

before it is too early:
    before:
        my life emerges from its sheath,
        its odoriferous existence full of anxious
        color, avid to give itself
        into all essence—and before
        it crowns the cradle of its leaves
        to rise into its splendor as a king—
        then close its face in death, rust, burn away

before I've lost the will:
    fully to know the journey I have done,
this astonishment . . . then going back!
        Because I will not sail now, on that ship
        those idiots sent for me,
        will not have skin cut down, sinews
        dismantled, bones carried me above the sea
        taken apart and boxed: a skull,
        trophy of tribal war,
        caught, shrunk and bundled into memory.

    but will have to fly
               back the way I came,
               the exact way I came,
               retrace each step,
               each thought, each action,
               action quicker than thought
               brought me to this success
               so near disaster I almost married loss
         and gain of all the world in one downing to land.

Before it is too late:
      before the will is paralyzed again,
      before all seems as futile as it did to me
      in that excruciation of my life
      kept me from final sleep below deep water,
      hour after hour fighting the iron sloth,
      no harder fight there is in all the world:
      this stupid human *maquina* required to stay awake
      all through the bleeding dawn, the hardest time,
      to hold the wings above that lethal surface.

Before too late:
           to launch this song of my ambition,
           born long ago, when I knew no desire
           except to be the first in some adventure
           and when it seemed impossible
           to fail as now it seems only too probable
           to do nothing but fail—at this late age
           when I go back over the traces
           to try to take all starts, all finishes
           up into air with me,
           make a last dash for that great sky
           above all weathers men will reach one day,
           lose themselves in
           long after I have breathed . . .

Before too late:
>to catch those ghosts behind my back,
>to hear their words again,
>study their talk this time,
>know what they say in breadth and depth,
>exhaust the tactics they describe, the falls
>of wing out of the sun onto an enemy,
>as well as endless journeys into night
>to link all parts of earth together
>into one kindness

>and above all, perhaps,
>how dream could turn to nightmare,
>so that we lose the very thing we strive to enter,
>destroy the breath we breathe just as we breathe it:
>trees fall; birds fall; fish; beasts; men drown;
>all species faint into the earth and color it no longer—
>because we spread the veil too thin
>over earth's eyes and rend it.

Before all this:
>before the will is paralyzed again,
>before I've sunk into depression
>for an achievement never to be matched,
>this I must do again:
>>to up again,
>>dispose the plane into her attitude,
>steady her attitude into extended flight
>as I would help some woman through her sleep
>back to the light she knew falling asleep,
>arrange her skirts about her—long ago skirts
>she could not quite escape to rise
>(freedom of legs and arms!)
>>into this empyrean—
>then ride her through the sky,
>her final ride
>before dismemberment.

      This I had dreamed,
     that life might after all continue,
     throughout obliteration:
     flaps lowered, throttles idled,
     sticks eased back,
     props feathered to a standstill,
     radios silenced,
     towers calmed, all controls at bay,
     runways naked, all lights blown,
     sky's highways drowned out one by one,
     the moon gone out over the earth,
     the sun preparing to collapse out of the day,
       swords into swords,
         ploughshares into ploughshares,
the last year ironed out,
       stars blind, over night's ocean into which
         I could sink down as into dream—
       (that last, interminable flight
      across world's rim into time's body,)
         be whole at last.

From there, rising with no obstruction
and lift without a ceiling,
   without a crown in sight,
     rising toward the steps,
       the thrones of heaven,
  wings throbbing without cease,
    voices nothing could override,
    life become flight without remainder—

   but then, over the thrones,
     here is this smoke,
thin smoke of people,
     ultimate people in this domain
    I shall fly through to understand,
to change the will to change
   where they fired flesh and bone

                into extinction,
this smoke thinner than cirrus to the eye
          thicker than thunder to the heart
we all shall fly through
                  for generations
        before it is too late to know,
to recognize, to understand.

II. A DISTILLATION, FROM SAINT-EXUPERY, FOR FRANCE

*Grass seems to flow like water in your wake,
then ground to tighten, to run like straps
under your wheels. You pull the fields
toward you, throw them behind, reject them
utterly. The air untouchable, then fluid,
now solid. A transform out of noise made
into matter.*
    *To tell of the real weather of the earth:
white ruin of waves, border of land & ocean;
at sea an opening, foretold because of spying
along the water a prairie-colored lead. The
clouds sit very low but light shines through
like a great smile. The sky an atmospheric sea,
planet at bottom lying on the sand. Earth
naked, dead at height—you drop, she dresses
up. Draw to yourself the distance like a cloth.
Slow earth bringing you towns as surely as a tide.
Towns seated in their plains, midst of their roads,
like stars open to nourish them, full of field-sap.
Then the undressing—from plains, from towns,
from lights. The night comes on, enclosing you,
a temple. Slow death of world as the night falls,
you count stars washed by rain. You count one
star too many: its search for bed & board among
the constellations. You dream. Little by little, the
plane may slope, lean to the left. You then dis-
cover human lights under right wing. But this is
sea, or ice, or desert: human lights? You level
out and smile: yes, village—but of stars. Dream
on. Sometimes a storm: a shadow from the origin
of worlds. You see three stars within a hole, you
climb toward them, knowing you cannot down,
no matter, up you are, biting the stars, hunger
for light so great you climb regardless. Under*

the sea of clouds, they told you once: remember lord eternity. Not enough height for you to shut the maw of mountains.

                    Then, land again, laughing to join again your shadow, pulls a man up as you down to your very own, your height, your scale.

III: AFTER THE FLIGHT:
TO SLEEP, PERCHANCE TO DREAM

How is it possible
I say to myself over and over
that your life might be divided so
                       by a single action
into a solitude so vast on the one hand—
that it is hard to credit such salvation
(no, I am not mistaken, this *saves* me *now*,
this has built up whatever trove of strength
I can shore up against my ruin) . . .
and, then, on the other hand,
into a company so large
it batters at my gate very like an ocean
several times the size of the one I crossed
into this madhouse. How do I hold
such axial solitude against this tide?
And is it the perception of that inner cloister
thrills them the most and draws them to me
much as a saint draws men by modesty?
The more she claims she does not merit worship,
the more they bring her food and treasure
and their knees. Sleep, jeeze, how I need sleep!
Since I missed that night
out on the field, New York, May twenty-sixth,
and nearly died of it at sea—not *all* the sleep
I've had in Paris, Brussels, London slakes my thirst
for sleep. Breakfasts, lunches, dinners,
        the speeches above all
where they expect a rhetoric from me they know
the codes of like the contours of their hearts—
but we Americans can never manage that fine noise
since we are used to things not to ideas:
                      No ideas but in things.

If I could tell them
who fantasize on flight as if it were
imagination: winged men, head up toward the sun,
legs trailing far below—always that upward thrust—
(look at the trophies they have made for us:
birds, horses, women—not a single bolt,
spar, elevator, rudder, wing—not one red cent's
worth of any true *machine* gets us into the air
and down again.) "My Lord," I said once to a colleague
"what are these things but lawnmowers with wings!"
and he "oh sure, but kill in overdrive!"
I never meant it, you know that, being too much,
far, far too much, in love
with the most beautiful *machines*
our engineers like Ryan can provide
to carry Icarus up to the sun.

              Wish I could tell them though
what it is like to hold the two in mind:
                        both the heroic climb,
and lyric lunge toward the sky,
the sovereign liberty in the air's empire,
as well as elegy sometimes, crash back to ground,
hard gaze at all the errors made in flight.
Tell them compassion for the land below,
sacred detachment as you see
all hills made into valleys with the valleys,
all earth a valley, borderless, no war, no conquest—
as it will be still more one day when fiercer thrusts
may let us see the planet in the round and grasp
at last the sum of maps as one blue orb,
        perfected as a bluebird in the morning light,
            angelic to the sun with sister planets,
we may yet visit, finding right there the dead
    we have lost so for such a lasting time
they far outnumber us by untold quantities.

                    Wish I could tell them *also*
not just the vision but the joy as well
of all the scholarship involved:
            yes, not to laugh,
learnthing I mean—from humble
                        lift/thrust/drag/weight,
                                gravity center,
in the machine you use—and on to motors,
fuels, oils, instruments, and on out to the
very curves the earth has in her distances,
   her winds, weathers high/low,
      mists, fogs, clouds, rains,
         and every golden warmth from balm to fire,
down to the touch of these over the distant valleys
   the rifts, lakes, falls,
      you hope to fly some day.
      Not to forget sea-valleys:
how you assess a wind the way it
plays with spume at the discretion of the waves.

                  But usually I thank them all,
harp on the theme of future hopes and fears
(if not the downright future of the industry)
mainly the thought we may all travel soon
            as safe and sound as bugs in rugs
relaxing back in padded seats and comforts
where he or she we feast today as hero
will not be more than wholesome busdriver . . .

Brussels, princes and king; London a prince, a king,
("Tell me dear Captain Lindbergh how do you pee?")
I seem to dream awake as if I flew
at wavetop with a heavy sky hemming me in
close to the waves. I guess it is those meals
with food so rich and varied I could croak
without some discipline. Damned if the other night
they didn't mock me with a jar of water

and pile of sandwiches on the fine ware before me!
A heavy belly is the mother of all dreams
        they used to say in the old airmail days.

What a surprise!
Why, she is standing there, my silver dream, as if
       I'd never left her. Up, up and out,
          before they get me and discipline again
catches my scruff and heaves me onto *Memphis!*
(It would hardly surprise me if our dear President
disliked some of my close intentions as to Europe—
that wire I sent to Rome, e.g., "Thanks for your call,
Long live *Il Duce* and Italian youth." And wished
to ship me back to Washington allegedly because
my country could not wait to honor its great hero:
in fact to keep my nose out of his politics. And
all those dumb *ententes*, treaties and paper scraps!)

      Now, hold it! . . . Paris or not Paris? I could
follow a *Handley Page,* Croydon to Abbeville, Beauvais,
into Le Bourget without a scrap of trouble. It suits me
better, this June third, to leap to Paris, then fly to Cherbourg—
from there without a landing jump to Guernsey, drop the *S.* and
          sail off to an island I was told about
at one of those receptions. Don't remember which.
Rest. Rest is what I need—just for a day or two
       before the next adventure. "Herm" names
         that island? "Herm" is for Hermitage,
they say. Is there no poem, part of which (or
am I . . . dreaming?) goes, if remembered rightly:

"There is an island set in a circling sea
of which it has been said
      (as of the paradise gardens)
'if there be any heaven on this earth
it is here, it is here, it is here!'"

Let me lie there couple of days. No *do!*
no one to talk with: not a single order.
Watching the gulls fly overhead, neck
pillowed on fine sand at the little beach
no day-trips have ever picked out yet.
Perhaps, at some much later settlement,
it would be good to own an island here.
May fly the coast a little before leaving
to see what I can raise out of the ocean.

IV: THE DREAM CONTINUES: OUT TO HERM

                 Asleep. Gotten the *Spirit* and away to Paris—using a passage in any *opposite* direction would seem the ticket! Taxi out slow, full fuel load, four-five-o gallons, zero wind, on good hard ground, and *UP*, thrown at the sky, my javelin, my purpose, to rouse the dead and let them fly along. Now seen entirely spirit, all body left behind, & one more time over the Concorde (where once a *padre*, assisting L.XVI, long ago cried "Look: Louis's saintly spirit climbing to the skies!) but *We* were *out* of sky, also St. Louis' spirit, come right back *into* France. Now it's recorded in the book of records—my *Roland* epic, a single deed never to be forgotten among the few: those single deeds set history on fire and men in joy at some unearthly *done* rather than not done, now to be done again, but modestly,
                                      against the current.

Noon. Mid-time. Clearing through which departure can be made. Up and around old B, direction Eiffel Tower, circle that peak, then, check out epic photo—the get away: plane just by fraction at the bottom of the farthest lower margin in the picture. Some other man above me taking pot shots I guess. Over the big bridge arched on Seine, its four heroic statues, twin exhibition palaces (*Grand* & *Petit*)—below the latter: fine, tree-lined avenues. To the left (not in the photo but not too far from it) the Champs Elysées: It was a Saturday *We*'d left for Brussels: it's Saturday (again) within this fiction. "We" 'll leave (again)—to clear the *Memphis* on a June fourth and clear the sea—my old love/hate—and crown the silver air.

Back out, within the night. No need to fight the darkness now: we go 'gainst sun, together now—as *"We"*
flew in together, not *I* nor *it*—but *WE*, a both uplifted
by achievement. Forgive my style: I guess I speak old-fashioned like *your* Dad might have done. I remember
Paris, mother goddess, queen of cities, rising over earth's
edge—a galaxy of lights, denying darkness on behalf
of us, we whole mankind. Riding along Seine's silver
highway artery draining the dark, to point straight at
the mother's heart. I can remember looking forward
at those lights as if I had transfixed the earth & seen
the heavens shine above its other side. Paris shining,
scarcely perceptible, as if the moon had gone ahead
of this time/space to see herself reflected in that city.
But, post that madding rush, I was no way impatient
to reach the ripeness of it, would have been satisfied
to sit more hours, still on the diamond throne of this
traverse—with no desire to sleep, no ill, eyelids like
swallows on some stream—back there in childhood.
   I had preferred the flight to the arrival:
   to find is death—plucking is witherall.
Now, in full sunlight though, enjoy the green and fertile
France—Burgundy's speech? —and greet those farmers
risen from food to hunt my noise as if they were old
comrades in a war. How green the France of early summer! Now leap the estuary of Seine, Le Havre out right
(maybe old *Memphis* in the sun down there . . .) Let's run
the coast: Deauville, Cabourg, on past Arromanches,
Trévières, cut off the head of Cotentin, zip on between
Helier / Pete Port and out to ocean. Old *Okeanos* ah!
One hour and bits from Paris and forward on to home.
The food better in Paris . . . I agree. Food to shame my
first lunch on board whose wraps I would not throw
out over fields: I would not let the cover of a sandwich
symbolize (you ecologicals to come: please note this
pride) my first embrace of a delightful nation. Home.
   On to Herm.

I think its name was once like Ithaka—
but no Penelope as yet.

V: THE DEPARTURE

The Blackburn Co. at Brough, U.K., has good facilities,
(their *Swift* had been competitive with our *NC4s*),
they gave my ship the fairest overhaul since San Diego.
Decide departure Brough June seventh, eighteen hours.
"Eternal summer daylight of the North" should be of use.

Now should be flying over Kirkwall in the Orkneys
at twenty-one, 06.00 hours after four hundred miles.
Ha! I'm at sea again & won't see land till Hornafjörd
five hundred sixty miles or so from here, three and a
half dead hours away. Something familiar now and
comforting, back over old Atlantic! I love the ocean:
that Channel dash was joyful—yet something short:
no time to match me against a seeming timelessness
of waters. Strange how some men will not dare fly
on any water: afraid to lose direction, even more so
to lose all possibility of landing in case of power out,
failure or some emergency. I've known them brave
great peaks where you could not put down to land
a kite in any circumstance—and yet not fly on water
for love or money. Why, further up this flight, you'd
think there'd be (in winter that is true) vast acreage
of ice on which, given some skis, or even with your
wheels, you could touch on quite safely and get off
again. Though what you'd find for eating . . . well, that
is half another question. Exhilaration of these northern
climes: the light so beautiful and various, expanse of
unknown territory; the sense that you can still explore
this shifting mass though all the rest of earth seems to
have shrunk. How I would like to come up here by ship:
at night on the deserted bridge under fierce stars pin-
ning you down to deck it seems—but the ship gliding
through the night, with distant lights perhaps, dancing
on water, or simply you, the stars and the immense dark

creatures of the deep traversing silently under your keel.
As now I pass over the ships, they moving slow below
my silver keel. The other thing I love about the North
is that you see so well the shape of the geography. You
can follow a coast in minute detail on the map and all
things correspond immediately: there's not too *much*
topography to overthrow the eye and topple it. Same
way I love the deserts for ease of circumscription: I've
since regretted that nocturnal flight, bringing the *Spirit*
over to N.Y.C., from San Diego, missing those deserts
    of our own Southwest.
    I shall go back someday. Be sure of that.

Next "stop" Reykjavik. Why, for ten pins, I'd down &
rest some here. I've read the scapes of Iceland are rich
and hot, with towering geysers, seething lava fields and
wildness fit to wander round in many days with no com-
    panions but the eagle and the fox.
      I'd like to see just once the vast plain Thingvellir
where the old parliament was born between volcanic
    folds. No trace of it they say: one solitary flag,
                        red/blue, remembers over it.

VI: ULTIMA THULE

Out there! Nothing but ice! Thule perhaps,
Ultima Thule! I remember reading, when was
it? long ago, in adolescence maybe, or was it
college, about man's own beginnings at the Pole.
Before the sun was born: a paradise up there,
temperate climate, ringed with ice walls—so
that you could not enter, or get out, but stay,
& first men stayed—& lived for aeons. They
claimed their land was on the Pole and, under-

neath, right underneath, the planet's crust let out—
you could fall straight into the lining of the earth,
where man first had his life. Out of which lining,
time come around, he flew into the sky for the
first trial—but *sans* machines for in those days,
you could not tell apart human from angels:
indeed, primeval man perhaps was angel. After
that age of ice, warmed by those fanning wings,
the sun is born, a tilt occurs and the symmetric
limits of the globe become perverted. Stars in
disorder, north abandoned, men move toward
the girdle of the earth to warm them at her belly.
Equator! Then arrogance, which first men had,
falling outside of wisdom, picked up again at
the sun's feet where they had left it rising, re-
booted and we bore a master race, us northmen,
blonde hair, blue eyes, radical bodies. All is
perverted now for power' sake and empire on

the broods of lesser men. Although, before that,
inside the paradise of ice, between the equinoxes,
"love" and "knowledge:" witness the roiling sols-
tices, the godly means to build a cross (call it the
bridge)—and the bridge "beauty", moving, now,

around the axis of the pole, its limbs ready to grow
both hands and feet—as if the cross were running
with the wind. This wind alone would take you to
the ends of all the earths you could imagine, give
you dominion over them, no matter night and mist
had downed over us all, we worshipped beauty, re-
mained attractive. Beauty, drawing us onward with
green eyes reflecting a green robe and a green veil
and the green heart of youth—where all is possible.
As we move forward, *Spirit* and I, a weathered pair
by now, grow old together, we see the great lights
of the north, born of the radiation of the arctic star,
swirl all around us like the old ice walls girding the

birthplace. And it is true. Had you been there, you
would have seen, below the *Spirit,* far to the north,
some green lights shining, as if inside the ice, as if
recalling a far more fertile season, as if the ice it-
self had turned to emerald. All this, if not for sci-
             ence, I would most willingly believe.

VII: THE VOICES

The silence. The sail up/down and through
the cloud pillars—down to the waves again,
up to a longed for sunburst high on cloud.
Vast funnels belting in my life, now vertical,
now horizontal between cloud layers. They
point me West, toward the Western wall,
our country figures in the scheme of things
(the land where earth sticks to men's feet
the ancients say; where men color of blood
guard like fierce mastiffs the wall of death).
I move now from this early present into far,
far longer futures: price of success in youth.
There'll be celebrity to cope with: an early
martyrdom to idiocy will veil over our day
till they'll have magazines for fame alone.
It's good I've had the shot of timelessness
I knew along the Paris route, when ghostly
voices started inhabiting this cockpit, and
wisdom widened like a gigantic sphere to
trap and deconstruct all contradictions. All
life inter-related, all death so linked to life
no way a chink of thought could interfere.
"Where self is not, there is no room for other."
Quiet. And now return. And now, my Lord!
the voices come again between my sleep/my
waking! Facets of being far richer than they
were; mirrors of being entertain each other
with infinite reflections of philosophy. Now
no surprise, no suddenness, no shock. They
glide in/out the fuselage, weightless, as if no
wall stood firmly between my seat and space.
I do not need to turn toward them : it is as if
my skull were one great eye seeing all things
without the burden of dimensions. Now we
have many, now a few—and all depending on

the nature of the story they seem so eager to
disclose. One will press forward, lean on my
shoulder to speak over the engine racket and
then retreat into the crowd behind me. Some-
times the voices near, sometimes so far they

      seem to sound out of "another world"—
as if there were such things within this unity.
Telling their story, they interrupt themselves
to counsel on my flight, advise, help, reassure
and with import of information not to be had
through fleshing. The mind loses its dualisms
from pain & pity. Despite the unity, I wonder,
nothing I touch seems to have weight or mass,
my flesh itself seems to evaporate. Attachment
to my life, the flight, grows ever weaker. Is this
the bridge to death I dream on—before I crash
into our Western wall? Have I gone now so far
there will be no return to solo manhood? O.K.

      Death is no longer wall, not barrier nor
end—but seems the birth of freedom. They say
that, dying over, the loved ones stand around
that final door with light to fly you in. So is it
with the voices. I trust they are not strangers.
They're more like long lost family, united after
lifetimes—even perhaps like friends from other

      incarnations. Who are they then? When
did they board this plane? As stowaways? How
long have they been with me into sunrise? What
is their link to me—and if they care so much why
did they not speak out before? Ah there I go again
with separation! The flight continues.I run the kite
over Atlantic—but I am living now in years much

further forward . . . I'll have a part in them for sure.
Among the louder voices, a single one much smaller
says it is out of some New Mexico. "Recall the march,
the Death March of Bataan, *Señor* Cal Lindbergh, re-
      member and repent."

2: THE PHONY WAR

With intrusions by Homer

I: A VOICE COMES FORWARD, ACTS AS PROLOGUE.
FIRST MOVE: AN ENTRY

It is as if
you were about to play
a game of chess
with boxes at your side
so full of pieces
you'd justly sense them as innumerable—
or, even if in number limited,
"to all intents" as countless.
The use of thirty-two alone,
however, would allow you to enact the game,
being the legal status of such matches—
the book of rules forbidding override
of battle's deepest structure—
sixty-four spaces outside the clouds
or perhaps three times that,
in three-dimensional
playing in air as you might wish to do.
The pieces by the hundreds, jumbled together,
if you are fixing to dream the whole scenario,
king, towers, knights, bishops and pawns,
(the queen here as the goal of the imagination)
in their equality of pieces, wood, metal,
ivory, as nothing more
than fodder to the game.
Yet each one piece,
at some break unforeseen,
some unforgotten moment (to be retold
time and again by future aces)
seeming to have total control of any circumstance
it enters into. And any piece, the point is,
as valuable as any other—whether it stays
the game through to the end

or slips in the first round
and breaks its face
before it's had a nickel's worth of chance
at demonstrating tactics.
A piece or more, boxed here or there,
may have been marked by players
as specially fortunate—to such a point
a book might have been written
about such pieces, their efforts recognized,
their valor chronicled in fullest detail.
Sure they will rise again in history
and strings of histories along the road
destined to copy a first history—
that way their fame will become myth
throughout the lands
of friends and enemies alike. But,
by common consent, they'll not be worth
more than the humblest silent piece.
All they may do
is stand in line for story
and for the other pieces
that don't get named.
Each piece, now rest assured,
will suffer equal fear before engagement,
and equal cold in the high air
of boards undreamed of in the early days
of the game's history.
They'll burn with equal speed,
should the board flame
and the whole shoot go down;
will die with similar delays or
selfsame expedition. The players at their war,
thinking of the whole game, never of pieces,
quickly determine first positions
and, based on this, you can already read
in many cases the fate of each named piece.
So, far from the first throw,

it's all a crap-shoot. Piece
triumphing today will die tomorrow;
piece dies today
who need no longer suffer
the constant shuffling of sorties—
but they all die or live by inches
so sharp here is the razor of their flights.
Stand here then for each piece,
behind each piece, the legions of unnamed
but brave combatants
and even those who fell
out of the game
for some defect of craftsmanship
in their apparent substance
figure as record also in this hoard of words.
For man, as the man said,
is born to trouble
as sparks fly upward—
life has no other duty than to kill us off and
suffering, the dream of queens among the kings,
intrudes upon us all in common measure.
We don't see it that way, becoming blind
and weary at the repetitions of the game—
thinking this man has a fate in store
that's better than our own—or this one worse.
Ain't so: all pain is equal in the match,
each piece will suffer in its very being
as much as the next piece. The quality
of suffering is all, the quantity
is nothing.

[Now, should you care to,
learn these games from me,
my fellow players, kind *lecteurs*,
who spend so many days in your own minds
rehearsing games without the use of pieces—
cry as you may for fact, you lose

the very signature of fact's
                    abyss of suffering

and thereby lose the *very name of action.*]

II: FIGHTERS

Fighters. Not long before the war, it's still not clear to pilots that biplane time is over. Biplane is top maneuverer. The industry, however, knows it's dead. Sorley, Ralph, trouble-shooter, decides the need for eight machine guns with unrestricted rate of fire required to enter fatal two + seconds burst, demands their being placed in strong and rigid wings outboard of the propeller arc. *Hurricane*, Hawker, conceived by Camm,

Sydney—out of his major line of biplanes. Switches from Rolls Royce Goshawk to a fine Merlin engine prototype in early '34. First *Hurri* up 11.6.35, fast, easeful flyer, agile in air. Largest of three protagonists (the British *H*, *Spitfire*, & German *Bf109*). *Hurri* sits pilot high: designer views! And solid as a gun-platform, cheeringly steady. Wide undercarriage for stability, excels in T.Os, landings on the roughest airfields.

Main contra: lack of a self-sealing fuel-tank in fuselage can flame the pilot live. Slower between 10/30 m.p.h. than *109*, (depends on height). Best up at 15 angels where Nazi bombers mainly to be found. Around this altitude, *Hurri* has turning radius advantage over *109*. (Turn-radii: *H*: some 650; *S*: 700; *Bf*: 850. Rest of the specs. Speed: *H*: 324 mph; *S*: 353; *Bf*: 348. Height: 31,000; 34,700; 34,450,

depending on a host of variable factors
and conditions. 111 Squadron, Northolt,
first to receive the *Hurri*, November '37.
Equips 2/3rds Fighter Command at time
of B. of B. and its real victor—despite the
overwhelming beauty, glamour, flash, of
one princess, that gorgeous silver seagull:
Spitfire, Supermarine's. Reginald Joseph
Mitchell progenitor, man of the Schneider
Trophy racing monoplane: for sheer good

looks best of the thoroughbreds. Goes for
high speed: thin wing, thin fuselage (& so
less stable undercarriage, less good views,
also less access to gun installations). M's
masterpiece: the wing, elliptical, featuring
"wash-out": at tighter turns, the wing-root
stalls before the tip affording warning to a
pilot of oncoming menace. Slight speed
advantage at low level, weaker at altitude.
(Mark II bests this—but not before 8.40).

Euryale at dogfights: *Spit* can reach *Bf*'s
tail in 7 and 1/2 turns (roughly two mins.)
within a shooting range of 250 yds. First
flight of prototype, March 5, '36, delights
all viewers: a star is born, a long enduring
star: the *Spit*'s the only Allied fighter in its
many marks to stay on line from day one to
the ending of the War. Now for the *Bf109*
by Willi Messerschmitt. The maiden flight
six months before the *Hurri*: May '35. The

proving ground is Spanish *Legión Cóndor*.
Willi picks smallest build will hold the finest
engine: fuel-injected 601 from Daimler Benz
(allows the plane to "bunt" causing negative

G in dive—while early Merlins will cut out). Cannons over machine guns in the wing are very powerful. The cockpit's claustrophobic, joystick movement is side to side restricted. Canopy's hinged and view even more tricky than the *Spitfire*'s. Excellent panel smoothly

engineered. Leading-edge slats on wings extend at their own will to prevent stalls. Great rate of climb, at steeper angle, shows a clear vantage higher than angels twenty. Fast and agile in combat. Despite poor radius proves well in dogfights. Wizard bouncer. Problem: the Daimler engine's ferocious torque pulls to the right which can, at certain times, make this beast tiring to fly. *Luftwaffe* also learned the need for a long-distance power-fighter to

open bomber paths: hence *Bf110*, *Zerstörer*, twin-engined plane with four mgs., two cannons in the nose, a major bomber-killer. But no match for the single-engine fighters: sluggish getaway, poorly maneuverable—and not enough defensive armaments as surplus to its speed which overtops a *Hurri*'s (though not a *Spitfire*'s). Sizable wings and heavy engines disable it for rolls, a job essential in a fighter. It's great worth was revealed after its failing

in the Battle: the role of fighter-bomber. If all had been employed as *Erp 210* employed them (see below) the Brit Fighter Command would have been much the harder off.

III: WHATEVER PILOT'S VIEW: THE LADY OF THE SPHERES

"And then went down to the ship—
A man of no fortune and with a name to come—
Set keel to breakers, forth on the godly air, and"

    She was the loveliest of man-made things
    hard as it was to see it at that moment
    busied as you became in combat rush
    though, afterward, after the savage battle
    that hardly gave you time to draw one breath
    between what there remained of life and sudden loss,
    she flew like bird in arctic air, pure bird,
    pure air, pure light surrounding bird in air,
    and moved with speed beyond all calculation
    and yet she never seemed to move, there—
    seated in your mind like you'd been seated
    on her heart, between her wings,
    moving and yet not moving, centered for life
    between the wings, those gravid and all-bearing,
                                       mother wings.

                For a moment,
                tasting the passing sweetness of life,
                impermanence of cloud
                and it is gone.

"His first one was a shield, a broad one,
well fashioned everywhere." But she was steel,
made with all ancient craft for your defence
to keep your threatened world from passing to the hands
of one new order on another, mad with desiring
conquest and dominion. For it was not alone
to keep an empire (lost in any case) but to hold back
the gates of a disastrous future from closing

on your past. *"But it was **gold**, all gold—
a wonder of the artist's craft."* No, this was steel
painted in *Gaia's* ancient tints, made of all metals
this wide world offered—the very first machine
that ever had a soul: you could have sworn it,
each one of you—and could not bear to lose her
unless she resurrected quickly into one more frame
you could weld your own body into, becoming part of her.

                    For a moment,
                    the body of this mount
                    winged so that *Pegasus*
                    would never need another feather
                    but ride these wings
                    metallic and elliptical
                    as if he had turned mare,
                    his body fertile
                    to give their birth
                    to hosts of flashing mounts.

And she was fast, the fastest thing afloat
inside the sky for that short day of hers
(because, from that day on, time began moving
faster than you had ever known it move
in days before): you lived your lives in seconds,
drew breath in milliseconds, rhyming with guns
split-breath maneuvers, kicked off a turn,
or climb, or dive, thrown out across the sky—
for you had height to lose and could afford to tumble
some several thousand feet before recovery. Imagine
here the lists of legendary arrows from time's dawn:
list of famed horses, races won and lost;
list of swift clippers running the sapphire seas (in calm)
or wine-dark seas (in storm) from old worlds to far worlds
much older still; list of fierce engines,
cars, trains, with all their records, trophies and awards:
faster she was than any other craft and terrible

"*as an army with banners*" when she ran in packs
Ouranos-thunder in her choir of voices
falling out of the sun or climbing all the stars
             as if she wished to reach beyond this climate.

                    For a moment,
                    sky full of roiling engines
                    snarling at each other,
                    pit full of hawks
                    changed into vultures

                    whose loss of sanity
                    darkens the sky to ash,
                    next moment:
                    sky sudden empty
                    and you alone as you have never been
             and somewhat thankful to be left just so,
         making quite leisurely
                    tracks back to base.

So, go, continue flying her, up from your birth,
up from these Eastern downs—green hills
and forests rain favors in your country,
each rise, each altitude, follow
each river in the world, each burning desert,
over each blinding ocean in all directions
up to this mountain in the setting sun.
Mistress of everlasting motion. Which
is illusion, naturally, because she drank
herself to a fast empty with such little range.
Flew her as boys, with all the lust
of youth, but aged in her
and fly her now as aging men
all of eighteen, twenty or twenty-two,
the urgency gone from desire,
a calm descending on the mind
in re all worldly things—except herself:

your carriage to your rest and all your memories
(they say fly through the mind before it closes)
here on the narrow rib cage in between her wings

where you have hardly room to move a hand
up to some instrument or where stick passes
over your knees and thighs with but a hair to spare
locked as heart-locket between the mother wings.

                For a moment
                stunned by the shock,
                concussion, fear of fire,
                terror of falling reasserted,
                reach up, tear at the canopy
                if possible before you suffocate,
                loosen all reins, up, bank, out,
                dive at the mother wing
                as if you were to lie on her—
                not up for tail to strike you.

Perhaps it was a special breed those days
who flew her: boys who were like dead men
in that, in combat, if only then, they had
abandoned all concern with self, every desire
for earthly things of any shape, kind, value
they would desire on earth between their flights:
but, up there, wanted not, and could not even
think of them, remember them at all
so busy were they at their matins. Those
still afraid in any way, would fall
out of the sky sooner or later
stalked by the billow of their lives,
flower of smoke, earth rushing up at them,
or sea to swallow them and their remembrance.
Some fell on fire, screaming into the ears
of fellows, some mute, merciful shot
or shrapnel having found their bodies

and brought them to their quiet, metal-sheathed,
a second body to their own and quite as fine
a tomb as any dust or water could provide.
But the daredevil leaders—those *sans* concern
except to kill the opposition, bring it down,
at any cost, out of the blue into the smoke: those
were the sky monks—born on either side,
by special favor, out of some childhood freedom,
gaining a kind of immortality among those archives
kept by *aficionados* in after times.
And they were known on either side of combat—
for it is said among the *cognoscenti*
that as planes passed each other, one on one,
in any attitude, any configuration:
they changed their liveries and crests in that
same moment, each ace becoming herald of the other
until the final pass and resolution. Whereat
the victor gained his colors back again—only
the shrunken ghost of his opponent's crest remained
       painted in miniature below his bat cage.

                For a moment,
                thinking how clear the bubble is
                above this seat
                as if your head were bare
                into the sky
                and you like Rilke's insect
                being air-born, breathed in the sky
                as natural to you as mother's womb.
                Thinking you could almost survive
                out of this cockpit—then the draft
                passing through one thin sliver
                left open in the groove between
                the canopy and this your inner body
                frightens, cold as the air is,
                brings back to you how much far up
                you are and out of reach of earth's

                        long fingers, their safe grasp,
                        or any Windermere that far below
                        and all the lakes of childhood
                        with their blue eyes.

"Sun to his slumber, shadow o'er all the ocean,
Came we then to the bound of deepest water"
below home cliffs. How sweet she was
as you sat anchored there between her sides,
those wide, comforting wings, hiding too much
of ground for utter safety—and yet,
in compensation, you were resting there
as if pillowed on air, deepest assurance
you would get back below. Sweet in
directional maneuver up / down,
or side to side, needing but one suggestion,
more sensitive to touch than any other bird
known to you then or now. Hey, even when the air
ceases to move over those wings, deprives
them of their lift, she does not buck
or shiver in the stall, but glides
obedient down the wind back to full power
and roars away again. How still all is up here
while you gather your way across this sky
far faster and more steadfast than a clipper, yet,
for the altitude, no sense, or hardly any sense you have
of any movement, sense of your fervent speed—
unless another crosses you, then relativity
shoots you as arrows past each other. Or, should you dive,
then the uprushing earth gives you your boost again
and you move all this awesome beauty through the air
as if a green-eyed goddess downing from the heights
were to bring message to a stillborn man
of what the speed of the girl's heartbeat is,
when changing from one state,
passing from her domain into another.

>"And on the shield
>the great bowlegged god
>designed a pasture
>in a lovely valley,
>wide, with silvery sheep,
>and huts and sheds and
>sheepfolds there." Back
>over your sweet shires,
>the evening light
>playing over your wings,
>how may you yet come out
>to yearn one day
>
>for the forgotten country
>you gave away in youth,
>and flying still,
>flying forever
>to keep her on your mind,
>singing in memory.

>"So down the ranks the dazzling goddess went
>to stir the attack, and each man in his heart
>grew strong to fight and never quit the melée,
>for at her passage war itself became
>lovelier than return, lovelier than sailing
>in the decked ships back to their native land."

It was a time in which you heard the stories
of how the world was to improve after your day,
after your war, if you could only win it, and you came
out of those narrations hearts electrified
and wills settled for sacrifice. As with all wars,
there's been no betterment. Perhaps the only legacy
you have from days of will—the need
to rise and rise and rise again, time after time,
leaving your dead behind you—is the ability
to last out disappointment. And to hold live

in the mind's eye, haloed, immortal beauty:
as if the bones and muscles of a goddess
had been transformed to steel inside her sky.

IV: RULES OF THE GAME, OR "BIBLE." (THERE ARE AS MANY "BIBLES" AS THERE ARE PILOTS.)

Whatever fighter pilot chatter says, it's an "ace-*squadron* war," not a one-upmanship forum for single *aces*. You live and die in a cohesion with your group. Your only job (whatever seems the case in the pursuit of "fame") is *go for* bombers when attacking, *defend* your bombers when escorting. All else is gravy.

Two things matter for combat: altitude / speed: you trade the first for speed when diving. If speed, no need maneuverability. Maneuverability not for attack: merely a respite-purchaser whose value lasts the time of the maneuver, nor more nor less. Also, you lose some speed in a maneuver. Always select to keep your altitude and thus initiative. Only maneuver when yr. ship is up against a faster one. The gist of it: come in behind an enemy, fire with sight on, stay only one good burst, break,

climb at your best angle—come back in. If you're attacked, make hard steep turn, (rudder plus-plus) and never stick around. Keep speed in dive (do not close throttle), & extra speed to re-climb. Caught unaware? *Always* turn in toward the enemy, always aggress, that fierceness pays. Even if no more ammo, turn in toward, watch for a useful moment, then spiral down (rolling straight down is good) and get flat out. If dived on from above, wait till the enemy is some 5,000 feet off you, then turn in

to attack. When enemy's on tail, always go with the turn as steep as possible: never slacken the turn, *never* reverse it. Don't stay on straight and level for more than thirty seconds at *any* time in the combat arena. Shooting: give yr. attention *totally*: brace body; hold two hands on stick; feet firmly down on rudder pedals and concentrate on sight. But watch when you set up, or execute, or break away from an attack: such are the three most vulnerable times.

In gunnery, you have a set of problems: distance from target; speed of the target; allowance time for fire to reach yr. target (given he's moving); angle your target's moving at related to your own oncoming course; the need to curve continually in follow-through to hold yr. aim and keep the fire pouring into yr. target: the fire-density constantly changing according to yr. and opponent's movements. On this base a "deflection shooting" art—a way you "lead" the guy (and it's a *rare* man gives sufficient lead). Never rely upon a pointing nose (either your own or your opponent's) to tell an enemy's direction: he may be being sidetracked by a crosswind, by combat action or rudder flying. Beware of skidding—not just your own but t'other's skid as well: accurate turns demand the indicator bubble has to stay dead center. Airflow also in up or down can cause a plane to skid. In combat you cannot rely on trim tabs: you won't have time to shift them in the heat of dogdom.

Remember: wing-guns are harmonized, i.e. set so as to deliver fire together at a given range (advise pair inboard at 600; next add on seven-five, & on outboard again). Do well to fire at yr. harmonized range. Remember gun-vibration scatters bullets. Remember to maintain your guns pointing up high (since they are mounted below your line of sight) but do not ease stick back when banking to ratchet up yr. nose since this pulls nose around, not up at all. Closer you are to target ("whites

of his eyes,") tighter diameter of strike & bullet-density within the circle: anything *less* than say nine hundred feet: bullets will lose their penetration shot ("gravity drop") —*anything* more than say four-fifty feet is dangerous to you. Enemy a/c carrying rear defence, do not go closer than three times fifty feet. Beware of too much "G" when body gets so heavy that you may pass out, (some say: use top pair rudder pedals, if two provided, to bring knees up to chest makes you less subject to the fade-away.

Others say nonsense to that & much else). Also of losing sighting if size of yr. plane's nose limits your vision. The "length-ahead" method is not a bad one: judging the length of E/A's fuselage, placing yr. fire ahead of that; number of lengths depending on these factors here defined. For all of this, you get

to learn the workings of a sight—both "ring
and bead" and then reflector sight—yet you
must keep the former: your electric systems
might wash out. Never forget to check your
bulb is functioning and that you carry spares.

Polish the windshield after every mission to
safeguard the reflection. Forever check fit of
your mask and oxygen supply—you'll never
know till doom that you have been deprived.
Just past your take-off, turn on the flow up
to 5,000 feet. Constantly check the oxygen
flow meter/pressure gauge: if reading drops
too fast you may be leaking and you had best
abort. Above a given height, let's say some
17,000, each move should cost more effort;
everything's sluggish, you and your plane,
so watch out for collision. The bird's more

apt to stall: don't move too slow or violent.
Add speed to indicated speed to find true
speed—take careful calculation of yr. height.
Always remain aware of cloud position so
as to stay at such a point, wherever possible,
as to attack out of the sun (c.f. *"Ware Hun
in Sun!"*): the enemy, looking for you, will
then be blinded. Practice as much formation
flying inside cloud as you can ever manage.
Send out a minimum of planes into attack,
keep maximum up-sky as a defence whose
job is *always* to defend the lowest. A boss

searches for quarry, navigates. Fl. leaders
hold positions, also search. Each searches.
Maintain yr. radio silence. Learn to shut up.
If cloud is heavy, do not concern yr.selves
with a top cover: the enemy's best visible

when breaking out of cloud. When on an
escort job, determine your own stations by
the bombers'. Do not be drawn away from
bombers: there's always more E /A around
than you'll find visible. Circle above those
bombers when they're at the target. They
fly much faster when unloaded and there's

more than a double chance they'll have to
face a great deal more of flack on homing.
Attacking bombers is probably best done
in flights of three to max distraction for the
defending gunners. Beam and quarter kites
do the distracting, while kite astern handles
the business. Against a flank, the kites fly
echeloned almost abreast, the C.O. closest
to the enemy. Opens. His no.2 & then his
no.3—with each next plane positioning it-
self upon the one in front. Attacks to be as
simultaneous as may be, firing together, out

together down and to the side of boss. Rush
first some eighteen hundred feet ahead of bb.—
turn in behind and come in from a flank. C.O.
disposes squadron so that he travels longest
from outside of his ship to outside of the E/A.
This will ensure he won't have stragglers. The
turn is done coming almost in line astern from
up in front of bb., switching into flat echelon
as turn completes and run on target starts. C.O.
instructs his group to attack and "go!," the rest
stay high on guard. So much for aerial combat.
Now, basic rules for strafing ground. Come in

as low and fast as possible. Hide behind land-
scape as the land provides. If one sure target is
selected, approach at 15,000 and fly five miles

ahead. Be sure to have your group in echelon.
Peel off in turn within some eighteen hundred
feet. Shut throttle back, losing altitude, make
contact with the ground two miles from target.
You're still valuably fast there because you've
dived. Approach. Climb to 400 ft. to check the
options, fire at about 1,200 feet way up to point
-blank range and turn immediately: don't block
the way of the next aircraft. Depart ground level,

get the hell out of there and always never fail to
$$\text{look behind you.}$$

V. TIME INTERLUDE: SURVIVOR

Out of the battle, white section two, alone,
gas low, making for base along the quiet
air, a summer's evening pooling toward rest,
and radiant light over deep-breasted England.
The canopy, open a little, letting in the air
on which you could imagine hay and grasses,
perfumes of hedgerows, a stream perhaps
where fishermen had gone for fish, not birds,
alone in peaceful sky which but a breath ago
had roiled with powerful machines swooping
at each other—suddenly sighted, single Spitfire
ahead a little lower. Perhaps White section One,
friend, leader. Thin trail of glycol streaming
from underneath: radiator hit. No radio talk,
no answer to a call. No recognition possible
from behind. Come up alongside, some two
wingspans away. No, not White One: a perfect
stranger, not even of the squadron. Close in.
Perhaps pilot still in there, the hit
unknown to him; perhaps he had baled out,
his plane left to herself. Coming up closer yet
and all is clear. Serenely sailing on as if
a master guiding her: a dive so shallow
seeming no dive at all, mere loss of height
toward a homecoming and rest. Like a green ghost
over green field, brown ghost over brown field,
combined, demurely gliding. And there's no mystery.
Boy's head lying against the hood in deeper
rest is motionless. Some rust under the head.
The wind, prying its way under the hood
a little opened, as if a baling out attempted,
had spread the blood right back along the cage
in which the boy lay haunted. One could imagine
in the last thought, not the whole life, things
moved too fast, but the last moment of the scrap

when, in some triumph, he was lunging down,
target in sights, all unaware of death behind,
coming to break a darkness on his eyes, him
carrying his kill into his own, the two deaths
intermingling. The plane sailed on in gathered
grey of twilight settling. Now and again some
small turb in the air: the pilot's head lolled
forward, then fell back to where it had been
resting. In trees below, birds congregated
whose noise could not be heard in this abyss.
But: danger here, flying too close. Some small,
involuntary movement of the boy, inside that cage,
some touch at stick or rudder bar could cause
your utter shipwreck: his fighter swerving
sudden, dead killing live, mid-air collision,
ghostly empowerment, revenge on his own
kind: not the disaster you would wish if you
could chose. Pull out, depart. His shallow dive
increased in angle, the glycol stream in volume,
terrible speed mounting to frighten no one
before the louder hit below, break and cremation.

3: BRITAIN

With versified intrusions by Sir Thomas Malory,
his "Le Morte Darthur"
and by Anonymous,
his/her "Nibelungenlied."

I: BUILD UP TO ADLERTAG

           End of the *Blitzkrieg:*
Germans stampede like famine across France,
swallowing roads and rivers. Bright, unstoppable.
R.A.F. delay action over France is unimpressive
against the German army. Bomber Command's
tiniest forces, are sadly nowhere with humbling
losses. Only the *Hurricanes* elicit action—but
R.A.F. desires to hold them back for the Defence
of Britain. So to the French: You have your own
                                  planes, fight!"

Plenty of reasons, it is said, for Hitler to hold
back and not provoke the Brits into humiliation.
Negotiated peace the true solution. Invasion problematic: the *Kriegsmarine* would not enjoy it.
Kept as an option to see whether the *Luftwaffe*
can crack the R.A.F. Meanwhile, play cool and
hope the Brits will join the Germans against Rus.
The only Dunkirk "miracle," some swear, is that
                the sea remained so calm . . .

One problem hovers: Britain is insular; *Reich*'s
continental: there's much about invasion from
the sea that Germans do not understand. And
there is endless misconstruction of each other's
forces: the Brits will overestimate German air
capability and German air force size . . . while
Germans underestimate the same in their RAF
foes. Also the task of German air force fleets
changes from ground support of Army—which
had lit up the *Blitzkrieg* on the Continent—to
naked one-on-one with yet another air force,
      this one prepared with air defence in mind.

It was the need, mind you, against powerful
tides of inanition, self-interest, isolationism,
both in the U.K. homeland & the far-abroad,
to fly a spotless moral standard in the wind
so as to draw the U.S. in eventually, sooner
rather than late, if at all possible—one man,
Churchill, Winston, had the Romantic *nous*
to pull it off. *Mater*: American, *pater*: a Brit
aristocrat. Churchill required that Battle bad
for a persuasion that Brits were fighting for
the immense wide world, not just themselves,
and holding highest our Western civ. against
the fascist tides would swamp our universe—
all Europe and beyond.

6.18.1940: The B. of B.
may now begin. "Their Finest Hour" and all.
Göring, the WW1 ace and *Reichsmarschall*,
(morphine addicted since surgery, 11.'23)
will offer safeguard to the Brits as long as
Deutschland has free hands in Commieland.
His *Luftwaffe*: much advantage. Experience
in Spanish Civil War with *Legión Cóndor*,
& much organization, especially by Milch,
Erhard, Secy. of State for Air, perpetually
in conflict with Udet, Ernst, Göring's ace.
The blitz in Poland, France etc.: a potent
myth of terror. But many problems: re a/c
production; training of crews; Command/

Control & a dismaying lack of stress upon
radio technology. Enters a war too soon
(re Hitler's plans as well as *n* surprises)—
minus enough reserves, some say absent
decent equipment (though many disagree)
above all: much fought over by jealous
generals, each clawing for terrain. These

primal problems will ever worsen as war grinds on & on—right up till Speer, Albert seizes the reins in '44. Whereas the Brits, reputed for a bumbling amateurism (one self-inflicted, & thus often acknowledged) in fact had, in the RAF, the most prepared of all world forces, especially for fighters.

The RAF reorganized in nineteen-thirty-six into Commands for different tasks (whereas the *Luftwaffe* had major Air Fleets—*Luftflotten*—mixtures of bombers, fighters, ff.-bb.). Fighter Command created *sub* H. Dowding, drawing the whole system together. Brilliant Command/Control—with Groups, Sectors & Satellites (Sectors with Sector Section fields controlling two or three, up to six squadrons), a whole tight web so as to know who / what was where & when. And to economize on sending up of intercepts—thus to preserve a Force. Plotting: "a system for the managing of chaos," something the *Luftwaffe* ignored

the Royal Air Force owned. Radar, a major feat, had by now solved range calculations, bearing, strength of attacking force & height though it remained a gamble between getting the info to the RAF and time it took the Huns to get athwart the Channel, clear off France. Transmit-Reception stations: "Chain Home" set up in '37; "Chain Low (-looking)" in '40. Germans had had some but never took it half as seriously as they might well have done. The *Luftwaffe*, built for quick wars, got slow ones. They should have hit again, three times daily, repeatedly, consistently, the radar towers, & Sector Station fields & factories—with ground attacks (something the pilots feared—& yet *Erp.gruppe* 210 managed: a model the *whole* force should have followed)—and only *lastly* the Fighter force itself. But lack of strategies lies over all: mist from a major want of clear directives: Army and Navy pulling different directions, the *Luftwaffe* has to divine its own. 8.1.1940; Osterkamp, Theo, the Fighter boss, *Luftflotte 2*: "This is utopia!" Not one clear aim for *Adlertag*: each leader has his whim! Each leader picks a different way of a/c use. And since they were the *only* ones with aces, a RAF would naturally agree to be defeated, its pilots quietly stay still to be brought down.

Kanalkampf over late July. The Channel virtually German: convoys are far too vulnerable. 7.21: Göring at Karinhalle changes the guard, promotes his young ones to head the fighters. Osterkamp, T. *Jagdfliegerführer, Luftflotte 2;* Mölders, Werner, steps in his shoes at *JG51*. 7.24: Galland, Adolf takes head of *III / JG26*. These latter rivals said to have *halsweh* bad: a soreness of the throat yearning for the Knight's Cross. Discomfort of the wingmen so often sacrificed to these experts' ambitions. A *"Cóndor Mafia,"* having been clandestine, has never had much use for radio. A.G. especially, is to frustrate all tries to fit air-to-air radio in his aircraft.

II: JUST BEFORE EAGLE DAY

August 12th, 1940, day before *Adlertag*. Cloudless blue skies— much like so many days before and after. *Luftwaffe*'s grown awareness of British radar prompts raids on stations. They're struck by *Erprobungsgruppe 210* with blows at Lympne and Hawkinge while radar's down. Damage is not in depth as was first thought by Germans and most will re-emerge on track some six hours later. The Manston story follows.

Finucane, Paddy, operational only since July 25th, in brand new *Spit*, flying Green Three position for 65 Sqdr., scrambled 11.00 hrs. at Manston. 11.30 over Channel, 26,000 ft., 10 miles out fr. North Foreland, breaks into thirty *109s* 2,000 ft. below. First try is interrupted: evasion violent, substantial loss of height. Climb back gets him an ideal tail down to some 50 yards. Return to Manston 11.45. Almost immediate scramble up again. Hit on the ground at take off. Then, at 12.50 Manston attack: *Erp 210*'s *Zerstörer 110s* &, simultaneously, eighteen *Do17s* of *KG2*. Wind had then veered: squadron in tough downwind take-off position. J. Quill, *Supermarine* test pilot, proves many a point *re* rapid T.Os out of that. Smoke clouds and chalk dust, as first bombs fall, adds throttle wide and fullest boost-up. Veers into wind:

peeps back at hangars up in flames, intense
surprise at being airborne. One after one

Spits float up out of smoke, mixed in with
109s, the *Spits* still slow. Paddy outs cloud
4,000, beyond Margate, sights Quill on his
right wing firing at *109* and chases, in and
out of cloud. Probable first at some 1,000 ft.,
then, swerving off under attack gives him a
chance at one more *109*—two hundred yards
and claimed as damaged. (In fact, P.F. up,
out again at 16 hrs. next day, scores other *Me*
off of Dover, plus one more, that a possible.)
All groups had been in combat more than once.

Deere, Alan, 54 Sqdr., up once (or even twice)
over Hell's Corner, ordered back Hornchurch,
sees Manston from above bombed by first wave.
Great deal of switching airfields between sqdrs.
Manston in use by many. 65 lands Manston not
long after 54 lands Hornchurch. Caught going
up again by that second wave. 54 Sqdr. sent up
again in afternoon. Deere gets a *109*, 17.30 hrs.,
an *Erp.110* fifteen minutes later. Back Manston.
Over the place, gutted and smouldering, a film
of chalk like a spring snow coats planes, huts,

armaments. Yellow flag rows put down to lead
planes landing among craters. Meanwhile the
Germans home after five minutes, convinced
Manston is done for and destroyed—though
field in fact is operational again after 24 hours.
Page, Geoffrey, 56 Sqdr., midday: to Rochford
forward field. Relax. Bell tent with solitary tele-
phone. Sleeping to birdsong. Tea. Wasps in the
jam: bomb them with jam. Deflected hatred of

that phone. Shrill call shattering silence, nerves
off and hand held out. Page sees hand shaking.

"Scramble! 70 plus approaching Manston,
Angels Fifteen!" A later strike. One foot up
stirrup step, second on wing, step set along
the wing, right foot fuselage step, heave into
cockpit. Chute straps on shoulders & Sutton
harness; mask clipped, oxygen on, priming,
switches, thumbs up and starter. The dozen
simultaneous lion roars. B Flt. Commander
out in front, leading the squadron. Page no.
Two. Swelter and sweat. Ten thousand feet.
Kent's northern coastline delineates the way.

E/A above, in midget swarms: some thirty
*Do215*s & forty *109*s. "Echelon Starboard
Go!" The *Dos*, also in echelon, turn north.
Hurris at the same height, can level off &
follow. B Leader rushes for a heading *Do*,
running rear-gunner's gauntlet. Look up:
no fighters coming down. Follow Leader
till he disappears, start firing swiftly at the
front machines. Race to destroy before yr.
own destruction. 17.39 hrs. Ten miles up
and north of Margate.

    And therewithal Sir Kay
ran fast as he might run
to join with one of them
and struck that king a cubit
thru shield and body also:
fell he to earth stark dead.
That saw Gawain and ran
unto another king so hard
he smote him down and thru

*the body with a spear: fell he
then to earth dead. Sir Arthur
then a third ran thru the body
& with a spear, that he fell to
earth dead. Sir Gryffelt ran
to a fourth king and gave him
such a fall his neck broke down.
Then ran sir Kay unto the fifth
smiting him hard upon the helm:
the stroke clove helm and head—*
  hard fell he to earth dead.

III: TIME INTERLUDE: PERSONAL. GEOFFREY PAGE: THE BURN

Three bangs in quick succession: a vacancy
gapes in the starboard wing. Gas tank explo-
des—volcano shatters cockpit. *Phlegethon!*
Bare hands, on throttle and the stick, shrivel
like parchment. Screaming, throw head all the
way back to keep from fire. Right hand reach
for release pin (Sutton harness). Fingers in
blind and bleeding grope. A sudden loss of
metal in between the legs. A sudden tumble
to cool air. (The estimate: six minutes to get
out; seven you're badly burned. Eight: dead).

Sky, sea / sky, sea / sky, sea. "Right hand
to ripcord, go!" Moistening eyes attempt
to fix an arm somewhere out there in space,
meatball extremity. Right elbow bends, hand
comes to ring, bounces away in agony. Fall
slows. Force hand to ripcord. Chute billows:
nothing is burned. Fear noise of guns, four
flashing wings—but friendly. Stench of burnt
meat flesh inducing vomit. No time to vomit.
Coastline of Margate too many miles away.
Look down and laugh. Clothing, blown off:
from both thighs down, includes one boot.
Foot rubbing foot, ease off the other boot.

Shock and the cold bring on shivering fits
to sway the chute. Chute turns around and
coastline disappears. "*Must* see the coastline!
Essential to survival!" Meatballs pull on the
shrouds, chute slowly swivels back toward
salvation's coast.

Water coming up faster. So much *too* fast.
Need to discard the chute but fingers will
not turn the disc. Effort still going on into
the belly-freezing waters. Kick blindly up to
surface, fingers still working at the disk,
flesh flaking off, blood coloring the water.
O.k. Fight free of octopus-the-chute. "Inflate
Mae West!" More aeons of exertion—oh hell!
Mae West shows a big hole: destroyed by fire.

    No longer visible from surface, shore
guessed at from the sun. Swimming toward
it: salt dries all over face, chin strap of helmet
shrinks right across raw chin. Buckle & leather
welded, single mass. Shudder. Joyous thought!
a Brandy flask! Fingers work, inch under vest
into breast pocket. Last button yields, flask
eased from pocket warily, hands dead. Slide it
between the wrists. Teeth to stopper, flask to
lips, pursing to drink. Flask slips and drowns.
"Damn!" Sob with rage. "Damn!" "Steady *on!*"
Fatigue, cold, pain, despair. Time starts to vanish down itself. Darkness? Eyelids descending?
How steer to light, to shore—if sun cannot be
seen? If sun invisible behind a pall of smoke?
Smoke? Smoke!!! What if it's self that is invisible? Yell, thrash and splash.

Last desperation to stay afloat before all
energy & will dissolve. Chugging of little
motorboat manned by two Merchantmen.
Copious questions: "You a Jerry, or one
of ours? . . . A Jerry, mate, or one of ours?"
Rage cocks and fires. "You stupid pair of
fucking bastards *pull* me out!" They pull.
"Minute you swore, mate, we knew you
was an officer." Clothing stripped off

with a large knife & body blanketed. Embarassment & speechlessness at so much pain. The *Hurricane*, P2970, had crashed two miles off Epples Bay. Two years in hospital with Doc. McIndoe, the famous surgeon-father, an early "Guinea Pig." Before a gradual return to action.

IV: THE EAGLE DAY ITSELF

                August Thirteen, 1940: *Adlertag.*
"*Studie Blau*"—the *Luftwaffe* report a month before
disastrously depreciating the RAF—left uncorrected.
Ignoring airfield structure, radar report co-ordination,
main Woolston *Spitfire* plant, Southampton, *und so
weiter.* Incredible misreads of photographs by four
Aufklärungsgruppen. Result: no target scheduled for
the *Adlerangriff* would have impeded Dowding in
                            any way whatever.

            Pre-dawn, 05.00 hrs. Seventy-four *Do17s*
(of *KG 2,* Johannes Fink commanding)—all un-
aware of a postponement to the afternoon, T.O.
from Arras, Epinay, Cambrai, out of France for
Sheppey in Thames Estuary . . . and miss their *Me*
escort. Weather control warrants a change: *Mes*
recalled but news don't get to Fink. R.A.F. (bad
reporting) sends only Malan (74) to them. *Dos*
claim ten *Spits* broken on Eastchurch airfield

(correct to *one*). Fink loses five a/c: of these
one falls to cannons (Roddick Smith)—one of
the very first to fall to cannon. Various other
sorties not prevented: on one a *Bordmechaniker*
told by his pilot to bail out, obeys too promptly:
his pilot gets control, making it back to base. It
was this engineer's first sortie: his first
                        and last and only.

                  Malan, Adolf, "Sailor,"
had led his Tiger Sqdr. (74) into four sorties on
the 11th., broke up an *Me109* at 08.00 hrs., one
at 14.00 hrs. while damaging another in between.
13th.: scrambled Hornchurch 05.55 a.m., Malan

discovers premier *Dornier* onslaught of the day. Five sqdrs.sent up fast to meet the big raid: only the Tigers find it. Tigers jostling to get at *Dos*. Malan leads pass within a 100 yards, pulls round to no.3 of Vic and sends him down on fire, 07.00 hrs., over Thames Estuary. Lead *Dornier* flames, & loses engine. Malan sends final compliments to *Dornier* no.2. Meantime, Piers Kelly blinded by glycol. The watchful Malan closes on Kelly's wing and gets him down, even avoiding brand new craters for him: Manston is excavated more than most!

Adlerangriff finally launched mid-afternoon. Mixed force (three hundred aircraft) intends to paralyze Group 10 in Western England. Some thirty 109s of the west flank mobilize land at Isle of Wight, sweep over Warmwell, make for the sea at Lyme. Sweep fails but quickens RAF fighter state, scrambles Exeter, Tangmere, Warmwell, plus Middle Wallop. Eighty *Ju*88s, mainly by force of numbers, get through despite the *Hurris* (43, 257 sqdrs.). Bombing is heavy. More 88s, ravening for Portland, meet R.A.F. (601, Tangmere) who shoot escort to rout: three 110s destroyed. *Stuka* component gets as far as Lyme, turns north for Middle Wallop, their escort out of fuel and gone for home. Struck by the 609, one *Staffel's* losses of two thirds.

Others lose bearings, jettison bombs at random.

One falls to Dundas, John, brother of Hugh, with one more damaged over Lyme Bay. The next day's catch is one *Do17*, near Salisbury, and half another bomber near Middle Wallop. On 9.15, he shares a *Do* with Eugene Quimby Tobin of U.S. "Eagle Squadron" 71. John will continue flying until 11.28 when, shooting

down ace Helmut Wick (of *JG2*), he will
himself be killed by wingman Rudi Pflanz.

Another flank thrust, 17.00 hrs., on
Rochester. Fails to find target, scatters bombs
all over Kent. With a free chase by *JG26*, C.O.
Handrick (Decathlon champion '36, who'd had
his fighter's schnoz Olympic-ringed for Spain),
forty more *Stukas* plunge on the Detling field
near Maidstone, Kent, at dinner time. *Mucho*
damage: C.O. and sixty-seven killed, twenty-
two planes destroyed and heavy cratering. But
Detling *not* a vital Dowding field.

II / *JG26*, drawing the British
off from the Detling *Stukas* in free chase,
cross coast at two-five thou., *I Gruppe*
under them. Borris, Karl, spotting three
Hurricanes below him. Makes for the left
a/c which banks a little left—and scores at
50 meters. Banks to another *Hurri* side-
slipping under him, and scores again. Fired
at by *Hurricane* below, inverts and leaves.
Home solo to Marquise: entire 6 / *JG26*
and four of his own *5 Staffel* lost in cloud,
run out of fuel, force-land around Verdun.
His kills the only aircraft logged by the
Abbeville Kids on *Adlertag*.

A limited success on both the sides.
Ragged defence in cloud conditions: a sign
of future danger should weather worsen . . .
and Germans use such weather.

Kent, John Alexander:
on this 13th., pushing his Polish Sqdr.
(303) toward ops. standard, Northolt.

Formation practice with two sorties.
On second: interception take off
called down as raiders had turned
back: Brits can be scrambled indivi-
dually but Poles continue practice for
discipline in English. (This drags on
'til the end of August, 8.30.40: F.O.
Paskewicz breaks off on practice to
down a *Dornier*. And 303 makes it
to ops. that very evening).

     Nightlight of *Adlertag*: raid on a
Spit plant (Castle Bromwich); a *Stirling*
factory (Belfast); various raids on towns
and rail. Meantime thirty-six *Whitleys* go
fifteen hundred miles to bomb *Caproni/Fiat*,
"cooling Musso's morale." August 14th +/-
quiet. Noon hrs.: large dogfight over Dover
lasts one hour. Some 200 aircraft in there,
32, 65 & others; *JG26* conspicuous. *II Gr.*:
Ebbighausen: one *Hurricane* (himself killed
On 8.16.); Krug: one *Spitfire* (himself down
& POW, 9.7.); *III Gr.*: Galland: a *Hurricane*
shot from great range going toward a *Stuka*—
the *Hurri*, diving through cloud, ups through
the cloud; G. follows, gets him there & then.
Müller-Dühe: one *Hurri* prob., (dead 8.18.);
Beyer: *Hurri* of 615 (down, POW, 8. 28.);
Burschgens: a 610 *Spit* (down, POW, 9.1.);
Müncheberg: one *Hurri*, 615, (dead 3.43.);
Schöpfel: one plane, probably *Hurri* (suc-
ceeds Galland 8. 21.). Of nine R.A.F. down,
six planes and seven pilots make it back &
into combat soon or late.

*Then put their spears into their rests
and came together with their horses
as fast as they might run, and one
smote t'other in their mid-shields so
both their steeds' backs were broke
and both the knights left very sore
astounded. Ever as soon as might,
they left their horses off and took
their shields before them, drawing
out their swords to come together
eagerly and one gave t'other many
strokes: nor shield nor harness might
hold those strokes. And so within a
while both had many grim wounds,
bled passing grievously. Thus fared
they then two hours or more thrashing
and slashing where they might hit any
bare place. Then at a last they breath-
less were the both—and they stood
hard and leaning on their swords.*

Barclay, George (249).
8.14, the squadron flies to Boscombe Down
out of Church Fenton. This after lunch with
Portsmouth line defences a priority. On 8.15.,
stays up an hour and twenty minutes on first
patrol (offensive), with fifty on the second:
no results. 8.18. one more flight. (Control at
Middle Wallop [sector for Boscombe Down]
works under many drastic strains: no informa-
tion given aircraft between first order ceiling
and return to land. Hence little chance of any
interception.) Number of men have blanks in
records during this period: luck of the draw.
    Bader, Douglas, of 242, among them.

    Manston again (*E.Gr.210*). Nine
more or less small raids on southern coast:
of these, two major penetrations had success.
1) *versus* Middle Wallop; 2) *v.* Southampton,
and on to Colerne, Sealand. First one: Crook,
David / Dundas, John, climbing out of smoke,
destroy one *Heinkel*: D.C.'s ten seconds burst
way down to thirty yards plus J.D.'s latter
coup de grace. Day over. With something
much like prescience, Dowding reformulates,
this very day, north / south, his Battle Order.
    The Germans more and more surprised.

V: GÖRING'S "BLACK THURSDAY"

8.15.40. German "Black Thursday."
Top brass commanders to Göring's *Karinhall*
for biopsy on *Adlertag*. Among a host of
things, Big Man questions the wisdom of attacks
on radar, idem on airfields for a second day.
Question insures 11 Group's infrastructure
survives throughout the Battle. Sky improving
over Northern France as well as England.
Deichmann, Paul, *Oberst,* in Bruno Lörzer's
absence (C.O. *II Fliegerkorps, Luftflotte 2*),
has to decide if massive launch over eight
hundred miles, from Exeter to Scotland, is
on or not. Target: airfields, Fighter Command.
     Not radar this time round.

   South, Tramecourt: some sixteen *Stukas*
of *IV (Stuka) / LG1* (von Brauchitsch) arrive at
Hawkinge 11. 35—plus massive *109* umbrella.
Eleven *Hurris* (501) thrown from that field
11.10. by sheer good luck (C.O. Grice, at Big-
in)! Idem twelve *Spits* of 54 from Manston.
Hurris, lower than *Spits,* attack the *Stukas*:
claim ten (actual two). Escort cascades on the
two squadrons and kills two *Spits,* two *Hurris.*
Hawkinge mainly protected from destruction
though major radar down:
     Rye, Dover and Foreness.

  South, Pas de Calais: twenty-six
Stukas, II / St.G1 (Keil) menacing Lympne,
11. 35. No contest. Same as at Hawkinge:
a use of 50 kilo fragmentation bombs to
shatter planes on the ground. But, as at
Hawkinge, no planes on ground just then.

Snap raid of twelve *Zerstörers*, Manston:
lucky that 54 did not refuel there.

          Deere, Alan, up with 54, meets
combined *Stukas* on crossing English coast
Dover to Dungeness. Given the numbers,
and the escort, only harassment possible.
Galland, Adolf, III / JG26, leads the screen
and kills one of two *Spits*. Escorts the
Stukas out some way, then comes right back
to England. Bounces squadron of *Spitfires*
now forming up again below him, flames one
and hurts another. Brits lost in the swarm of
109s. Deere gets one *Messerschmitt*, backs
down, ammo exhausted, into Manston. Cau-
tious approach: when just about to land, airfield
defensive guns explode. Sneaks out under an *Me*
nose, close to the tree tops, drops back right in
when guns calm down. Rest of that day (Man-
ston is left alone), A.D. is up six times—total
four hrs. air & four rearm/refuels: total six hrs.
twenty out of a total eight. Won't condescend
to mention he gets a *Heinkel* damaged, Dover,
and one destroyed at Maidstone—and yet an-
          other probable, also at Maidstone.

    North. Shocked by south's excep-
tional response, *Luftwaffe* thinks north un-
protected. Did not appreciate Dowding's ro-
tations: exhausted sqdrs. sent north to rest.
Sixty-three *He111s* of *I* and *III* / *KG26* (Fuchs,
Stavanger / Sola, Norway), preceded by a feint
of seaplane *He115s*, with one and twenty *110s*.
Mistakenly, bombers follow the seaplane track,
ruining the feint, raising Brit radar counts.
Seaplanes turn back some forty miles or so

from Scotland. *Heinkels* appear to drive for Edinburgh, but suddenly swerve south.

Twelve *Hurricanes* (79), resting at Acklington, moved from "release" up to "available," 12.15 hrs. Twelve *Spits* (72) to "readiness" at Acklington, 12.20. Six *Hurricanes* from Drem, 12.25, a rushing climb for intercept at 50 miles south-east. Radar now much confused by friendly kites. 72 arrives 12.30 for a five minute rumble at eighteen thousand feet off Isles of Farne to meet their bandits—not the reputed thirty but upward of one hundred. Approach head on (400 mph.), 3,000 ft. advantage. Make for the seaward side, with sun behind, dive onto *110s* and down into the *Heinkels*. Kill two *Zerstörers* (including Restemayer). Several *He111s* discharge, diving for cloud. *Spitfires* sense these as "damaged," claim eleven total (actual: *Heinkel* one, plus *110s*).

Out of the northern Group 13 into Group 12's preserve: their fighter state advanced. *Defiants* sent to cover ships: "Arena" convoy just then out from Hull (13.05). Around this time, some fifty 88s of *KG30*, direct from Aalborg, Denmark (C.O. Loebel), minus escort, cross coast at Flamborough Head, making for fighter strips Church Fenton / Leconsfield. Met by 12 *Spits* of 616, 6 *Hurris* of 73, scrambled from Leconsfield 13.07. E/A follow south-west—then, of a sudden, swing into Driffield bomber station. Ten *Whitleys* smashed with more severely

damaged. Seven *Ju88*s destroyed, three
others crumble on landing back in France.

    Dundas, Hugh (616), bored at Leconsfield:
nothing but convoy duty day to day and envy of
south sector. Too little time up / too much down.
Morning, 08.15 hrs. begins quiet. Stood down
from readiness at noon to thirty minutes standby.
Lunch. Unheard of "scramble!" to all aircraft
while having *lunch*! Urgency everywhere. La‑
conic clerks jump up and down. Pilots leap
into cars, race and run out to *Spit*s, take off
in twos and threes, scream out to sea. South
of the Head: enemy planes approaching coast.
Control repeatedly: "top speed!" Ram throttle
through the gate, no forming up, just race
across the coast and over waves. *Ju*s east of
Bridlington some fifteen miles, loose. Switch
on reflector sight, set range *circa* 250, guns
to "fire." Wheel down in diving turn astern
of nearest Hun. Rear gunner's tracers. Own
guns switch gunner off. *Ju* turns, height lost,
falls steeply to the sea. Another curling back
seaward. Hot-headed goes for it, instead of new
one coming in. Knocks that down further out.
Back to Leconsfield with total air flying time
twenty-five minutes. Claims one and one half *Ju*s.

The great spear flew across the field,
the hero's heart-blood flowed out loud
and when Lord Siegfried felt the wound
mad with high rage he bounded back,
the spear shaft bristling from his heart.
He hoped to find or bow or sword but
was left nothing save his shield. Snat‑
ching the shield from river bank, he ran

at Hagen. Wounded to death, the hero
struck, with such a might that many gems
flew from the shield as it broke into
shards. Hagen fell pitching at the blow;
the riverside roared loud. Ld. Siegfried's
face had lost its color—he was no longer
fit to stand. His strength had ebbed. Over
his shining countenance now showed he
forth Death's blason. Siegfried fell low
among the flowers and you could see his
blood wash over them. These fiery flowers
allwheres were drenched with blood. Ld.
Siegfried now was at his grips with death,
yet not for long—Death's sword was far
too sharp. For now Ld. Siegfried, brave
and joyful, could breathe easy no more.

    A total loss for *Flotte 5* of near one fifth
    with aircrew 80 plus, or killed or missing.
    Northern attacks no longer so attractive.
    As a result, some of the *Flotte* moved to
    Flotten 2 and *3*—but Dowding not
    clued-in. It is supposed he could have
    switched some squadrons north to south
                  had he been well informed . . .

VI: INTERLUDE: PERSONAL. BRIAN LANE

Weather hellacious. Towers of thunder cloud,
base varying from five to ten. Travel patrol
from darkness back & forth to light. Lead bunch,
diving away into black crevasse, now disappears.
We chase. Come out at last into cloud circus,
some sixty enemy in there for twelve of ours:
a bit beyond me. Circle around arena walls up to
their altitude. My people follow, break, dive in.
Five more grey dragons spew from cloud funnel
top right and then one more. A *109* tickles my
nose. I follow him, another follows me. My guns
shoot slow, in spasms. Half roll and cataract a-
way until the clock reads at 400. Slowly ease out.
Climb the great wall of darkness out of darkness,
eyes coming back to focus, wall flooding under nose
as we go vertical. Tilt head to watch opposing cloud
pour slowly down like waterfall to splash the nose
as *Spit* flows over on its back at the loop summit.
Then ease stick forward, roll out level.
Such moments precious in the flare of battle
as if the sky were slightly less than neutral
and we not just kill-counters now, but summer
boys still joying in the heights we knew in peace,
ever so slightly lifted, or so we thought
                        above the earthbound legions.

VII: THURSDAY STILL BLACK

South. Afternoon. Very inscrutable, with many feints and doglegs by the Germans. Well over eighty *Do17*s of all three *Gruppen*, *KG3* (St.Trond, Le Culot, Antwerp) with fighter screen of eighty *109*s (Pas de Calais), confuse the picture. During confusion, *Erp.Gr.210,* with sixteen *110*s and nine one-seaters (Rubensdörffer), designs a cool attack on Martlesham, putting the field out for a two day stretch. Three *Hurris* (17), Martlesham, and nine (1), North Weald, will intercept. Of these, one is shot down with rescue, two get killed. The *Erp* suffers no losses. Twelve *Spits* (19) from Fowlmere come in late.

Cox, David, 19 Sqdr.: Group 12 called on too late many a time. Fowlmere to Martlesham is sixty air miles. At 300 mph.: twelve minutes needed to get to Martlesham. *Spitfire Ib* can only reach 300 at 19,000 ft.: this flight could only rise to some 2,000.

South, 15.30 hrs.: the *KG3* planes (Wolfgang von Chamier-Glisczinski) with escort now of hundred thirty plus from *JG51, 53, 54,* near Deal. At the same time, the *109*s of *JG26,* some 60 plus, sweep over Kent on either side of Dover. To these, Grice, Richard (C.O. Biggin Hill) sends out twelve *Hurris* (111); 12 more (151); 12 *Spits* of 64—already airborne. Four squadrons more are scrambled fast and try engagement.

But *109s* too numerous. *Dorniers* suffer two
losses (never filed—so victors must have
died immediately). *Schlageter* field day: Beyer,
Henrici, Krug, Ebersberger, Ebbighausen,
Blume, Müller-Dühe all claim successes
and write up kills.

Gleed, Ian, "Widge," 87 Sqdr.
circa 17.00 hrs. out of Exeter. After much
waiting: at super-readiness—pilots sitting
in cockpits. Lovell-Gregg, "Shuvvel," C.O.
to lead from B Flight for the bombers; Widge,
A Flight, 1,000 ft. above for fighters. Bandits
one twenty plus. Widge climbs behind B Flight.
Control: "Crocodile calling Suncup Leader.
Are you receiving? Over." "Hullo Crocodile,
Suncup Leader here. Receive you loud & clear,
Over." "Hullo Suncup Leader: Patrol Portland.
Over." "O.k. Crocodile. Listen out." Red Two
is grinning. Red Three making rude gestures:
both tucked in fine. At 15,000, two-finger sign:
"Open to search formation" (swing out abt. two
spans and weave). Sun blinding. Bandits just

south of Portland, fifteen & up to twenty-five.
Widge opens glasshouse. Sees bandits. "Suncup Leader! Tally Ho! Bandits just to our
right. Line Astern! Line Astern! Go!" Slams
shut the canopy. "Steady! Work round into
the sun!" Bombers 10,000 ft. below. Starts
dive and shoots a *110* out of the sky. Banks
into turn, greys-out and moderates to forestall
spin. *Hurri* ahead at a *110*, another *110* on tail:
two splashes in the sea. Widge gets another.
Steep turns. Sees three more down: five in a
second. Keeps turning, arm tiring at the stick.
Too crowded. Over banks, stick right to bottom

starboard corner: roars to 400 on the clock. Flashes by *110s* and heads for Portland. *109* cannons back of him. One overshoots. Gets him from 50 yards, oil blacks his screen. Another three behind. More aileron and down. Pull out over the sea and rush the beach. Wreck bits over the water, cliffs smoking. Waving from streets of a small Devon village. "All a/c back & land." Roars home. Shuvvel & Comely dead.

South: *JG26* free chases, round 18.20, cover a bunch of *Dorniers* penetrating Kent. Fifteen double (*110s*) and single-seaters (*109s*), acting as fighter-bombers, come in at Dungeness for Kenley Sector Station. *Erp.Gr.210* again! The *Dos* would have been told to go for Biggin. Herr Rubensdörffer misses his escort: fearing for *Dos*, he goes without them. Comes in out of the north on Sevenoaks in diving turn for Kenley. 18.59: Croydon reached, *not* Kenley. Murderous bombing. John Thompson (111) had scrambled nine *Hurris* secs. before: just time to get to line astern and turn around. Nine more from Biggin (32) engage the *109s* while 111 pins down the double-seaters. These, as of one accord, break for cloud. Thompson & three go for the Staff Flight, sending out Rubensdörffer over Rotherfield in raging fire. The Flight nearly wiped out. Meantime, Biggin not hit *but* Malling West, a field at that point insignificant.

The Rubensdörffer lineage killed in command: von Boltenstern (9.4.40); Lutz (9.27.40); Weimann (10.5.40). Von Ahrenhein stays to the Battle's end.

Galland, on yet one more self-
service hunt, supporting *Do*s over West Malling,
returns with wingman Müncheberg to Caffiers.
Deere, chasing one of *Erp*'s one-seaters back
to France, reveals himself by opening fire.
His prey dives for a field buzzing with *109*s
& raises G and M to him. They turn to cut D
off. Turn after turn, fire after fire, D dives—but
holds for the White Cliffs with slip and yaw.
Spit flames and D bales out, landing near
Ashford. Five miserable hours in ambulance
looking for Kenley and ending up at Queen
Victoria, East Grinstead. On another side *Staf-
fel 7* encounter single *Spit* near the French coast.
Low level chase, the *109*s quitting for lack
of fuel. *Spit* lands Wissant: Roberts, Ralph (64)
much confused, had thought he was on England.
Spit taken clear with lots brand new equipment.

Luftwaffe sorties north and south:
two thousand plus. Fighter Command: nine
hundred seven four. The RAF claimed 182
destroyed (corrected to: perhaps some 80).
Luftwaffe found no weakness in the British,
especially up north—and *Flotte 5* was never
sent again *en masse* against the kingdom.
All vital Sector Stations carried on scot
free. The *Luftwaffe* lost near fifty aircraft
on fields irrelevant to the F.C.'s defences.
Thus broke off a black day for the attackers,
should have seemed whiter to the U.K. team
if that defence had been more capable, spite
weariness, of noting white or black.

VIII: AUGUST 16

August 16 of '40. Firstly: three little raids,
10.45: *Do*s (*KG2*) onto West Malling. The
airfield out for four more days. *Do*s go a half
hour later while R.A.F. refuels. At 12.15,
three groups over three hundred total:
eighty-six British planes climb to attack.
1st): twenty-four *Do*s (Weitkus, II / *KG2*) for
Hornchurch. Nine *Spit*s of 54 engage over
the Thames, 12.25. Main raid prevented.
*Spit*s harry escort back to France. Gray,

>Colin, claiming two. 2nd) a hundred fifty cross
near Dover, fanning out north / north-west.
Some thirty *Spit*s (64, 65 & 266), twenty-one
*Hurricane*s (32 & 111) are ordered up. *Hurri*s,
pit-bull head on, break up formations. One
Hurri (Ferris, Henry) smashes a *Do* that way:
two planes fall flaming into Marden. Scattered
Do bombing kills fifteen civilians, wounding
another fifty-one. Seven *Spit*s (266, Wilkinson,
Rod, Sqdr.Ldr.) surprise a *Staffel*, II / *JG26*,
another nine *Me*s join in. Ebbighausen killed.
Roch gets one *Spit* (but killed 9.3). Marz gets
to home and safety. Phillip destroys a *Spit*
(later, still N.C.O., totes one and eighty kills
and the Knight's Cross). Wilkinson dies at
Eastry, near to Deal, in flames from a *109*.
Body of Bowen found near Canterbury. Baz-
ley bales out, severely burned. Greenshields
is killed by Müller-Dühe on the Channel (the
latter killed just two days later.)

3rd): more to the West, one
hundred a/c of *St. G2* and *JG / 2* plus 88s
of *KG54* & some *Zerstörers* of *III / ZG76*.
Eight squadrons raised from Tangmere
and some fields further west. At 13 hrs.
the German force hits Isle of Wight's
east end. Flares fall from the lead plane
and raid splits into four. The largest bunch
of *Stukas* goes for Tangmere. *Hurris* of
1, 43 & 601 fail to reach *Stukas* before
the bombing but meet them on the field,
while *Spits* of 602 fight off the escort.
Stukas successful hitting all the hangars,
stores, water plant, sick bays, officers'
mess and transport section—as well as
seven *Hurris*, several *Spits*—18 men killed,
40 severely wounded. The *Stukas* pay with
seven down and three messed up. During
the bombing, a damaged *Hurri* picks its way
home among craters. Rolls to a stop . . . and
strafed into a roaring fire. The pilot dies of
burns on the next day: race ace Bill Fiske,
(Le Mans in '30; Cresta Olympics '32),
American, "our first to buy it over England."

[Not quite:
James William Elias Davies, born in N.J.
(though parents British) joins R.A.F. in
'37. Achieves first kill of Sqdr. 79 and
all 11 Group, 11.21.39—then further hits
until he dies himself June eighth of 1940.
One Palmer also, Cyril Dampier, Ohio-born,
flew for the R.A.F. (1 Sqdr.) in '39 & '40.
Of the Yank earlies, within the R.A.F., be-
yond the starter "Eagles" Tobin, Mamedoff,
Keough, you should know Davies, J.W.E.,
with Sqdr. 79: has victories from '39, No-

vember until June '40 (k.i.a.). You should know C.R. Davis (601) also from '39, November to September '40 (k.i.a. then); O.J. Peterson, in 1 Royal Canadians excels from roughly Davis's death until he dies himself September 1940. In '41, there's Donahue, A.G. of 91 and Dunn, an "Eagle" (71) and Peterson, C.G.; McColpin, C.W. (both 71): these two go well down into '42, become survivors, forerun the deeds of Blakeslee, Don & t'other Don, Gentile, to '43 & '44. Told altogether, some 244 Americans flew with the "Eagle" Squadrons before becoming part of the USAAF, September '42.]

Five *Stukas* go for Ventnor radar and take it out for seven days. *Spits* (152) intrude but get put off by escort. Section attack at Lee-on-Solent naval station wreaks some damage. An intercept by 213 squadron from Exeter loses one pilot killed. Meanwhile, twelve *88s* and eighteen *110s* go for the Navy airfield at Gosport. Some *Spits* of 234 Sqdr. fail to make contact. Three *Hurricanes* of 249 sight the invading E/A. Had been installed at "readiness" on Boscombe Down at noon and scrambled up to check a Poole / Southampton line soon afterwards. Fl.Lt. James Nicholson, leading Red Section, attacks the *Me110s*. Bounced by some *109s* above / astern. All three *Hurricanes* hit. One breaks and heads for home. One goes a flamer, pilot bales out —but his chute fails him. J.N., on fire, continues his attack and gets his *110*, bales out and then is shot by friendly fire on his way down. Hits ground alive to his amazement: Fighter Command's only V.C. in the whole

war. Critiqued by some as a P.R. endeavor,
by the young Nicholson himself and by some
other fliers who felt no single one should ever
become "chosen." Couple days later, repeat
performance: Connors, Stanley of 111—but
no combat report as Connors died—and so
no Cross. (J. Nicholson missing and down at
       sea off Burma, 1945.)

'Now truly' said King Arthur to sir Gareth,
'you say so well and honorably have done
unto yourself great honor. And all my days
of life know well that I shall love you—and
trust you all the more. For when seen in great
danger, it ever is an honorable knight's to
help and succor another honorable knight.
For ever will an honorable man be loath
to see his like hurt and ashamed. And he
that is all honorless, meddles in cowardice,
never shall show true gentleness nor manner
of true goodness were he to see a good man
in some peril. For then would cowardice
scarcely show mercy. And always will a good
man do unto another as he would be done to
       for himself.'

    Late afternoon: eight *109*s strafe
Manston. Steinhilper, Ulrich, *1 / JG52*,
in a first major action. Ordered transferred,
while airborne, from bomber escort into
ground attack on Manston. *Schwarme*, all
at same height over the Channel, each
Rottenführer flanked by his *Rottenhund*.
Roaring due south, cross in near Margate,
soon topping Manston. Flips flap on top

of joystick, thumb on the nose-gun's button;
forefinger over flap hits the front insert
button to fire the wing-guns. Drops height
to lower shots' downward deflection & burn
a fuel tanker, then hits two *Spitfires* parked
out at dispersal. Banks left and flies from
Manston at hedge level. Just minutes later,

over and out. Then, *inter alia,*
careful premeditated raid by two *Ju88s,*
sighting Brize Norton, approach in haze,
wheels down, hoping to pass for *Blenheims.*
Reaching the field: wheels up and drop
thirty two bombs. Get forty-six a/c,
trainers for the most part, and damage
many others, including *Hurricanes.*

Lane, Brian, at Coltishall
from Fowlmere. On 8.11, new *Spit* X4231,
two cannon, four machine guns, had been
delivered to 19, replacing cannon-only kites
which had proved problematic. August 16th:
so little action, flights toss for taking break.
B Flight goes off into the huts for tea & rest.
A Flight stays "ready." Order for Sqdr. to
home back to Fowlmere: A Flight leaves by
itself. Near coast, five *Heinkels,* then five
more, & more & more—like chorus coming
on the stage. Approx. one fifty: *Hes, 110s,*
plus the top escort. Germans sight R.A.F.,
turn back full throttle. *Spits* catch up faster
when *110s* come back to shield their *He*
bombers. The big ones impossible to get at.
The *110s* attempt to get behind the *Spitfires.*
Lane executes stall turn, dives after one but
misses. A second *Spit* comes in to finish that.
Lane holds another in his sights—one of his

cannons jams (six out of seven *Spits* involved have cannon stoppages). Another circles to him—but breaks away in opposite direction, absorbs Lane's lead. Fight over. Dives to the water and swallowed in white mist. Artificial horizon (L's) left upset by combat. Manoeuvers blind. Then lines up wings to coastal cliffs. Flight record: three destroyed, one probable. Score would have been far greater if cannons had not jammed.

IX: A REST, THEN ALL HELL LOOSE

        8.17 is almost uneventful,
though men continue dying in these intervals.
18th marks one final defeat: that of the *Stuka*.
Two hundred eighty-one on hand two weeks ago.
Since then, fourteen big raids: thirty-nine lost.
On this 18th: seventeen more. The totals mount.
While this is not the end, they are not seen
        again *en masse* during the B. of B.

        18th: a little after noon, the largest stack
of enemy yet on line: a full three hundred.
South sector menaced some. *III / JG26* led out
by Schöpfel, Gerhard (Galland with Göring
at Karinhall), gets choice free chase assignment
25 m. ahead of the three hundred. Near Dover,
sights a sqdr. climbing far below: *Hurris* of 501,
homing to Gravesend, suddenly told to climb to
20,000, patrolling Canterbury. Schöpfel figures
the *Hurris'* spiral will soon give them the sun
and puts his men up in that light, trailing the
RAF alone. Dives to gain speed, pulls up below
the tail-end Charlie, blows him to bits. Repeats
three times, his foe still unaware. Fourth kill,
however, from too close, sprays oil and blocks
his sight. Breaks off: the whole endeavor had
lasted but two minutes—a record feat till then
unheard of [—but heard of later, most remar-
kably, near Bir Hakeim, 6.6.42, when five *P40s*
fell to Marseilles, Hans Joachim, the "Star of
Africa" with a sixth damaged]. British pilots
down: "Hawkeye" Lee, wounded (baled out
free-fall a record six six seconds); Kozlowski,
wounded bad; Bland, killed; McKay, burned
bad. (Later that day: Stoney, killed; two others
                    down unhurt.)

Tuck, on a visit from a post in Wales,
bobs into Northolt for a friendly lunch.
Raid warning sounds. Tuck scrambles solo,
on own initiative, picks up Hornchurch control,
crosses the coast and sees, far to the north,
the biggest dogfight ever. Far below, two 88s
making for home at sea level. Long, shallow dive
brings him ahead of them. Turns in again for a
head-on attack. Left one rears up, centaur-like,
broken, to cartwheel to white water. Half loop,
roll off the top, hard dive, pass over second,
round back head-on. The other's forward gun-
ning more and more precise. And so is Tuck's,
to nose and canopy . . . Bluff on for an eternity.
Stick/rudder. *Spit* rasps on the *Ju*'s right wing,
belly exposed. Shells slam into Tuck's cowling's
throat. *Spit* shudders west, 88 east—neither is
certain of the other's fate. *Spit* somehow nursed
to coast; blows up; hot oil jets to Tuck's face.
Grabs cockpit side, hauls up and pitches out
head first—somewhat unusual, but down too
far now for niceties. Lands "Plovers," aristocrat
estate. Bathed, bedded, driven back to Biggin.
Invited "to drop in for bath any old time."

Circa 17.00 hrs.: Crossley, Michael,
leads 32 into the *Dos*. The *109s* of *III / JG26*
to them. Brothers, Peter, breaking formation,
turns sharply starboard to a *109* as he is over-
taking. The *109* crashes inverted to a field: it's
Müller-Dühe, dead. (Claim too by Wlasnowolski,
Bolesław.) Top of the Elham Valley, Blume also
downed, his plane hitting a pasture at a shallow
angle, arrows back up in ricochet. There is just
time to jump and open chute. Severely injured.
Just after this, Crossley, de Grunne, Pearce down.
Two *Dorniers* down, two crash in Channel, three

force-landing in France. In one of two to land,
pilot killed over Biggin, the kite brought in by
Ilg, a young flight engineer, for which he is K.C.'d.
The *Ju*88s, to enter with the *Do*s, arriving into
Biggin after, cratering the field. Park, furious
at London naked, orders new dispositions re
neighbor Groups at times of systems saturation.

At 15.30, brief Manston strafing raid
by twelve hedge-hopping *109*s. Destroy two
*Spit*s of 266. At 17.00 hrs.: five separate
formations over Kent. One flies the Estuary
and wheels around for Croydon. Worried about
his field, Beamish, Victor, goes up with his a/c
out of North Weald. These *Hurri*s catch E/A
just as the Hornchurch *Spit*s make contact too.
Beamish's *Hurri* damaged, loses two planes,
one pilot killed. Germans miss Croydon
and loose their bombs on Kent and Surrey.
Fifty-nine casualties in Medway towns alone.

Townsend, Peter, 85 Sqdr. circa
17.00 hrs. scrambled from Debden to
Canterbury. T. instructs: "in scraps with
*109*s, no climb/no dive. Just turn: *your*
turns are tighter." Over Thames Estuary:
column mile and half high: *Stukas* at base;
*He*s above; then *Do*s & *Ju*s, then *110*s &,
up at 20,000, *109*s. Close in on bombers:
Stukas & *Heinkels* turn away seaward. T.
gets a *110*. *109*s cataract. One attacks T.
who turns toward it. It falls below, to climb
in wide left turn. T. easily enters its turn and
burns it. Repeat. The second *109* keeps turn-
ing. T. fires and hits, pilot bales out and sags
irrelevant among this gale of wings. Dick Lee
chases a plane home toward France, though
T. orders him back, and he is lost.

             Then, after dark,
some 50 bombers rise again
for widespread tedium and
                botheration raids

X: NEAR TRIUMPH, AFTER WHICH THE SWITCH

          In three out of four days
Göring gives up fifty plus planes per day.
                    The Fat Boy summons
his officers again. They're rabidly accused
                        of not protecting bombers.
Now dive-bombers are unprotectable; others
                  want cover to the limits—
but ff. have to disengage and make it back.
                Add to the mix
the stress of over-water flights and homings
                  with fuel-warning lights.
Kanalkrankheit, Channel fatigue,
                has made appearances.
The *110*s and *88*s still fine! Cut out
                the *Stukas*! Cut out free
chases! Cut out the older *Kommodores*:
                push up new blood—Galland,
Trautloft, Lützow & Schellmann! Only *one*
              officer per crew: we lose
too many! Let *109*s protect the *110*s (fighter
              protecting fighter!) Move any
*109*s that can be spared to help the Channel units.
              Choose your own targets
at your will. London & Liverpool however
                must not be touched. They are
                    allotted to the *Reichsmarschall.*

*Now Rüdiger was giving ample evidence
of what an iron man he was by the great
list of foes he killed—when one of such,
none other than our power-man Gernot (he
noted that) flew into a great rage &, from
that moment, Death stalked to hound Lord*

*Rüdiger. Hailing that Margrave, Gernot
bellowed "You will not let my good men
live, Lord Rüdiger—and this distresses
me far more than I can tell! Your gift I'll
ever merit to your own dismay." Then, mad
for honor, sprang at each other, working
to shield the vital parts—for swords were
keen and nothing could withstand them.
Ld. Rüdiger split G, his adamantine helm,
so that the blood gushed forth—Gernot
paying him back forthwith. Fatally hurt,
G, raising R's blade way up high, struck
clean through shield and helmet-strap:
the fair wife's lord died there. In one &
the same while, Gernot & Rüdiger gave
to each other death and fell in war, each
slaughtered by the other. As men saw this
great ruin they lusted hot for vengeance.
"Death has been busy to swell his reti-
nue and robbed us foul", said one, "now
let us go out in the air so that our weary
bones and armor may cool down."*

      Park, on his side, to his Sector
Controllers: German attack now switched
          from coastal work to
raising us inland over our own defences. Fight
        over land or within gliding
range of coast, *not* over sea. Too many
         pilots lost at sea! Stop
sending fighters over sea to catch a reccy
          plane or small array
of Huns. Let fighter pairs intercept reccy
         singles; if clouds allow;
patrol the vulnerable fields when E/A might
         be nearing them through

cloud. Send as few sqdrs. as you can versus
      mass flights inland, *and
get the bombers*—especially the ones
      under the lowest clouds.
If all 11 Group is up, ask 12 to shield
      Debden, Hornchurch,
North Weald. If masses have already
      crossed the coast, put
kites under the clouds over each Sector
      field & even use a Sector
        Training Flight if necessary.

A quiet day, 8.20.40, Churchill
orates his famous speech about the Few.
      The Few joke it's a
matter of their unpaid mess bills.
      German Intell. now suspects
that British industry's in better shape
      than thought, so they
will make for factories with many feints
      to trip the RAF.
They try a new one: fly planes out to the
      coast, scare the RAF up,
then turn around and come right back
      while Brits refuel.
Life on defence is nerve-wracking. Pilots
      dead beat. Ground
crews slaving all night in total blackout
      on planes and runways.
Plus all domestic worries, the
      constant, nagging worries
        of a hard war thrown in.

Almost unnoticed, 22.00 hrs. on 8.24:
one hundred bombers tracked to London—
      the East End cops it.
not Göring's option. Next day, eighty

                    RAF bombers at Berlin:
boosts U.K. spirits, dismays the Nazis.
                    London is but one hour
from Channel bases, Berlin some four
                    from British ones. This
is the time when cannons fail for *Spits*;
                    when night fighters
achieve almost zero success and the E/A
                    confuse British defences
by split ups overland. Park now demands
                    coherent sighting talk
before the "Tally Ho!": position/course/
                    strength/height of enemy.
This too's the time of "Big Wing" arguments:
                    Leigh Mallory of 12 backs
Bader's sense that squadrons should form up
                    by threes to catch
the bombers—but problem is this taking
                    too much time. Besides, 12's
                    tally is damnably uneven.

Next German tactic is to dispatch
big fighter masses with small bomber groups.
                    British defences cannot
always prefigure this, send up their planes
                    and get embroiled
with German fighters—combat *the exact kind*
                    Dowding feared most.
The *Flotten II, III, V*, with radio beams
                    improved, jack up their
night attacks on British cities behind
                    smart pathfinders.
Without a great success in fighter traps,
                    Germans switch to free
chasing. Tempo increases on August 30th:
                    climax intended by
Luftwaffe to coincide with *Seelöwe*,

                    the great England invasion.
The raids in seeming endless phases bring on
                    a bigger day than 8/15:
1,054 in sorties, twenty-two squadrons up,
                    some four and almost all
two times. Both factories and fields hurt
                    grievously. RAF seems
    to some to be damn near
                            final exhaustion.

September 1. A long hot broil seems
longer far by dint of waiting for invasion.
                Plane reserves low
but the main danger is lack of pilots.
                    Of 46 Sqdr. Commanders,
11 killed or wounded. Among 96 Flights,
                    27 dead, 12 wounded bad;
7 promoted to lead their squadrons.
                This rate of loss below
the rank of Sqdr. Leader strains the RAF
                    systems hardest. South
squadrons too experienced,
                those resting North
have not enough: both suffer casualties.
                    Six squadrons' worth
destroyed in seven days: 1st to 7th
                    September. Milking
from resting squadrons of their better men
                    raises the anguished
protests of those squadrons. Germans, mean-
                while, pioneer bombing
stages (fires and high explosives) which later
                    will be turned on them
                            to end the war.

Fighters fly higher,
                falling on British fighters

far better and more often. Attackers
               have the choice of time, place,
frequency and strength defence don't have.
               Defence has lack of certainty,
fatigue, nervous exhaustion. Göring is not
               aware of this, nor too aware
of his own men's frustrations and their losses.
               RAF has a closer sense
of purpose. When a Brit falls, he mostly
               falls on home; Germans
on enemy or out at sea. German abhorrence
               of the Channel grows
extreme. They kill more planes statistically
               but that is unknown then.
September 7th. Göring takes his own lead,
               gilt like the lily
                      (a uniform pale blue & gold)
in all his obese splendor: imagine the effect
               on battle-weary leaders.
Park gets his own planes to be vectored
               lower in recent days:
the bombers insinuate themselves too far
               while his planes climb
(though fighters do not like to fly too low:
               too easy to be bounced
                      by a high escort.)

Meanwhile, our heroes very like
to disappear in all this action. Among the
               "few," (who really aren't
so few when all accounts are made that can
               be made without a register—
and when the few that mattered on the German
               side are factored in), we
see fly by some men we've followed.
               8.22: H. Dundas, downed by a
109 near Dover. Lives. 8.24: One P.O. Pniak

down 15.17 hrs.; crashes
again at 16.30. Lane, Brian with a six-cannon
Spit claims *110*s times two
close by N. Weald and Mamedoff, an early "Eagle,"
shot down unhurt. Count Manfred
Czernin, later of S.O.E. in Europe, claims
three *Zerstörers* on 8.25.
8.28: Al Deere bales out once more, hit
by a *Spit* this time. His new C.O.
is Donald Finlay, Olympic Silver '36: bales out on
the third raid, same day. Townsend
kills too on 8.29, Hillary, Richard gets one and probable.
Tempo heats up 8/30:
Deere is involved at dawn against
a reccy.; Tom Gleave, finding a "Balbo"
of *109*s, claims five.
8.31: Townsend down with hurt foot
defending Biggin—where Grice blows up the only hangar
left . . . . . . so bombers won't return!
Gleave is shot down and badly burned. Later that day,
Hornchurch hit: Deere and two more
a'taking off, enjoy miraculous survival! (witnessed by
Hillary). RAF's highest losses in one
day of all the Battle. 9/1: 43 Sqdrn.: (2 C.Os., 4 Comdrs.,
14 pilots lost) gets famous Caesar Hull
—dead a week later. Bürchgens (*JG26*)
down, taken prisoner. 9.2.: Hillary
gets a *109* (—shot down 9.3 with appalling burns.) Tony
Woods-Scawen killed (43)—brother of
Patrick (85) dead on the day before—day of a gong an-
nouncement and of the finding of his bro-
ther's body. 9.4: the genial *Erp. 210* loses von Boltenstern.
9/6: Beamish faces some *Stukas* by himself,
claims two. Poles' 303 will lose five *Hurricanes*.

The story of a meteor: Hughes, Paterson,
Australian—Cooma, New South Wales (234).

                A dark blue uniform: thick stripes at
sleeves. Three combats: 8/16, 18 and 26 bring in
                two *109*s from each with brilliant tactics
and firing at close range. September 4th gets him
                no less than three twin-seaters, while 5th &
6th chalk up some three more singles. Sept. 7th:
                Hughes is extinguished because of his great
talent: work at close range. Sqdrn. finds enemies
                at 18.00 hrs. or so. Order had been to
work at angels 10 but sqdrn. led to double that.
                Leader tells H. to go for homing bombers
then falls to a *109*. Hughes closes in to *Dos* (quar-
                ter attack) and shatters one to pieces. At
first seen broken by a piece of *Do*, now possibility
                got by a *109*: Blue Two sees him go down
after the *Dornier* with one third wing destroyed.

XI: SEPTEMBER 7: LONDON BLITZED

September 7th: a turning tide invisibly brings fortune to the RAF's orbit. An early reccy. over Liverpool. First use of *Spits Mk.II* by 266. Then: puzzling six hour lull in favorable skies conjures "invasion!"

    15.54 hrs.: First plot of day for Bentley. Powder Blue Lord watches his hordes set off. 16.16 hrs: hundreds times hundreds nose in to coast 'twixt Deal / North Foreland. Total almost all *KG1, 2, 3, 26* & *76* plus *110s* of *ZG2*, plus *109s* of *I* & *II* / *LG2, JG2 (Richthofen), JG3 (Udet),*
                  JG51, JG52, JG54 (Grünhertz)

and *I / JG77*. Nearly a thousand aircraft, stepped up in one huge bloc, in thousand feet fourteen to twenty-three, a front of twenty miles.16.17 hrs. Park flies eleven squadrons. By 16.23, all *Spits* & *Hurris* at the ready. By 16.30, twenty-one sqdrns. in reach of London up/on T.O. First fighters see a tidal bore break from the mist east of the isle of Sheppey: high by one mile one half, over eight hundred square. Not since the thousand spirit horses with raven wings inserted into Troy was such a coming seen: survivors have been haunted
                    by it through their lives.

The first four squadrons in go for the southern flank. Park, thinking London, unworried for his fields, sends their patrols to meet the Germans. A rain of bombs on London's poverty, and Babylons of smoke, clouds of foul vapor color of tar nearly obliterate the sun. The *110s* break south and circle Croydon to herd their bomber

friends back over Kent out of harm's way.
Nine *Hurris* (111) strike . . . & find themselves
too low. Always too low: a constant plaint to
all controllers! North flank attacked by 41:
           pinned down by *109*s, lose three.

Rabagliatti damages a *Do*. Over London N.E.
the south flank bombers feel 249 but see no
losses—whereas Brits suffer six a/c down.
From Middle Wallop, the *Spits* of 609 rush
in where angels . . . get three *Zerstörers*, two
Dos, a *109*. Nine *Hurricanes* of Tangmere
(43) lose Caesar Hull, & also Dick Reynell.
Stones, Donald, "Dimsie," (79), just before
15.00 hrs., sent up to 24—to hold a sky be-
tween Biggin & Thames. Patrol north/south,
south/north. At 16.00 hrs., *jefe* sends sqdrn.
          down for quick refuel. Before return,

Nazis approach at speed. D. going north and
leader south. Leader dives vertical into a mass
of *Dos*. D. turns to join, spies second lot close
by. Figures a loner must stab frontally to kill
or cripple leading plane and split the bunch or
cause collisions. Go-through and turn brings
him a chubby *110*, a perfect sitter. But racked
from tail to cockpit by a *109*. Spins with hood
jammed. Mercifully . . . the spin resolves itself.
Big gap right side of cage, leg shot up, rudder
and tail plane battered but gets the *Hurri* down.
              Johnstone, "Sandy," (602)

ordered to safeguard Hawkinge, angels 15.
Heat haze to 17. Climb straight up out of
Tangmere and soon catch up their *Hurris*.
Top of that haze: the tidal wave. An Escort
cataracts: sudden harsh shouts of everyone

at once, flames flashing by, anthologies of
aircraft pieces swirl around the sky. Nose
out of haze: the wave surges to London un-
perturbed. Or seeming so. J tries move east,
hoping to hit the flank. Shoots at a brace of
bombers. Fires coming up from Tilbury by
now and other docks. Fuel low.

Three *109*s meander by—J gets in a shot at
one which flips and vanishes. Tailed by two
others down to 1,000: the Huns then quit on
seeing Slough balloons. Johnstone, approa-
ching A4 road from London, figures balloons
unlikely on the road, holds back, downs flaps
and curves along the road, beyond the barrage.
Four lost, two pilots killed. Barclay, Dick
(249), out of North Weald, scrambled as
sqdrn. after lunch to check out Maidstone.
Sees house of godmother & cat at Rochester;
Burnham-on-Crouch with schoolboy

thoughts—and Clacton Pier with childhood's
home (Great Holland) not far off. Meets 15.
Then: "*109*s behind us in the sun!" Looks hard
into the sun, cocking one wing to cover it and
shield himself from glare. Sees nothing. Hard
climb and turn: thirty-five bombers in a tight
formation, a hundred little dots for *109*s. Then
beam attack on bombers with *109*s now coming
down. Two *Do*s lag back leading white smoke.
No other *Hurricane* in sight. Two *109*s go by
under his nose. Perhaps. Another *109* on tail,
cuts out, finds bombers now 7 above,

climbs to their altitude. Formation turns toward
him: head-on attack occurs. Gets a third probable
and turns away, windscreen devilled with oil and

engine dead. Lands with wheels up four miles from field. Four others out of action. Wants to go up for a second scramble—but there is no machine to spare. Has to stay down and lump it. That constant passing—from the rush of battle into the quiet landscape, from the high cage up there into the deck chair on the floor below and now the wait begins over again, no news, no joy,
no further action . . . "out of epic."

16.55 hrs. Bader, angry at being loosed so late, ordered with Duxford Wing over North Weald. Told to fly angels 10, Bader goes to 15. Bombers 5,000 ft. above, and above that, higher than ever, the fighter escort. 17.10: Wing must attack now or draw a blank. Fast battle climb in line astern: his people lose cohesion. Bader, Red One; Cork, Two; and Crowley-Milling, Three, take fire from bombers as they climb while escort dives to them. Bader & Cork skid left at forward beam of nearby bombers, fire 100 yds. to 50. Bader, already hit, tailed by a *109*, loses his undercarriage levers and engine priming pump. Misses the *109* but sights a *110* below and sends it down. Cork gets a *Do* and

a *110*—then, nearly blinded by glass in eyes, goes back. C-M., thwarted for the most part, is hit and must crash-land. Blown from his *Hurri*, Koukal of 310 survives atrocious burns, twenty-eight major grafts. In all, Wing counts up twenty wrecked, five probables, six damaged. Bader lands furious. Told he was sent only when Group 11 had asked for 12. This was the Wing's first action all together. Leading 19, Lane's lowest in the Wing formation by some five thousand feet. Eight *Spits* climb to engage Germans at 15,000. Climbing, Lane spots a *110*, attacks, follows it down past his other *Spits*. Two *Hurris* join the chase: The *110* from *Stab IIb* / *ZG2* loses pilot and gunner both to bailing out. By 17.45, *Luftwaffe*

heads south and east for home. RAF arms, refuels. A girl in town sees a *Do*'s gunner's chute caught up with a barrage balloon. He has to be fished off by complex means: it's a whole story! A second gift from powder-blue Pandora: the greatest flowers of fire ever recorded rated at higher than a thousand pumps. Over three hundred planes with fire bombs devastate London for well over six hours: three o six killed; one three three seven hurt real bad, one four two dead in burbs. Thus was fat Göring's face saved for his bombed Berlin, the fatal fault enacted: let the RAF rest and start to kill civilians. Though in hard fact, civvies had died for quite some time: it was impossible for either side, despite all theory, not to murder civilians. "It was on fire all down the river,

a horrid sight. But I looked down & said 'Thank God for that' (Park). The Germans had performed their switch, some say saving the RAF. T'was wonderful, among the hordes and conflagrations, they were not frozen in astonishment. The people start to figure out the RAF's ordeal: affection grows. All night, 7th to 8th, invasion looms. Dowding and Park begin to see the change. Park compromises on the Big Wing question: sends out sqds. in pairs whenever fit. Now moves: 43 & 111, in tatters, packed off north. Tuck, Wade, Kingcome & Kingaby of 92 from Wales to Biggin—tally first fifteen days: sixteen E/A for nineteen *Spits* lost (five pilots dead/five wounded). Big raid once more on night of 8th: second of fifty-seven nights, one after t'other. Hitler persists in damning

London & Göring goes on thinking Dowding's finished: pure self-deception as the 9th will show. Part due to fact that switch had left the RAF surprised, on top of that bothered by cloud as well—so that Hun losses were not massive. *Luftwaffe* figured the RAF had left about two hundred kites. In actuality, on 9th September, an anniversary let's note, they had plus seven fifty left with pilots thirteen eighty one— about two thirds of whom flew *Spit*s or *Hurricanes*. Dowding had wanted a full establishment, meaning fifteen eight eight—thus, from *his* point of view, he lacked two hundred pilots. Park changes tactic once again to meet high-flyer bombers. Sends *Spit*s out in reconnaissance high up will tell patrols at lower altitudes to start their climbs. Pilots send out false alts. on radios to lure the *109*s down to a more comfor-

table level. Nazi astonishment at this disastrous
                              turn is boundless.

XII: TIME INTERLUDE: PERSONAL, THOMAS GLEAVE IN THE GOLDEN CAGE

Gleave, Thomas Percy, 253, with Brown and
Francis, late a.m., ordered toward the East
after their squadron. Just close to Maidstone,
angels 17, across their front, 500ft. above,
like flying phosphorescent fish skimming the haze,
as far as eye could plumb the sky, a mass of *109*s
bound south / south-east.

                            I think my trio dives
straight into their flank—but Brown had wandered
after a stray only to go astray: shot down near
Maidstone. Lives. Riding the waves of *109s*,
I turn to them and aim for the nearest plane.
At near 20 to starboard of his arrow flight,
a bit above, I fire at yards 175 on a mild
right-hand turn. Tracer runs parallel a while
then curves leftward to him into his cowling
and his cockpit. Pneumatics hiss, odor
of cordite, sense of my nose dipped slightly
at the recoil. Curious tracer magic seems
to go in at right angles. The *109* flies straight
a little, turns gently on his back. Fire again.
In the light, jewels of sharded perspex spiral
        to his wake. Goes on straight down.

Whistle of tracers overhead. Someone chasing
my tail, 200 yds. Jink, dip and turn to right,
pull up—sharp climbing turn to left. No sign
of my companions but lots flying at different
levels, much firing wildly over all of us. Climb
up into the *109*s again: one goes across my nose
from left to right seeming without concern. Short
burst from me, turning with him: black smoke

from his right branch about a yard from wing root.
Goes down under his rising smoke as I pull up
to stop from entering another *109*. Flies past
a few yards out and unaware. Rush him. At
sixty yards or so, turns slightly to my sights.
I turn with him: three seconds burst. He pulls
his nose up, fast losing speed and drops out
of the sky. To my astonishment, his cockpit

looks quite empty: appearance only we need
hardly guess! Back in the thick of crowded *109*s.
Some try to keep formation. Tracers swing
on, above, below. Impression of deep flight
through a huge cage of golden wire. Look for
another target. One passes as I turn toward
the sun just to my right, slightly above. Up

nose, turn slightly with him, fire at seventy-
five. My shots look to me as if they get his
belly but then my guns begin to click: I'm out
of possibilities. At that same time, the *109*
rolls on his back, careening to disaster.
The mirror tells me I am fair to three
more *Messers* in fine line astern. Flick on
my side, forcing the nose well down, and
skid, and turn, until I'm gone flat out.

Because of claims submitted—compared to
wreckage found—my claim for five was
changed to one destroyed / probable four.
But I have always held to five and I believe
research postwar now lets me claim them.
They all belonged to *JG27* moved to the
     Pas de Calais some few days before.

XIII: SEPTEMBER 9

September 9th. Kent, John (303, Polish).
    Day quiet till 17.00 hrs. Sent off with
1 Canadian. Forty to fifty bombers backing
    south-east for France, with escort. Follows
an 88 with override and gains on it. A *109*
    dives from the escort: race to the post.
About to break off with the man too close,
    a *Hurri* flashes out across the *109*, forces
pilot to slow. K. chases bomber while
    Hurri works the tail. 88 hit & goes for cloud.
K. follows but, breaking cloud, no 88. Going
    for France, encounters different plane. Pretty
exchange of tracers. Quarry turns sharp: a *110*.

    Follows it down to its explosion. First kill
confirmed. His friend had kept *six* escort off his
    tail! Somewhere in here, K.'s Number 2, Jan
Zumbach, follows his double of the 7th with
    a *109*. Czech František, a *Heinkel* down and
Me probable, loses his radiator,
    churns up a cabbage patch,
force-lands near Brighton. His great delight:
    a bar of chocolate, donor
anonymous, while waiting for a train back
    to the base. McKellar,
Archibald (605 AAF) tackles a gaggle of *111*s.
    Blue section dives head-on

out of the sun. Mc.K.'s Glaswegian, as thick
    as he is short, leaves each to
his own target. Sets to the leading *Heinkel*
    of a Vic of three and fires eight
gun salute. Wings spurting blood. Switch fire
    to left-hand *111* while leader

flames. Third *Heinkel* flames as well, turns on
        its back and falls. Then left-hand
111 loses a wing and falls: all three gone down
        in one attack! Later Mc.K. claims
a *109* to bring the day up to a kill of four. He'd
        been the pilot to down the first E/A
on Britain back there in one nine thirty nine:
        those days now seem to all
a hundred years ago at the dark gates of Eden.

The Duxford Wing, in a successful 9th, suffers the
        worst mid-air of the whole Battle. Sinclair,
        the Yellow One of 310, turns his men starboard
to the bombers, but sees a host of *109*s swan down
        on them from their port side. Sinclair swings
to the opposite to check out the fighters. Boulton, as
        Yellow Two, keeping on course, rams into
Sinclair's wing and his rear body. Sinclair's
        port wing tears off. Boulton's right wing folds
over cockpit, his plane bounces into a *110*. Sinclair
        gets out but Boulton and the German men are
lost. Their chutes fail to fill out over the quiet fields
        and the green land rushes to fold them in its
quantities. The wreckage of their aircraft scatters far.

        German invasion set for the 21st September
but with this news and weather looming, they yank
        clock back three days. Not a great deal
of action over England. 9/10: The RAF bombs *II / KG4*
        at Eindhoven, destroys nine
Heinkels. Also Berlin: Germans admit considerable pain.
        The Palace hit in London: now none
can say the rich don't suffer too. 9/11: Sixty RAF
        planes fall on the *Heinkels* of *KG26*
and get 10 down. 41, 92 and 1 (Canadian), sent in
        too low, lose some twelve fighters.
        9/12: in the night raid, the

first civilians win their George Crosses. Malan,
    "Sailor" (74), the Tiger Squadron. Moved

to the Duxford Wing on 10th September. Sent up
    11th with 19 and 611 as rearguard over city.
Malan to go for bombers, the other two
    for fighters. Circa 16.30 hrs., long wedge of
88s at angels 20. Malan orders attack head-on
    but is cut short by *109*s descending. Drops plan
and turns immediately to bombers. By chance,
    delivers beam attack by turning right against the
front. Rakes them from hundred fifty down to fifty
    yards, damaging two. Continues down in spiral
to 13 and pulls back up to 20. Sees two formations
    at 22, one of thirty, one of fifty. But catches sight
of single *88* back down at 20. Heads into him
    and wrecks port engine. Pulls round to go for him
again but *109* zooms in, follows him down to angels 10

    Malan pulls into black-out turn and gets away.
Lane, Brian, leads 19—thirty-six *Spits* mounting
    toward the aging sun, sees the same lot in a superb
position—the sort of interception pilots always
    dream of. At them head-on, slightly above. First
Flight's forty-eight guns to shake them. Lane
    takes the right-hand one. Hard round return but
they are gone, utterly gone! And flight and squadron
    gone! Then sees septet of *Heinkels* turning home:
perhaps, with leaders dead and four more down, they have
    lost steam. Two *110*s form up each side the bombers.
Shoots up on one of them, the other runs. Then goes for
    bombers, now down to six (never accounted
for the seventh one!). Attacks the last and
    then the leader: no response. Gets number six.

Later that day, Beamish with 249, goes down on 60/80
    *He111*s at angels 17 above the London Docklands.

 Hindrance from friendly Anti-aircraft fire.
   Climbs up, dives down again and bags a *Heinkel*.
13th: The Germans put more anti-aircraft guns
   on to invasion barges. Six *109 Staffels* withdrawn
to guard them also. But R.A.F. hits Calais, Antwerp
   & Boulogne over two nights. Ginger Lacey (501)
destroys a *Heinkel* and is downed as well: the *He111*
   had bombed Buckingham Palace through
the clouds. On 9.14: activity *reprise, Luftwaffe* jams
   defences, a new technique but four days
old. Neverthless, invasions clock put back once more.
   On 9/15, climax of B. of B., Göring's
proof of the pudding one last time.

The RAF had not sent all its planes due south, nor had
   fields south of London been abandoned.
     Luftwaffe suffers doubts and low morale.

XIV: SEPTEMBER 15, "BATTLE OF BRITAIN DAY"

Day starts peaceful, weather good. 11.04 hrs.:
first index of big raid. Twenty-five *Dos* (*KG76*, Lindmayr, Alois in lead) assemble, wait too long for escort—
instead of meeting on the way. Posse of twenty *Spits*
greets them at Dungeness, circa 11.35, then more and
more. 11.55: London in sight—nine squadrons strike
the *Dorniers* all at once. Twenty-three *Hurricanes* go in
head-on. Bombers dispersed/escort frustrated. *Dos* drop
on London randomly, flee for the coast. Huge battle
follows: massed one-on-ones. Holmes, Raymond (504)
dispatches *Do* into Victoria Station, bales out himself
into a Chelsea dust-bin. Or it was Ogilvie, Keith (609):
claims are disputed. Queen Wilhelmina of the Netherlands
witnesses the deed, sends her congratulations to Ogilvie.

Barclay, (249), clad in a friend's
warm Irving trousers, can fly with cockpit open,
climbs to 16. Meets eighteen *Dos*
flying in vice versa. Follows three of his
Hurris port up to bombers for a
head-on. Impatient, turns to effect a beam, nearly
collides into a *Hurricane*. Dives
from above the *Dos*. No escort opposition, so comes
back up to try again. And yet again:
has to break off: a *Spitfire* "glamor boy" making a pass
at him! Bombers too far now. Down to
Thames height and loosens gloves—fingers get frozen
if rammed in too tight. Pete Brothers (257)
gets two this day; McKellar (605) two and a probable.

Bader, Douglas at Duxford. 11.22 hrs.:
242 scrambled. Four others follow: 19, 302, 310 & 611.

Total of fifty-five a/c available form
upstairs Duxford and move on south. Bader curves Wing
south-east, puts it up-sun and set for stern attack.
Levels at 25, sends *Spits* (19 & 611) to 26. Now
move north-west: 242 leads, then 310 & 302.
Above and right: 19. Higher, at 28, the *Spits* of 611.
Atop the latter, some thirty *109*s, deeper into
the sun. As long as 611 position's held, B.'s *Hurricanes*
o.k. Bombers had flown over the London heart
at 17: squadrons engage on Hammersmith (in west) at 22.
Bader prepares attack: sees *109*s in dive,
warns *Spits*. Fighters are shocked and break south-east,

abandoning their bombers. Bader delayed again
by 257 and 504: attack head-on at Germans. Then "Line
Astern!" Germans turning south-east. Bader
picks west formation; Jeffries of 301 picks east and
Stachell, 302, goes for the center. Bader
(Red One) falls vertical to the tail trio; takes center;
Cork (his Red Two) takes right; Campbell (his
Three) hits left. Bader's prey's wing flames up. He runs
on by, attacks a *Do* ahead. *Spit*'s in the way:
breaks off. Another *Spit* smashes into a *Do*. Both down.
Bader singles a crippled *Do*. Someone bales out
and tangles with the tail. Now out of ammo, Bader
homes. Cork hits successfully, breaks down and
right, climbs for another pass: his enemy on fire worried

by *Hurricanes*. Breaks low and left joining three
other *Hurris* to send down a *Do*. Campbell smokes up his
bomber, loses it. Yellow One Ball hit by return
fire, hushes his engine and goes for land. Stansfield (his
Two) finishes off a *Do*. Blue Section (Powell-Sheddon
One & Tamblyn Two) claim two shared bombers
with other *Hurris*. Turner & Richardson arrive
the last, emptying out one bomber. But Hart, sensing too
many fighters on the scene, continues down to

fifteen thousand, etches a *109* into the sea. Next, 310,
cutting their target's turn and topping it,
find themselves parallel to the lead formation. Jeffries
lights up one *Do*, empties another, hits a third
but as the crew escapes, a *Spit* goes into it. Of Czech

310, four claim *Dos* shared: Kauchy & Kuminex;
Hubaček, Puda. Satchell with Poles of 302 dives seven
thousand onto the middle group. Leader's two
probables damage his *Hurri*. Chlopik, Red One, goes for
the rear from port; his Two from starboard:
sandwich a *Do* and eat it. Blue Two & Three, Czerwinski/
Wedzik, share a *Do*, one from the back, one
from below. Green One, Chalupa, closes to 30 yds. into
a *Do*, then fells another from 100 yds.
Sindak, the Yellow Two, slices a *Dornier's* tail with his
own wing. Palak, Green Two, shares that, then
climbs into the fighters for a probable. No. 19
Sqdrn. with Lawson in the lead attack some
twenty *Dos* in line astern at 18,000. Then go for bombers

and their fighter escort. Lawson, Red One,
attacks head-on at front, then comes in on the stern,
hitting the rear port *Do*. Around again at the
same plane which sinks down smoking. Others of 19
sqdrn. account for four. At 611, the *109*s
abstain. McComb calls Bader and comes down ten thousand.
Two *Dos* go down—another's flaming.

Bigger raid yet from *Flotte 2*: Fink's *"Holzhammer;"*
Stahl's *"Condor;"* with *KG26* (their escort *"Schlageter"*
and *"Grünhertz"*). From 13.50 to 14.28, the pepped-up RAF
scrambled to meet them on a ten mile front. Even St. Vincent,
of two world wars, Northolt C.O., clambers to strike head-
on and throws a *Do* bunch into confusion. Two hundred thirty
RAF fighters milling over Kent; then the Duxford Wing—over
East London. All three groups scattered, bomb randomly and

flee, their escort impotent with red lights winking. Shock of
280 fighters in twenty minutes, after two months, must have
been horrid to the *Kanal* hoppers. "The RAF down to its last
four dozen *Spitfires*" they would hear and still limp home
day after day. Churchill visiting Park: "Reserves?"
      Park back to Churchill "There are none left."

Park meant none left 11 Group—but this was less "dramatic."
12 Group and 13 Group still there for back-up & the rest.
Real problem for the Germans: city under some 9/10 cloud.
Also: the *109s* obliged to fly full-throttle: four times the
rate of normal fuel use. A 90 miles per hour wind delays
them over target—though speeds them on their way when
   veering round, ("Thank God!") and flying home.

     This second wave came in soon afterward
to catch the Brits refueling. Quick form up, crossing.
   Barclay back up at 14.00 hrs. Claims *Dos*:
one dead, one probable, one damaged. Tobin, "Red,"
    (City of Angels), after a morning *Do*, has
the strange luck of flight in interval between
    two mass assaults: T.O. 13.15 and back at
13.40 to hit the Middle Wallop crashvan cross-
    rushing from behind a hangar. Totals his *Spit*.
Elsewhere that afternoon, Galland of *Schlageter*,
    protecting *Dorniers*, ballets around with
British fighters for ten whole minutes without result.

    Then shocks a *Hurri* sqdrn. in stepped
formation 800 meters down. Fixes the far left rear man,
    then does the right hand a/c of the leading
flight. Panels break off. Two chutes appear. For
   Staffel I of *JG53*, two Poles of 303 fall down
to Heinrich Koppenschläger and Heinrich Ruhl: the last
    kills of this bunch for nine whole months.
   That morning, they had moved Neuville-Etaples and then
    flown out at 11.03 hrs. Leader Hans Ohly's radio

fails & he goes back. *Deckungsrotte* here: Koppenschläger
& Tzschoppe, Herbert—own plane unserviced yet
flying an unfamiliar. Bombers exceptionally slow: fighters

fly with flaps down. Attacked out of the sun.
Tzschoppe is hit and separated. Decides to home. Stalked
by the *Spit* of Lovell, Tony (41) for 15 miles.
Tzschoppe's wings hit; he opens canopy and frees his belts.
Instrument panel hit; face & hands burned.
The *109* explodes and throws him out: freeing the belts
had saved him. Two *Spits* circle his chute:
one RAF pilot salutes him: he greets the compliment.
(Marriage postponed. Proxy in '41. Wedding in '46.)
Almost immediately this time, 11 Group calls 12.
Four-seven fighters now. *Hurris* climb faster than
the *Spits* on this one. Bader, rising through

16,000 feet, sees enemy at angels 20: he's at a
disadvantage. The escort pounces. Bader
orders the *Spits* to go for bombers just past 15.00 hrs.
Upset now, breaks angrily, greys out, nearly
collides with Yellow Two (this flight it's Crowley-Milling),
bounces off slipstream, spins—exits at angels
5. Climbs back, fires at a bomber, stalls again. Rage.
C-M., startled by Bader, tails a *109*, lights up
its cockpit and sees it crash. Stansfield, now Yellow One,
reaches 21,000 to hit a *Heinkel's* second engine—
the first already dead. Blue Three (John Latta) hounded
by several of escort: one overshoots him:

he bites it down. Blue Two (Stan Turner) spins out a *109*,
another spins *him* out—but he gets a *Do*. Blue
One (Powell-Sheddon) quits the field to deal with thirty
*Do*s going north-west for London. Dives on
a bomber out of the sun and on the beam. *Do* goes for
cloud: a probable. P-S. turns home, bounced
by a *109*, loses control, inverts the *Hurri* and pours out.

310, Jerrard Jeffries led, behind the 242,
reach angels 24. A group of enemy turns west toward
the sun and J.J. waits. Charges head-on.
The squadron claims three victories. Satchell, with 302,
climbs after hard. Satchell attacked from high

behind, hauls *Hurri* up: the *109* draws him an underline.
Satchell snaps forward, rubs him out. Pilch,
the Blue Two and Chlopik, the Red One, tag on the *Dos*
right into cloud, wait for them out, get two.
Blue Three & Four forced out by failures. Chlopik makes
good again with *Dos*—Lapka, Kowalski,
Two & Three, join up with him. Chlopik is hit. His
chute will fail to open. Lane as Red One (19),
gets interested in the high escort: angels 30. Climbs up
to 25 when escort breaks on Red and Yellow.
Makes for a squad of *110*s who go defensive circle. Tries
to insert himself in the reverse direction but is

too far below. Gets out. A brace of *109*s descends
on him, pass alongside. Leader then turns port but
his Two starboard—unwise across L.'s nose. Full inside
rudder turning, the *109* skids under him. Lane
rounds half stalled and fires. The enemy flies rough: will
his wings last? Lane gains: the *109*'s slots open,
ailerons snatching too, wings dipping strongly in alter-
nation. The *109* flees out of turn, inverts,
maybe blacks out. Lane shoots him from the quarter. Dives
down inverted into cloud out of control.
Sweat pouring down, oxygen mask humid, gluey, right
arm exhausted by the stick, Lane follows down

to check out *109*, sees *Dos* flying south-east and seeming
unescorted. Attacks, sails back and forth,
but the *Dos* tighten. Ammo goes dry: Lane's out. Red
Three, George Unwin, follows a diving *109*
from angels 25, falls off at 6 when the *Spit*'s screen

freezes inside a cloud. Climbs back to 25,
picks a *Rotte*: runs into both at Lydd. First goes down
vertical and, seconds later, boy two kisses
the sea. H.E. McComb's *Spits* (611), after 19, go for
top cover, ignoring bombers. But *Spits* have
reached retiring age and cannot make it. Back down into
right echelon, cut up some *Dos* at leisure.

Leigh-Mallory continues grumbling at 11 Group but gets his kicks from the Big Wing. While Osterkamp tells Göring afterward the RAF surprised his pilots. Major achievement of Duxford Wing was to impress the Huns with numbers well beyond their nightmares. Lane scrap: the only one recorded, took more than the duration (twenty seconds) of a standard dogfight.

For this, the day is named "Battle of Britain Day," as famous now as Crispin's. Rest of the month, Göring insists on wipeout, ever misreading his intelligence. British ff. production continues rising. France-rested pilots come back in. Park re-examines kill figures: not enough crashes on British soil to justify them. Downgrades. Orders Biggin & Hornchurch *Spits* to hurt top-cover 109s; *Hurris* in sqdrns. three—should time allow—to go for bb. at medium angels. Germans ordered to hit weaker British groupings when feasible. 9.16, a princely Mölders (*JG51*) destroys a *Hurri* of 605. 9.17: II & III "Pik As" bash 501, then caught by 41 and Duxford boys for heavy pain. The RAF continues striking barges hard: sink about 12% and also maims Dunkirk & Antwerp docks. Germans, trying new tactic, send a few bombers with massive fighter groups.

XV: TIME INTERLUDE (No Date): PERSONAL. ROGER HALL, THE HEINKEL

Hall, Roger here: 152 sqdrn.,
                        Nizam of Hyderabad's,
[what Nineteen Forty]. One hundred bombers
approaching Warmwell, west of Isle of Wight,
at fifteen thousand up. Flight Leader Cox, C.S.:
"For Christ's sake, A Flight, off the ruddy deck!"
Now Yellow section off. White Leader's trouble
with his engine. Fight down passion to take off
without him, given approaching bombs. At last,
follow in starboard V. White One: "Hey, Maida
Yellow One / Where the hell are you? / This is
White One!" "Yellow One / Due north of base/
Four Angels high / Pull your finger out!"

Full speed, three thousand feet per minute,
Yellows way out ahead of us. Need boost.
Pull throttle back, push red half-lever in,
open up throttle. Plane leaps and slams my back.
Shakes engine, black smoke out of each exhaust,
whole plane vibrating now. Harsh with Control
who should have scrambled us before. Reach E/A
level in twenty minutes, angels sixteen, behind
to starboard. Some eighty bombers: ten eights,
stepped up from front to rear. Up there, some
twenty *109*s: two rows of ten. Yellow & White
starting to overhaul in line astern. "Prepare

head-on attack!" Goggles. Slide open hood
to help bale-out and keep hood splinters off.
Four against eighty: not a good average. Still
vague about the break-away head-on. Cannot be
helped now. Boost on too long but hardly care.
           Three miles ahead of them. Yellow One

leads with steep turn to port. Goggles mist now
prayer arises. The role of God. Slide out to echelon,
starboard of my White One. Firing immediately
at the whole compact target: hard to see light
between the bombers. Us four in shallow echelon
to starboard, steady and cheek by jowl. Only these
seconds left to fire: thirty two guns at thirteen
hundred rounds a minute. Reaching six hundred mph.
See no results yet. Glimpse Yellow One swivel port
wing below lead bombers, followed by Yellow Two.
White One starts turn. There is a bit more time
to hit the bombers. Push goggles up. *Freeze frame*:
nose of an *He111 right in my face*, stopped dead,
right in my face, dead still, right in my eyes,
 Collision!
 Black-out. Body shrivelling in, perishing
scorpion. Hit enemy machine? Own wings fall off?
Jolt around tail: hit bomber? No . . . Still blind . . .

Hands dead as lead on the controls. Stall shudder.
Spin to port. Sighted again. England down there.
Just let her spin. Thumb still on trigger, firing
at England. Eight thousand on the altimeter. Stop
spin, forget to quit opposite rudder pedal, spin
starboard. Forget again. Spin port. More viciously
each time. Check out machine: all seems in order.
Grip on myself, pull out of spin, dive on a little
to flush out stall, and level out around two thousand.
 Shaken, fly aimless. Alone. Need obvious
to get back into action a.s.p. and rub that *Heinkel's*
imprint out of mind. Climb north. Dead duck: No

clouds or cover, glare intense. Slow climb is easy
target: no sudden turn *sans* stall, no move without
a loss of altitude, no guarantee of camouflage
if ground is wrong below you, the hidden menace in
the sun—all this leaving you naked. Every excuse

to home in now: technical failure, oxygen failure,
wireless dead, engine too hot or no more ammo. God
looms, cramming the solitude. Height regained. Take
back my speed and throw the *Spit* around all over sky,
regaining confidence. Nothing in sight. Call up,
return to base.
        Flight Leader: "Roger the Rammer! Well I'm

damned! Fancied a posthumous V.C. no doubt!" Nearly
awash with joy, explain apparent braggadocio as nothing
                            more than downright clumsiness.

XVI: SHELVING INVASION

    Hitler decides to shelve *Seelöwe* on the 17th.
Weather is getting worse. Dowding, noticing time
it takes for fighter climbs to the top escort sweeps,
puts up some spotting squadrons: dangerous work.
Fortune moves back and forth with many dreadful
shocks for both the parties. But *Luftwaffe* loses do‐
minion over the skies of England during September.
They mourn four *Geschwaderkommodore*; thirteen
Gr.Kommandeure; thirty-one *Staffelkapitäne* killed /
missing / POW in thirty days. The *Stuka*'s out. The
110 has distressing losses. Obsolescent *Do*s are bad‐
ly wounded. *He*s come in: also riled. Even fast *88*s
run into trouble: forty lost to *KG77* in half a month—
which is a hundred sixty souls. In strategy to tactics,
a fade of purpose, sargassoes of confusion. The RAF
meantime sticks with the system . . . Dowding created
K.G.C.B. on 9.30 of '40. Retirement had turned out
so many times postponed. But, in his going, he was
scarcely honored—and nor was Park: too many intra‐
service rivalries, too many personals, as with every
                                             commander.

            Battle continues into October's end
                      especially the Blitz. The boys
                      dying one after one in the
gilt cage. By now, whatever joy the Germans had
                      of their successes no longer
mattered: Many in *Luftwaffe* feel their waves
are far too regular against the capital: all
            R.A.F does is sit up high
                      and wait for them to show.
      Their enemy could not be beaten in
                      this three-act Battle,
      this small stage set of great particulars.

And still the count continues in universal language.
There is no other calculation for the fighter pilots.
One kill, a personal. One kill, a shared. One kill,
collective. How many kills the pilot, how many kills
the flight, how many squadron, how many Force,
or *Aviation,* or *Luftwaffe,* or *Reggia.* How many kills
toward a decoration—the Flying Cross, *Croix,* Ritter-
kreuz, *Medaglia.* The kill marks on the kite—on rudder,
below cockpit. The kills on landing for the Intelligence.
The kills Intelligence reports up to the Ministries. The
people bombed and comforted with kills—in papers, on
the radio. The kills often inflated beyond any measure.
The bright smiles of the young, the knightly, among all
the nations. The hidden terror. The immense fatigue.

'Ah Launcelot!' he sayd, 'you were
the head of all the chivalry.' 'I now
dare say,' sir Hector sayd, 'why you
sir Launcelot, why there you lie, that
never equaled were by any hand of
any knight on earth. And were most
courteous knight that ever bore his
shield and truest friend to lover ever
bestrode his horse and truest lover
of a sinner that ever loved a woman
and kindest man that ever struck with
sword. Godliest person that ever came
among a press of knights and meekest
man and gentlest that ever ate in hall
and sternest knight to mortal foe that
ever bedded spear to rest.' Then there
was pain and weeping out of measure.
Then kept they this sir Launcelot out
of the earth for fifteen days and after
      buried him with great devotion.

In re the "knightly" among British flyers,
also a class matter must be put on record:
how a line ran between the officers, for ins-
tance, and the flight-sergeants. How it was
felt among the senior bureaucrats that only
"public school"—read "private" in U.S.—
backgrounds of hunting, shooting, fishing,
could give birth to the men with the "right
stuff," not subject to the dreaded "lack of
moral fibre;" how birth imported insofar as
"heroism ran often in lineages of heroes."
How ancient feudal customs among "lords,"
—as Osterkamp was fond of calling them—
recruiting "decent" men from areas and
regions, clubs and associations, in which
the blood stood a good chance of running
blue, gave rise to the "Auxiliary Air Force,"
(A.A.F, 1935), its "pampered pimpernels;"
its "weekend flyers;" and "Brylcreem boys"
as distinct from, let's say, the 'Volunteer
Reserve" (R.A.F.V.R., in 1936). Triumph
of rank sometimes over long expertise in
leading battle groups; separate messes, not
much fraternization until the war had worn
down some of it and expertise began to find
a voice. And, here, of course, we
talk of flyers only. Even, as on the ground,
another kind of war ran against "aliens" &
"extra-territorials:" rumors of Jews, for ins-
tance, running foremost and first away from
war—East End of London most especially—
(which, as it happened, many inhabited) or
sitting all day long in air raid shelters. As li-
beral a writer as George Orwell decides to
test the case: "War Diary," 10.25.40: "*Not
all Jews*" in them "but, I think, a higher pro-
portion . . . than one would normally see in a

crowd this size." Adds "What is bad about
Jews is that they are not only conspicuous,
but go out of their way to make themselves
so." Fact: Blitz sent out *all* people in their
thousands from many cities into the tents,
camps, boarding houses and the fields as
          far away from bombs as possible.

XVII: IN THE FORM OF CODA

        Who wins, if there was winning,
loses if there was loss: an open question.
This not the only Battle at the time: add in
the Med to cope with Mussolini, plus the
Atlantic with the U-boat plague. America
had not come in, despite the admiration
(that wartime version of old Anglophilia):
she would await December's "Infamy."
A stalemate in some sense: Germans cld.
not get into Britain's pants; Britain not
thrust her way back to the Continent.

Brit fears do not die down immediately.
Invasion, poison gas, a back-up secret
air force waiting to shock-bomb England
into a one-raid stupefaction: rumors
abound from every quarter. Unlikely
as it sounds, new men claw up into the
Victors' seats: Newall & Dowding go
without a smidgeon show of genuine
honor, and Park leaves Group 11—later
to rise again defending Malta. He the best
man perhaps among them all. The sense
of victory, momentousness, true myth,
ups slowly. March '41: a governmental
pamphlet sells by the millions to tell of
people's war though, here, the win had
been attained by a small group—at cost
of dead two hundred eighty four; wrecks:
hundred fifty nine. Compare the stats of
Stalingrad and Kursk. Orwell: "Britain
could not be conquered at one blow."
One liberal presence left in Europa still
could yet move later back to Normandy.

This was most to the purpose purposive.
This was the "Victory."

AVIA

PART TWO

4: MALTA

with intrusions by Samuel Taylor Coleridge, poet,
Secretary to the Governor of Malta,
1804-1805

"But if it is because you see us well clothed, riding on great chargers and having everything for our comfort, then you are misled, for when you would desire to eat, it will be necessary for you to fast, and when you would wish to fast, you will have to eat. And when you would desire to sleep, it will be necessary for you to keep watch, and when you would wish to stand on watch, you will have to sleep. And you will be sent here and there, into places which will not please you, and you will have to go there. It will be necessary therefore for you to abandon all your desires to fulfil those of another and to endure other hardships in the Order, more than I can describe to you. Are you willing to suffer all these things?"

Tuitio Fidei,
Sovereign Order of the Knights of Malta.

I: MALTA: THE VIEW

> *"Insula parva situ sed rebus maxima*
> *gesti Africae et Europae ac Asiae*
> *contermina, Pauli Hospes, et alborum*
> *procerum gratissima nutrix."*
>   Vincenzo Littara.

"Small isle—yet great by illustrious acts,
joint neighbor to three continents, host to
St. Paul, sweet nurse of White Cross nobles . . ."

    The island flat, without an elevation,
        "a leaf over the sea"—
or handkerchief, seen from the air,
hard target in emergencies, ('chute:
thistledown on winds from Africa)
with the apparently interminable ocean
        bridal around it—
                tide-fashioned caves
eating into the limestone.

North side, there is a cavern where
"the nymph Kalypso has him in her hall"
and thrall at that, great traveler,
exploits unmatched two thousand years
downstream, remained to view the battle
        after his mishap under Gibraltar
                (pronounced *españolando*)
cave planted round with death plants,
herbs will sleep men into most other worlds.

        Night hunting birds,
     birds of the drowned,
           perch among trees

shade on the sprouting dead.
        Four springs, shallow and clear,
                lift oblivion water
out of four island-bearing columns,
        roots from the depthless ocean.
Sea monsters: sharks to submarines—
        only predators
that could bring down the island.

        In depth, the pillars correspond
to another four, upholding, in the north,
a city cut by rivers wider than the sea
some other fleets may dream of drowning.
A midnight sun lies low in wartime's June
skulking back of the Baltic winds.

        But here, where sun is burning
and ceaselessly illuminates the world—
though the world wavers
        in the shimmering dust—
the cavern is an ancient temple
made of colossal stones the oldest folk
down home raised up together,
        first among men,
once linked to all the major continents,
thus mother to them in our western world.

        And all the temples linked as well:
stone veins and arteries,
        shifting over the sand
        great currents leeward, windward,
with corresponding stations in the sky.
        Such temples,
lit through the heart valves of the sea,
where long-extinguished herds once swept
from continent to continent,
        laying their bones

on rocks still hold their imprint,
project upsky such radiant power
as make men stronger than any known
        in any war before or since.

        In this midyear, a morning fog
might keep the days from off the sea,
wide veil over an entire continent,
        blinding all birds and airmen,
blending with smoke stilled
              between north and south:
a smoke fed ceaselessly
        in feudal ovens: blood, bone and fat,
a fossil people's at the west's heart
offered in sacrifice to war's own gods
like the seared bulls to ravenous Olympus . . .

Saw the limb of a rainbow footing itself
on the Sea at a small apparent distance
              from the Shore,
a thing quite of itself, no substrate cloud
or even mist thus visible, but
              the distance glimmered
thro' it as thro' a thin semitransparent hoop—

A brisk Gale, and the spots of foam
that peopled the alive sea most interestingly
combined with the numbers of white Sea Gulls;
so that repeatedly it seemed, as if the foam spots
had taken life and wing, same-color Birds rose up
so close by ever perishing white wave heads,
that the eye was unable to detect the illusion
which the mind delighted in indulging—

The Sea is like a Night-sky . . . . . as if
the Night sky were a Thing, that turned around
and lay in the day time under the paler Heaven

When first an Ajax from the Apennines:
Musso more bloated than any previous
         pumpkin known to men's annals,
decided he would join this *krieg*
rather than lose his jackal's share,
he felt the little jewel of an island
known as Melitta in the ancient tongues
(for the abundance of the honey it provided
Athens or Rome) might well become inserted
in the long necklace of *mare nostrum* isles
his country had assembled.

         The island had no more than
three old biplanes forgotten on stone fields
         and with these *Gloster Gladiators*
                  "Faith," "Hope," & "Charity,"
miraculously held the Roman hordes at bay.
The Romans, tangled in Greek mountain webs,
         failing to quell their Abyssinian lions,
their neighbors on the northern Axis spike
had to fly down to help. Somehow, the Brits
fed the Melitta winds with *Hurricanes*—&
         these, with latest tactics yet unlearnt,
though tried almost beyond endurance
by faster, better-managed Teuton birds,
         "miraculous" to speak it
                  (the word will have long play),
kept them at bay through two long years.

As for the population of this fortress,
prey to more bombs, trials and hungers
than almost any in the central sea's
long history of battle,
         they hid among their stones,
their caves carved out of immemorial rock:
dark-eyed undead among the megaliths
of their Phoenician, Jew, Greek, Roman, Arab

lines, collectively fought on to be awarded
a decorated praise, unique among the annals,
named to an entire nation: "Malta George Cross."
Meantime, war's tides along African shores
from Dido's home over to Pharaoh's Egypt
(some in Italian hands and some in British)
swept to and fro, one side's triumphant surge
and then the other. Only little by little
did both sides fathom that the small isle,
this tear of Sicily, held, with its fighters,
bombers, PRU blues, subs and destroyers
the key to whether Axis needs could reach
safely from Europe into Africa. The island's
chiefs sent message after message—to Alex
and to London, unheard for the most part
   with seeming almost criminal neglect,
until the strangling of the island Britain
      had loomed less probable.

  Now stands the wind
     for Malta—as for France
the RAF had swept in forty-one and two—
and with the month July in forty-three,
    chosen somewhat at random,
(for to tell truth the record cannot be
    entirely changed to verse
      lest **hypocrite lecteur**
be whelmed and overwhelmed) the story
can begin again of how our era's air
   renders transpicuous
      the archives of the grave,
   crafts myths to make
      mythographers run wild—
aged ten or seventy, it little matters.

*11 Jan. 1805. Convoy has been far off
these four days: and still it cannot beat
into the Harbour. But the boat will go off
for the Letters. —O my poor anxious Soul!*

*Of the feelings of the English at the Sight
of a Convoy from England—man cannot be
selfish—that part of me (my beloved) wch
is distant in space excites the same feeling
as the "ich" distant from me in time! (I have
the same anxiety for my friends now in England
as for myself that is to be, or may be—two
months hence. My Friends are indeed my Soul—)*
                                            19. Jan. 1805.

II: MALTA: THE PROGRAM

Friday morning, ½ past 6, May 18th, 1804,
in full clear sight of Malta . . . . . Friday
afternoon, 4 o'clock, ... dropt anchor in
the Harbour of Malta—one of the finest
in the world the Buildings surrounding it . . . . .
of a neat even new-looking Sand-free stone.
Some unfinished, &, in all the windows,
placed backward looked like Carthage
when Aeneas visited it or a burnt out place-
. . . . . . and when you begin to understand a little
of the meaning & uses of the massy endless walls
& defiles . . . . . . the houses looking new, like Bath;
all with flat roofs, the Streets all strait
& at right angles to each other; but many
of them exceeding steep and none quite level;
of the steep Streets some all stepped up with
a smooth artificial Stone, some having the
footpaths on each side in, stone steps, the
middle left for carriages; lines of fortification,
fosses, Bastions, Curtains, &c &c endless, endless-
with gardens or bowling Grounds below the high
ones; for it is all height & depth—you can walk
no where without having whispers of Suicide, toys
of desperation. Explosive Cries of the Maltese
venders—shot up, broad and bulky noises, sudden
and violent . . . . . The language Arabic corrupted
with Italian & otherwise perhaps.

Sudden Bellow . . . shot high up into air
with bomb-like Burst—Maltese crier.

. . . . . . even in Malta—jack asses—Cats—Cocks—
Bells—Day cries—Night bellowings—Guns.

Found myself light as a blessed Ghost-
brought my Things from the Boat

                       Program:
supplying Malta once problem recognized, responsibility accepted. June '41: the Germans leave for Russia. Same month, over two thirds of ships from Rome to Africa sunk out of Malta. In 5, 7 and 9/41, convoys break through to Malta. December, forty-one: Field Marshall Kesselring returns to Sicily, six hundred aircraft strong, to "neutralize" the island. Hitler agrees to *"Herkules"* invasion. 3-4.42: more bombs on isle than bombs on London in a year of Blitz. Ten thousand houses out, double that damaged, one hundred churches wrecked. Over a thousand civvies killed: shelters in daily use. Too few Axis ships bottomed. March 7, '42: first *Spits*,
     so often urgently requested, take off from *Eagle* A/c Carrier out of Gibraltar.

4.20.42: Churchill's appeal to FDR yields USS. *Wasp*. "Op. Calendar" gets over 40 *Spits* to isle (with much-loved Jumbo Gracie's famous "red on black" [heading the wrong direction] and U.S. Sgt. Walcott's weird defection to North Africa). Security not tight enough and too much time taken to pen *Spits* safely. Germans forewarned, "spitcher" thirty-nine planes out of a total forty-six. A second try, "Op. Bowery," May 8th one nine four two, with complex stages led by expert Malta pilots, makes it to isle. Turn-round, rapid as kingdom come: the *Spits* o.k. Canadian Jerry Smith's performance on this lap is famous still. His 90 gallon belly-tank breaks off on take-off. Scorns options (eject or French N. Africa) lands

back on deck: first *Spit* thus on a carrier without
arrester gear. Down in "dry" *Wasp*, D. Fairbanks
Jr., liaison man, slips him the largest scotch he'd
         ever seen; later, a pair of U.S. Navy wings.

A.O.C. Lloyd and "Woody" Woodhall, greatest
controller of the war perhaps, can now ignore
the fighter sweeps and concentrate on bombers.
"Ultra's" special liaison unit, unbeknown to air-
men, "Y's'" saturation information: both masked
by Photographic Reccy. Unit's blue, high, lone,
unarmed *Spits* (a knightly Warburton, a systema-
tic Coldbeck) lead to many a perfect intercept.
Ground crews working "for life," "to keep the
effing birds on the effing line," perform their jobs,
their miracles without complaint. The regiments:
Manchesters, Buffs, Dorsets, W. Kents, Devons
& Inniskillings build 27 miles dispersal tracks &
260 d. points. As in the Huns' fatal decision to
stop attacks on stations and go for London, old
Kess is blind to RAF's respite and *"Herkules"* at
                  last loses its whole potential.

         Convoys continue hair-raising. Ex-Gib, con-
voy "Harpoon": six merchantmen—two only make it
into harbor. As for "Op. Vigorous" from Alex, Italian
fleet driving eleven ships and escort back. Six weeks
again to the next convoys: rationing peaks, electric
blackout, the frantic efforts to unload boats destroyed
even in harbor. Evolving talent of anti-a/c guns, like all,
toiling in broiling heat. Ongoing: snail Navy biplanes ver-
sus Axis shipping, plus *Wellies, Blenheims, Beaus,* against
                  the coasts and night intruders.

         Most of the Malta combat considered worse
         by many than the B. of B. One: Malta's small
         compared to Britain: tonnage of bombs acutely

concentrated. Two: replacement a/c for B. of B. quickly available, & thus delivered. Three: B's pilots fought with fullish stomachs; Malta's in state of slow starvation. In B. amenities survived. Malta: the whole of life went by the board, save kills. Everything else till then—including Channel sweeps, "child's play" compared to this.

III: TIME INTERLUDE: PERSONAL.
THE "KING OF THE MEDITERRANEAN"

The time he's christened in a sub at Malta,
his father being a submariner.
The time he photographs Taranto before
the Swordfish raid.
The time he finds the fleet for Matapan.
The time he photographs the whole Via Balbia
   (250 m.) & shoots up 3 *Savoias* on the ground.
   The time he dives to bomb a convoy & "clean
            forgets" to pull out.
The time he extracts a fat bullet from his chest
            while up and flying.

The time he visits Gib to collect a plane,
spends evening out in civvies (neutral Tangiers)
with some *Luftwaffe* men, also in civvies.
The time he runs into eight *109*s, crash lands
at Bone; persuades French admiral to fly
Algiers; picks up a *Halifax* to Gib and gets
arrested as a spy (unorthodox appearance);
getting *Spit* back to Bone to retrieve camera.
The time he snaps Pantelleria so low, the
            anti-aircraft fires *down* on him.
The time he photographs obliques of the
                        invasion beaches.
The time he entertains the U.S. Navy and
a Russian colonel upon the same occasion.

         The times he smokes cigars in planes
         & leaves his chute unstrapped.
         The times he flies through flak with cap
         above his helmet, stub drooping from
         his lips, one elbow on the cockpit rim.
         The times he frats with airmen & air

      marshals both—but little in between.
      The times he flies abroad to score
      both booze & eats for his men's fiestas.
      The times he downs 20+ aspirins a day.
      The times he disappears into the blue
                      on unofficial missions.
      The times he "always gets his pictures."
      The times he never learns to take off
      or to land—while master in the air.
      The times he held in love the greatest
             beauty in the island.

The time his kind of flying came to an end in Malta
with the invading hordes making for Sicily.
The time he broke his pelvis in a jeep, feared for
his manhood, was reassured by a "lady doctor."
The time he flew his *P38F5*, paled over Europe
           like Saint-Exupéry, never sighted again.
The time he may have crashed Comiso, trying to
                  make it back to Malta.
The time, as myth would have it, he may have been
          returning to keep in love that beauty.
Also so many other pilots, doing suchlike things . . .
(Wingco. Adrian Warburton, Two D.S.O.; Three
            D.F.C. & D.F.C. (U.S.).)

Yesterday . . . . . the Thermometer was
at 88 in the Shade, 134 to 140 in the Sun
& today the Heat seems equal or greater.
The boards fly, with perpendicular Cracks,
with frequent and startling Sound the
Mahogany & stoutest woods . . . . . literally
explode & burst the instrument.
. . . . . not a board in the beautiful new
dining Room but split from top to bottom
in two or three places.

(. . . . . *I have the prickly Heat on my Body,*
but without prickling or annoying me
and I am better than I have been for a long
time . . . . . —In short, if my mind & heart
were at ease, ... I should be more than well
I should luxuriate . . . . . in the Oven of the
Shade & Blaze of Sunshine.)

July. A relatively quiet month, compared to March & April—but the time picked to write this episode. In Sicily, II / JG53, set up with elements of *Stab & I / JG77*, leaves Russia & Rumania, arrives Comiso 7.3.42. *Kom.* Ihlefeld posted to *JG52*: replaced by "Pritzl" Bar from *JG51*. C.O.s of 249 change at Takali field: Stan Grant follows Stan Turner and "Laddie" Lucas follows Grant. Raoul Daddo-Langlois, a "Daddy Longlegs" to all his many friends, is Laddie's Flight Commander. Lucas, in logbook, joys to quote a Bard: "This blessed plot, this seat of majesty, this Malta." D. Douglas-Hamilton on board: comes in 4.20.42 with 603: mixes his boys in 249 to gain the Malta "form." With 126 & 185 at Luqa, the isle, tho' bushed & dogged by sandfly, dysentery, enjoys a possible July. Beurling, Canadian ("Screwball" for his prolific use of word), in with a middling reputation for disobeying orders—he'll prove himself precision flying master: superman-eyesight, great shot, instinctive feel for distance and position. Fasts flying —he thinks the eyesight sharper. He kills by single short bursts & almost all deflection shots.

July 4, '42. A "grandstand interception" (says Laddie) right over Island center. Choice Woody Woodhall show—"a few big jobs, some 70 or 80 smalls, at angels seventeen to twenty. Get off at once, up fast to south, angels two-four / two-five, stay S.E. of Grand Harbour well up sun," etc. Woody's plain talk, clear data, visualization, foresight out of "the Ditch," the comfortable sound of his deep voice, the normalcy of it! L. pushes to twenty-seven north at roughly 5 o'clock, Grand Harbor. Prey dead ahead some seven thou. below. Three *big Cant Z1007* bombers in a tight Vic: (decoy should tempt defending *Spits* to lunge at escort *109*s) and, well astern, Italian "after-thought:" *Res.* and *Macchis*. Unseen, the 249 "diamond-sharp bounce" right through the escort, get the three bb., down fast to deck. Screwball, free on the day says: "Boss, no way I could fault *that* one." Next day, Lucas goes into hospital. One man, Pelleschi, holds his arm up toward him. Hand missing. Found floating, appeared to hold up a white handkerchief. This was his shattered hand washed clean of blood. A violinist. His plaintive eyes. Lucas haunted for weeks, forbids his men to visit with their victims. Yet intercept, he thinks, had clinched his D.F.C. and so he felt July a fortune for his life. "For I can say with truth I longed to get it, and worked like hell to earn it."

IV: INTERCALATION FROM:
SWEET TOWNS I HAVE NOT KNOWN...

Click to: small town, now fist of bronze,
raised on the countryside, now pectorals of
stone, host to successive
meddler waves and waves of names,
small, yet head-town, since at least
Carthage—
Melita of the honeys;
Medina of the walls; Città
Notabile of banners, and Città Vecchia
once white cross knights had built their capital;
Palace of Paul and Peter in these present days
our home on earth while we are down from skies
briefly to rest and freshen.

From here
it could be watched, as Laddie speaks of it,
one five six five a.d.:
the first great siege in which, despite the odds
(some 40,000 men at ten to one, before the *Gran
Soccorso*, huge hordes of Janissaries, tidals
of Islam under the Ottomans), Malta
of the white cross held firm as Rhodes had held
three times;
as *Crac des Chevaliers* had held in the Crusaders'
time, forts' fort, castles of castles.

Here is Imdeena looks over Ta'Qali
our point of take off on this present siege
where I must go to justify this work.
White-out continues. The music sung.

V: LUFTWAFFE STEPS UP PACE

July 6: *Luftwaffe* steps up pace to multiply *Ju*88s by two. 603 meets them without much action. 603 lands, 249 up: fast in to greet the next lot. Italians. Lee, Norman, rushes for *Cants* head on—they jettison their bombs into the sea. Italians, whom, Beurling swears, the *Luftwaffe* will blissfully allow to do the fighting for them, engage the *Spits*. Beurling deletes Pecchiari, Macchi (352a *Squadriglia*, 20o. *Gruppo CT*) and Pagliani, Rom., *Reggiane*, (152a *Squadriglia*, 2o. *Gruppo CT*), dropping fr. 20 down to angels 5 where it blows up, the pilot in small pieces. Early post-noon, escort duty for Beurling: rescue launch to pick up fallen. A host of claims on either side—but killed seem only two: Edwin D. "Alabama" Moye, American, of 185, & Peter Wilbertz, of *KGr* 806. Another raid at 18.40. *Ultimo* raid at 20.30 sees I / JG77's maiden flights over the Island. Lord D-H. leading 603: all bb. said to be shot down by Glen, Swales, Irwin, Lévy-Delpas—though one seems to have gotten back. *Always that dumb discrepancy from claimed to credited!* Beurling gets Toni Engels, I / JG77. July 7: a harsh day w. costly losses for defenders: Terry & Haggas killed (185). *May seem like Rosencrantz & Guildenstern to us but, here, each man is treasured.* Tale of Ron West's. Receives a bar before a medal: joke-wears rosette without the ribbon, provoking icy wrath of A.O.C. and prompt express delivery of ribbon.

Eighth of July with four more *Spitfires* lost, three pilots killed. King, Neville (603), once London bobby, at wave-level: wing dips too low and he goes in. Berres of *I / JG77* runs Saunders (603) over all of Gozo, many hits. Saunders opts for Marsalform Bay: hauled out by fishermen with black eye only. Beurling claims couple *109*s that day and one *88*. July 8. Screwball: "Willie the Kid came close to hearing harps that morn." Puts a *Ju88* on fire. Hangs round to see his plane go down— foolish because a flamer hollers at unwanted sharks. Beurling spots the Kid's buzz around his burning bomber "seeing the sights," oblivious to pouncers. B goes head on to get the *109*s off from "the blue plate lunch" the Kid was offering. "Who do you think *I* am," says B: "your mother?" "Hi, Mom!" says Willie. Walk home to hear Smith (Smittie), Carlton Gilbert (Gil) dead. Because of ratios, British pilots alone most times, must fight, and flee disaster if they can, alone, "split-assing over all of heaven, to entertain the Huns." *Dixit*. That day, "hurts a *Ju88*, flying in tracer all the time, diving at some 550 m.p.h. right "down the hill." Go for the starboard engine on the *88*: plane can't keep height if hit there. Its whole hydraulic system, controlling undercarriage, is hitched to it. July 9: Lévy-Delpas, Guy André (A.K.A. Carlet, 603) last seen diving after an 88 (*Croix de Guerre, Légion d'Honneur* posthumously). On his first sortie ever, he'd gone and downed three enemy.

July 10th & 11th, Beurling builds up his score. Early on 10th, he sees a *109* about to kill a *Spit*, comes up below it and sends it to the sea: Frodien,

Hans Jürgen (*Stab / JG53*). Smith, Jerry, caught it happening from the ground and took the tail wheel as a souvenir. Niclot, Doglio, code name Furio, & Tarantola, Ennio, of *20o. Gruppo,* also around in there. On second raid, Jerry chalks up an 88—tho' shot up thrice, the third time by his target, & must force land Hal Far while Luqa field is bombed. "B" dives through a bunch of *Macchis,* glues onto one who acrobats. On final loop, "nailed him just at its top: two seconds burst broke cockpit right apart:" *(378a. Squadriglia, 155Gr. CT. Frco. Visentini.)* Pilot gets out, B radios in—"specified gent Italian, not one of ours." This day, Italians begin to notice compressibility vibrations: a plague in coming weeks. Carlo Miani: them so bad he thought his tail had gone, bailed from his *Macchi* over Sicily and into hospital. Next day, Jones, Varey, Lucas all have claims; Yarra his twelfth— & Paddy Schade a sixth in just one week, bringing him up to leader in the top-gun stakes. Daddo-Langlois achieves a one (Heinz Riedel's): *exactly* one year later, loses his life
                                          over invasion beaches.

On Wed. Morning July 11th, ... observed & tasted Locust Tree & Fruit . . . . . . deepest verdure & most efficient shade of any . . . . . . Pomegranate, prickly pear, pepper Tree, Oleander, Date Tree, Myrtle Bowers, Arbour of a scented Butterfly-flower, Walnut, Mulberry, Orange, Lemon, ... &. Banana

A deadly chess game July 12th. Raid on Takali not found by 603—they told to land & when the raiders hit they lose six *Spitfires* damaged. As bombers dash for sea again, 249 follows—but held in by a mighty

fighter curtain. Beurling's one second burst brings
down an *Re2001* of *358 Squadriglia*. Same plane
is hit by Hetherington. Berkeley-Hill, Owen (India)
tells H. he's seen it fall, then is shot down & killed.
Vichi, Francesco has to bail out (*358a. Squadriglia,
2o.Gruppo Autonomo CT.)* Quarantotti, Aldo, bra-
ving bad weather, takes four to search and two have
to turn back. Beurling and Hetherington (looking
for Owen) see Q, also Seganti, Carlo, in cloud. H
covers; B sneaks to the back of Carlo, burns him out.
Whips round on Q, closes to 30 yards at angle of
15. Q looks at B and is decapitated. While some
reports claim B cold-blooded here, others drown
                     him in nightmares weeks thereafter.

*On Hearing Of The Death By Drowning of John
Wordsworth, MN, Captain Of The* Abergavenny,
*2.5.1805. Dear dear John! These tears tho'
from eyes that throb & smart are pleasure
compared to what I've felt, to what
I shall yet feel.—Methinks it is
impossible, to live I shall hear next of Sara's
Death no, not of William's—
no! no!—sure not!—no, surely, if there be
a will in anything, or goodness
in Providence God forgive me!—myself
despair of ever seeing home. They are
expecting me—did they not so expect him!—
O God have pity! O may Almighty God bless you,
Friends! and comfort you . . . . . Ah venerated William*

*O dear John! and so ended thy dreams of Tairns
& mountain Becks, & obscure vales in breasts
and necks of Mountains! . . . . . O Heavens! Dying
in all its Shapes; shrieks; and confusion;
and mad Hope; and Drowning more deliberate*

than Suicide;— . . . . . Never yet has any loss
gone so far in the Life of Hope, with me.
I now only fear.

. . . . . whose last words were—"I have done my Duty!
let her go!"

. . . . . and all these being but Decoys of Death

Italians seen by some without respect. Others find their small tight formations competent and brilliant with defensive acrobatics. These often mask awareness of the truth their kites are not as good as those of enemies and allies—a truth unsafe for high morale. 7.13: Jack Rae with two kills on that day and Allan Yates follow a single *Re2001* heading home. Then shocked by the most complex flying they had ever viewed: almost impossible to follow. The *Re* starts to smoke, the Brits, too far from home, turn round. The *Re* turns with them, making a final dash at the two *Spits* as if to thumb his nose at them—and goes for port. Same day: on the first raid, Doglio, Niclot, homing *sans* ammunition, frees wounded 88 from a *Spit* couple, escorts the bomber safe back to Sicily. Pilot lands bomber at D.N.'s base to thank his man. Meantime, at Malta, Lucas falls to a trap, dives on lone *Macchi*—to be bounced in turn by two brace *109s*. On fire at 18,000 over sea, five or six miles south east of land. Cuts every switch, grabs toggle on the canopy, toggle snaps off. Astoundingly, after a while, fire heat abates. Height seems sufficient to squeeze in a glide. Undercarriage works; flaps also. Misses two Navy biplanes taking off toward him, avoids running into a hangar by just a bunch of yards.

Juillet 14—last day of third and final summer blitz. Italians, stunned by loss of Quarantotti & many others, regroup, await new boss. Keith Park, famed at 11 Gp. in Britain's Battle, in as new Chief. Lloyd, Woody, Turner leave: all three Leigh Mallory's; (also posts Lee, Daddo, Lucas & Gracie home) then quick (*dixit* L. Lucas) to lay on Sicily Mallory's tactics! July 15th: operation "Pinpoint." Thirty-two *Spit*Vcs T.O. from *Eagle*: four Yanks—but mostly Commonwealth. Smith, Rod, a new Canadian, meets brother Jerry and joins him on his squadron." T. O. from *Eagle*, ran 500 ft. and second off. Flew in first eight to Luqa. Looked on Algeria, made landfall passing over Tunis, changed tanks in sight Pantelleria, landed still in a group: Jerry at Luqa! Oh small, wee world!" Jerry: "Marvel to hear that Rod had landed here. Saw him in car of A.O.C. and chatted with him till he left for mess."

July 15: Beurling gets D.F.M. "the one gong that means something. (It means the years spent drudging to buy flying lessons; failure to get to China or the Finns; refusal by Canadians for lack of education; a trip to Britain minus certificate of birth; & back to Canada (convoys bombed both ways) to grab certificate; the training time seeming like years; the many nights of homework on shooting and deflection, the chance to get here and to *do* some shooting—*that* is the real one, that D.F.M: rest comes along when and as best it can.)"

July 18th: afternoon raid, everyone up again; the 126 boys join in the action some ten miles west of Malta. Jerry and Rod see a lone 88 on deck, heading for Sicily. Send the plane home, lolling along, glycol from starboard engine streaming, tail down, rear gunner dead or out of action. (R.S. records a near fatal mistake, arising out of training: to break away from bomber *downward* & to one side. He'd shot at 88—from some 250, one cannon stopping & spoiling aim. Pilot of 88 tries pitching up & down. R's second cannon out. To break on *upward* would cancel speed in own relation to target's forward motion, giving upper rear-gunner access at one's belly to rip it open. But R sees just in time that *this* a/c is right above the water: a *downward* break would be

a final dive.)

Park, for his part, tells Middle East H.Q. he wants no fledgelings on his beat. July 21: Operation "Insect": 4 men sent back to Gib to lead the flight; bring off twenty-four *Spits* from *Eagle* plus their own. One lost on take-off. Planes get off faster with wooden hydromatic props and pilots lighter as per a Malta diet. Fake "Social Democratic Cambridge accent" from Sicily attempts to lure them on a fatal course but Woody, not yet faded out of earshot, promptly will rally, capturing them back. July 22:

Jean Paradis (French Canada) of 249 & Shorty Reid of 185 destroyed by Schlick & Berres (I / JG77): JP. a friend of Beurling's. Last call: "I see the 88 bomb airs. I go up there." July 23rd: Mitchell, the new C.O., leads 249 into mid-morning raid, sends down one kite. Beurling, with Hetherington, disturbs the health of two, later blows off the wing of a *Reggiane* with a deflection shot. July 24: Rod S. gets his first single.

July 25. Park issues "Fighter Interception Plan" to catch the bombers out at sea (now there are plenty *Spitfires*) over the Malta Channel instead of on the isle with planes destroyed on ground. Great 27th for Beurling. Spots four *C202s* in line astern, takes on the fourth. *Macchis* pull into climbing turn to right. Gives straight deflection booster into the starboard

quarter of his quarry. Quarry flicks into spin, pulls
out over Victoria to belly slap a rocky field & slam
his face on instruments: Gelli, Faliero *(378a. Sqdr-
glia., 155Gruppo, 51Stormo.)* Beurling immediately
turns to another. This is Niclot: Furio Doglio, Com-
mander, *151a. Sqdrglia.*, 34 years, Turin, test pilot,
six victories and three more shared. *Medaglia d'Oro*
(posth.) N. waggles wings . . . to indicate—but what
exactly? then blows to pieces in the air . . . Screwball
moves on to the next customer but spies below two
109s. Half rolls, gets under them & sends one down
while knocking wing & tail bits off the other. (There
have been queries re Beurling's own perceptions of
this double whammy . . .) Later that day, B. once more
kills a *109* and damages a second. Preu, Karl-Heinz,
Stab / JG53 probable victim. Beurling is top scorer
on the island now and never forfeits this exalted rank.

VI: TIME INTERLUDE: PERSONAL.
ROD SMITH: TOO HIGH TOO FAST

July 26th.
126 Squadron scrambled at 16 hrs. to intercept
seven *Ju*88s with *109*s.
I am no. Two to brother J.— as usual.
Bounced by some *109*s homing from previous raid
but no harm done. The squadron separated.
Climbing alone the two of us.
For once, the German leader makes the *mistake*
of rising to his 18,000 much too soon,
so: he is early visible to radar.
In turn, we two can reach to angels 25 some 15 miles
north of Bay of St. Paul, west of Valletta.
Spot raid in front of us, the thrill of seeing
all *109*s below us: mounted behind the *88*s
back all the way up to 24 thou!
No diving turn into the *88*s: the *109*s can speed up
in a dive faster than tropicalized a/c all weighted
down with clutter. Jerry decides to turn 180
at their present height—behind the topmost,
backmost *109*s of the close escort. Careening
to the *88*s, we split the fighters right and left,
thus to delay their chase. One of *top*
cover *109*s spots us and circles them but pulls back up
(to my eternal puzzlement).
Just before last and highest *109*s arrive abeam of us,
turn to the right brings the two *Spits* behind,
a bit above them: now flying south as part of the
procession right into St. Paul's Bay!

Dive starts, myself on right, a little tad behind.
Witness the *109*s in fours, in line abreast, seeming to rise
out of the backs of *88*s like a great staircase—
or like the tails of whales about to disappear

in the last stages of a plunge. First section breaks—
left to the left, right to the right.
Same with the second down.
Third down: the inner pilot's unaware.
Too close for proper aim,
shoot anyway since *he* will shoot a moment later:
no hits. Ten feet over the *109*'s right wing,
look down into his cockpit,
get my first glimpse of human enemy.
To spoil *his* aim, raise the left wing, skid left and up,
skid down again, continue dive. *109* sections further down
break as before.

I dive right on and do not care whether followed or not.
Euphoric situation.
The thought "Don't give a shit who gets destroyed
as long as someone does!"
Speed tops 400 when we both realize
we're overshooting *88s* so fast there is no time for more
than a short burst—
plus ailerons freeze with speed: so no corrections
for a proper aim. Each gives
a frantic burst: Jerry feels single strike on left; I note
nothing on right.
Gunners of *88s* loose streams of tracers.
To frustrate gunners, turn steepest we can manage,
out and away. Then whole procession moves,
unshaken as a pod of whales unwounded by harpoons,
leaving the *Spit*s alone at 18,000.
Jerry is streaming glycol. Switches off engine now
and starts to glide toward his third
forced-landing of the month. I weave to cover him above.
Jerry requests location landing; controller judges
88s are bound to go to Luqa, tells him Hal Far.
(Two minutes later, the *88s* break up a *Spit* on Luqa,
three *Beau*s, a *Wellington*.)
Problem of judging landing on dead engine.

Too high: crash to stone wall *beyond* the airfield boundary.
Too low: crash at 75 to wall *before* the boundary.
Jerry continues weaving to lose height.
1,000ft.: lowers his wheels and flaps
en route north boundary Hal Far.
Late sun adds on a running shadow to his left
and closing in on him as he is sinking.
Not far off wingtip as he nears last wall.
He levels off, shadow slides under him.

Moral for wiser piloting. We should have settled
for top close *109*s
instead of being blinded by their initial height
to disregard the draw-backs of overtaking speed.
If *109*s had then driven us off,
we could, assuming ammunition left,
have dived to east and met the enemy home-bound
                                        some minutes later.

VII: TO MAKE AN END OF IT

Gardens, say rather Garden pots—beds
at least with Stone borders.
> *The Maltese Fields.*

. . . . . barrenness every where staring out,
& every where conquered, or a-conquering—
the Sea like a blue wall around—

July 28th. 08.50: first defence bounced: two pilots down, one killed. 11.30, five *Ju* 88s, escorted, well north of island. Only two 88s get through to bomb Hal Far. Several claims against bombers and escort. Late afternoon: 5 *Spits* from 185 sent on patrol; still up there when eight fr.1435 Flight & eight fr. 126 are flown to catch three 88s (*II / KG77*) wanting Hal Far. Several *Spits* hit two on left which both go down. One credited to Basil/Guthrie (185) and Tiddy/Park (126). Second to Jones, Thompson, Thomas, Farquharson, Jerry Smith of 126. Smith hit—to force land yet once more on his return. Rod Smith, the one exception to the ganging up, takes on the far right aircraft, gives a 12 second burst 250 to 150. An engine flames, then all the rest, until engines fall out and wings fall off. After this prize, RS. would always seek to hunt the furthest planes, often unvictimized. This time, another *Ju* was struck by Lovell, Mejor (1435), Stainforth (89 C.O.), of Schneider Trophy fame, who'd joined just for the ride. This his first combat at 43! Bauer, a baby P.O.W., complains he's ever on the outside flank and thus the first to be attacked and
> shot at!

That day, a group of *Beaufighters & Beauforts* attack Italian shipping off Southern Greece. A *Beaufort* forced to ditch. Men: Strever (SAAF), Dunsmore, Brown, Wilkinson, get into dinghy. Italian floatplane picks them up: wine, brandy, cigarettes as they are whisked to Greece. Here given clothes, huge plates of macaroni, steaks, brandy, smokes. Ping pong in mess, rest & pen home to folks. Next day, another *Cant Z506B* is due to take them to Taranto. Mastrodicasa, pilot; Chifari, 2nd. pilot; two others—plus one guard Taranto-bound. Italians due to start their furlough there. British unhandcuffed so not to put their lives in peril if the *Cant* attacked. On cue, after 45 mins., Wilkinson shouts *"Spitfire!"* points out the window. Guard's pistol grabbed and thrown to Strever. Pilots and crew tied up with their own belts. Rough map brings plane to toe of Italy and course is set for Malta. Waggle their wings to a *JU52* snailing by, get back same greeting. Free up Italians. Mastrodicasa, guessing at terminus, swears they'll not manage because of *Spits*. 603 *Spits* (four) attack indeed but *Cant* lands safely with a scratch or two. All nine perched on the wing enjoying wine & brandy brought for furlough when launch arrives half an hour later. Italians jailed for generosity, British bemedalled.

> July 29th. Beurling suffers a canopy shot-off, attacks a *109* (Witschke of *1/ JG77* in "Yellow 2") and sends it to the sea. In its new colors, the *Cant's* a Malta rescue craft. Smith, Jerrold Alpine, missed August 10th '42 chasing an *88*. Helmut Streubel's plane of *9 / KG77* does not reach Sicily. It may have stricken Jerry, or else a *109*. The sea

was searched in vain—by Rod and others. Rod D.F.C. October. On 10/14, Beurling, hit in right hand, left arm, left leg, helping Willie the Kid tidy his tail, for once forgets own tail. "Spang in the middle" of a German skyfull and now "my motive power's gone!" Holes. Controls shot out. The throttle jammed. Full power spin. Resigned to die but climbs onto port wing at about 2,000. Tries to bale out inside of spin, slips off at 1,000. Ripcord: 500. Homed out of Malta last day October on the ill-fated *Liberator* flight to Gib. Bad crash. 15 dead/missing: including Hether, also Willie the Kid. Beurling gets
out.

October '42: El Alamein. The last air spats fought in October. November convoy raises the siege of Malta. That very month: allied invasion of French North Africa. May '43: *Afrika Korps* capitulates; Malta bars way to their evacuation. July '43: invasion force proceeds to Sicily. Sept.9: Italian Fleet gives up under the very guns of Malta. A Virgin Mary Feast Day (as one day, August '42, had been when *Brisbane Star*—and the half-sunk *U.S. Ohio*, strapped between two destroyers, had made it in two weeks before an "unavoidable surrender.") *"Il Convoy fa' Sta. Marija."* Add day of Turkey's rout in the first siege of Malta.

...... —a few minutes before 4 o'clock— the morning two shocks of an Earthquake very strong for Malta ...... 11 July, from near 10 to past 11 in the evening saw the moon full or very near it, ... of the strangest

*appearance the Stars were bright in the
Sky, the air even cold, the milky way very
full, yet the moon like a new-moon with the
old moon in her lap* . . . . . .
*When it first struck my notice, the moon was
all like a round of silver completely lost
in egg-tarnish or sulphuretted hydrogen gas-
After some time the Seaward Edge was
brightened as by laborious Scouring till it
became a crescent as before described* . . . . . .
Most ridiculous! it was a grand Eclipse; . . . . . .
*I am not sorry it's a good instance how a
tolerably observing man would describe a
total Eclipse of the moon, who had no idea
         of an Eclipse in Mind.*

Beurling goes on to Western Front, cannot adapt; fails in civilian life, unable still, dies Rome, co-pilot too, ferrying plane (suspected sabotage) making to fight for Israel in '48. At end of '90, Rod, who'd also finished on the Western Front and shared in downing an *Me262*, answers a phone, finds himself speaking to one Heuser, his victim's navigator on July 24th. As P.O.W., he'd gone to England, on to Canada. Rod told of an ex-friend born in Heuser's town: turns out she'd gone to school with Heuser's wife. Few months later, Heuser dies suddenly. *His* wife asks Rod to visit all the same. He does so, w.
          his sister Wendy and they enjoy the trip.

Make no mistake—this craft of narrative, the task of linking, splicing, bridging & relating one to another thing: in *war*, the link is plane to plane, bullet to bullet; survival if at all—on the rim of chaos. "Did I kill him? Did he survive? Who could he be? Still think of him all our years after"—and maybe take him to the cemetery.

Twins underground? Attempts to meet, sometimes with fair success: "It's a small world!" The joy of finding an erstwhile opponent: incomprehensible to those who were not there. Or else: "Did he kill me? Did I die then? And how? And when? That too is possible." Pure plane doing its work of murder. Innocent pilot, doing his work of murder (whatever ideology he happens to be serving? We can never be sure . . . *Luftwaffe* said to be the most politicized): but brothers in the craft, most certainly. Few clearer ways to die—perhaps that end much envied? Up there, relationship is all; the human bond & comradeship of work deeply abstracted. These children murdering each other, a purge of rival innocents? Cause and effect stretching way back in time, propelling them, no hatred in the heart for the most part, up into sky toward each other. Most different on the ground! Moment a foot hits ground, it bares responsibility. We die the moment we are born, except perhaps in air. Up there, the body fades and when it breaks it falls while myth holds up the spirit of the dare, accomplishment, a model of the done. Sweet metaphor of flight—as vain as that which sings it, but without which we perish a fiercer end than death,
             all hope's disaster!

Tho' It Is Also Said
Like the Gossamer Spider, we may float upon
air and seem to fly mid heaven,
but we have spun the slender Thread
out of our own fancies
and it is always fastened
      to something below.—

The Sea stretched out in a long width before me,
   almost a whole turn of the Head
Horizon dusky crimson,
   of the same height & degree of color

     along its whole extent—
the half of the Sea nearest it was smooth,
   the hither half gently ruffled,
. . . . . . with curves and semicircles of smooth water—

. . . . . . When little more than a quarter risen,
the Ship streaked it with a transverse bar—
     but when almost full risen,
& standing on but not having yet left
     the surface of the water,
it appeared like the short, straight, stiff Stalk
   of the beautiful Water Melon of Light

   I quitted Malta on Monday 23 Sept >1805<
at 12 o'clock or past
   and arrived on Tuesday morning
tho' but for the night
     we might have been in the same day-

   (I was standing gazing at the starry Heaven,
       and said,
  I will go to bed the next star that shoots)

    As often when the Sun
   rises in sand- or brass-colored Vapor,
    we see him only by the greater Brightness
       of his Shekinah . . . . . .

5: RUSSIA

With intrusions by Count Lev Nikolayevich Tolstoy
& Danuta Czech:
*"Kalendarium wydarzen w obozie Koncentracyjnym
Auschwitz-Birkenau 1939–1945"*

"Judge for yourselves. All the children of the Party leaders were pilots. They participated in all the air parades at Tushino . . . . . . Both of Stalin's sons—Yakov and Vasily—flew professionally. Mikoyan's children flew. Frunze's children flew. The fame of pilot Chkalov eclipsed that of Alexander the Great, Napoleon and Tamerlane; it was beginning to rival the sacred reputation of the divine leader himself."

Maya Plisetskaya, Prima Ballerina Assoluta, the Bolshoi.

I: UPON THIS ROCK: LENINGRAD, 1941-1944

Thus, just as in the mechanism of clocks,
so in the mechanism of military machines,
	the impetus once given
leads irresistibly toward final results.
But till the moment when this impulse
is transmitted to parts the action has
not yet attained, as in the clock, they
	stay quiescent, stationary.
Wheels rasp on axles, cogs grip, pulleys
whirr with the speeding of their motion,
while neighbor wheels are calm and still
as if ready to stay so for a hundreds years.
Yet the moment comes when the level catches
responding to this action, creaks,
turns and partakes of the common movement,
	the end result and aim of which
		are beyond its ken.

And then Petropolis
	"Northern Palmyra, Northern Venice,"
		known in those days
as Leningrad, City of Lenin,
	but, for this reason,
(paranoid fear of one more revolution),
poorly trusted by Stalin—
and may, when all is said and done,
		and mildly said at that,
not have been helped
	as much as possible by Moscow—
Petropolis of stone
		had then been changed to stone.

On war's first day—June 22, four one,
                Op. Barbarossa,
the day that Stalin had forbidden
                      to be set down in belief's annals—
        speed of German attack
caught Russian airmen on the ground.
              In Baltic Military District, all aircraft force
crushed in the first two to three hrs.
Rychagov, A.O.C. Baltic, called up
to Moscow, shot. Kopets, Sov. Chief,
Bomber Command, a suicide. By 13.30,
                    June Twenty-one, eight hundred planes
          lost—for ten by Nazis.
                All-Russia loss on the first day:
900 ground, 300 combat. By end of
the first week, over four thousand.
                "An aerial Pearl Harbor" *dixit* Paul
Carrell.

                Elsewhere,
      in all the Arms, commanders
shot. The bleeding a continuation
of purge before the Finnish War,
           Nineteen Three Nine, when
half Army Command,
       suspected crazily,
              had been eliminated.

At the skin factory, fat factory, smoke
factory, date 7.14.41, one of one thou-
sand eight-hundred fifty-two delicious
days in this fine world, god-loved and
god-perfected: J. A. Topf & Sons reply to
C. in C. *SS* & officers with operating data
triplicated—stating these should be posted
in places visible inside the crematorium!

Also state: In the coke-heated T-double
muffle incinerator, 10 to 35 *body* can
be incinerated in approx. 10 hrs. This
quantity can daily be incinerated with-
out a problem and without overstraining
ovens. These may be operated day and
night, if need be, since the fire clay
lasts longer at even temperature.
On 17th, *SS* Lt. Gen. Heydrich, Reinhard:
SIPO & *SD* Chief's orders to shoot
all *Russian* P.O.W. who are or may be
a danger to the Reich. Concerns all
State & Party Functionary; all Com-
missar of the Red Army; all member
of intelligentsia; all *Jew*; as well as
all the *Red* fanatical. July 18th: Some
hundreds *Russian* P.O.W. put into Block 11.
Excavate gravel pit behind the
kitchen. In a few days all shot there
with short guns (small caliber),
or smashed with shovels. They seem to
be first *Rus* at Oświęcim-Auschwitz.
     Subtraction due to death.

Eight hundred eighty days—"Nine
Hundred Days" for short—city
encircled,
   an iron strangulation,
the belly of the city circled
and the soul. Bombed, fired,
   & every perishable thing
inhaled by fire up to the point
where all things turned to stone—
     even the stone.
Leather was eaten, plaster, book-

binding paste, sweepings of every
kind, chaff, linseed oil, mice, rats,
birds, cats and dogs, favorite
cats and dogs, zoo animals
     and also humans—
by "those who walked with healthy
cheeks," kept shops of body parts
behind closed doors—the meat
   cut to two classes:
     "ancient" corpse-cuts
and "fresh" corpse-cuts
    for the discerning.
And there were the inventions:
    the earth below
Badayev storehouses, tons of molten
sugar which had been bombed into the
ground : so many rubles for a top-
ground cup, so many less for earth
      from lower down.

Anna Akhmatova, poet, divorced by a police
decree from public speaking since 1925,
asked to address the city, August '41.
9.1.41, on radio too, Dmitri Shostakovich
announces the completion of new symphony,
part two, then backs to his apartment
     for ARP duties.
  Bombings, worst of the war, Sept. 6, 8,
9, 19 & 27: twenty-three raids in all,
(counting only the big ones). Two hundred
shellings. Explosives: a cool thousand;
incendiaries fifteen. Badayev warehouses:
stench of roast meat, carbonized sugar,
oil, flour, grain, lard & butter: the city's
major stores—oil smoke signifies famine.
Later, between September & December:
twenty-four thousand shells; three thous-
and, one hundred thousand incendiaries.

Sept. 16th, One Nine Four One. Kaberov, Igor, 5th IAP, the Baltic Fleet. One of four *LaGGs* together with two *Yaks*. In cloud-blue smoke the battleship *Marat* lies in the sea canal off Strelna. There with the *Kirov, October Revolution, Maxim Gorky,* their massive fleet guns pound the approaching Germans. At strike time, left undercarriage leg falls loose and hangs below the wing. Told by radio to turn back. Tries keeping thumb on button: u/c up—then falls again when thumb gets tired. Orders ignored. K joins the scrap: ratio is one to ten. Follows a *Ju87* and, despite swinging of his aircraft, forces it down. The *109s*, attracted by the wound, are hounding Kaberov. K side-slips deep and kills his engine. A *109* falls by on fire, pursued by *LaGG no.63*, buddy of K's. Shoreguns have hit *Petropavlovsk*, *Marat* which takes a shell right through its deck.

Same day, Rudel, Hans-Ulrich, *Stuka* man, briefed on incoming bombs with special detonators for deep trans-deck explosions. Further attacks. New bombs arrive. On 23rd foul wall of flak ten miles from Kronstadt. Flying in this, time seems to stop. The ships hold fire back until the dive. Rudel goes in with his Flt. Leader Steen, angle of 70 or so degrees. Steen rushes on, dive-brakes are surely off. Now R cuts his. Steen's gunner's face frozen in horror. Rudel at 90, streaking past Steen. *Marat* up in his face. Told not to let go bombs below 3,000—but drops at some 900, pulls up sharp (a more objective source reads drop 4,000). *Marat's* foremast slips sideways to water, sinks in a huge explosion.

Then forward guntower breaks. Whole nose
of battleship with leading funnel disappears.
Over 200 sailors dead or wounded. Yet parts
of *Marat* do survive and do continue firing.
Later Steen takes Rudel's aircraft & gunner
to attack the *Kirov*. Hit at 5,000. Steers right
at cruiser with ailerons but misses into water.
His bomb hits *Kirov* seriously. Somehow
    October Revolution left as sole survivor.

       When snow began early that year,
               11.00 hrs. fourteenth October;
when ice came early to Lake Ladoga,
                   fifteenth November,
almost all fuel drained
              out of the city,
corpses began to line the streets, especially
on the approaches to the cemetaries. Apartment
blocks were like huge chests of drawers; each
you would open: there you would find a corpse—
the corpses moved from relatively warm
to colder rooms, colder to icy: it was as if
it had become important to preserve the dead
there being no more live. But the truth was
no one had strength to move them—might
harm themselves trying to do so. At Pisarevsky:
800,000 in mass graves; 300,000 at Serafimov.
Sergey Davidov, poet, at the former:
                "Here lieth half the city . . ."
    —and a frozen body
as they discovered later (Stalingrad) could not
be pierced by bullets: its value then a rampart
                 for the live sniper.

The child Savicheva (11) with her child's
                alphabetic notebook
    records the passing of a family:

"Z: Zhenia, 28 December, 12.30 hrs, 1941.
B: Babushka, 25 January, 15.00 hrs, 1942.
L: Leka, 17 March, 05.00 hrs, 1942.
D: Dedya Vasya, 13 April, 02.00 hrs., 1942;
D: Dedya Lesha, 10 May, 16.00 hrs, 1942.
M: Mama, May 13, 07.30 hrs, 1942.
S: Savichevs, all. Only Tanya remains."
     House Thirteen, Number
Two Line, Vasilievsky Island. (Tanya,
    evacuated, dies summer '43.)

  Sex disappears, menstruation stops,
breasts shrivel, faces sag, lips remain white:
lipstick and face-powder eaten as well. Birth
rate 1940: 25.1 per thousand; 1941: 18.3 per
thousand; 1942: 6.2 per thousand.

     And mind
begins to fade: among two thousand people
in palace cellars (Hermitage), some carry on
research but many die each day. The packing
cases for evacuation become their coffins
until the day the coffin maker dies (only
the Hermitage has packing cases, and there-
fore coffins).
     There'll be a concert,
eventually, (dead Philharmonic) with a septet
or so of players. And empty seats for yet another
    hundred missing now.
 "Nothing to eat here, except poetry . . ."

11.7.41: the anniversary of Revolution. *Luft-
waffe* rains down leaflets days before: "Women,
go to the baths, put on white dresses. Lie down
in coffins, prepare for death. On November 7th,
skies will blue—with the explosions of German
bombs." Small force of *Shturmoviks'* spoiling raids

October 30 and November 6. Night of November 4,
"Hindenburg" Staffel over the city: Sevastianov,
Alex, Flight Commander, 26th Fighter Regiment,
a candidate to Party membership, later an HSU,
a *Heinkel 111*. Bomber falls with a giant
bang into Tauride Gardens. Both sides down in
by parachute; the Germans nearly lynched.

                  October '41 to April '42:
          One thousand seven hundred Russian
soldiers on each day reported sick or wounded.
Dead in the streets, buried in ice & snowdrift,
courts, yards, doors, cellars of great apartment
blocks. Fires burn everywhere (one month alone
seven hundred plus) for lack of water (water
pipes ruptured) to put them out, and lack of men,
and lack of energy. And sewers frozen: in Jan.
'42, temp. clatters down to 30 below zero.
        Official totals, six hundred eighty
thousand—of which six hundred forty thousand
dead of starvation. More informed estimates: a
million of starvation, a half again from "other."
                Total ten times that of Hiroshima:
"We're all one family in here,
                          baptized by the blockade . . ."
Coldest of winters in modern times: no
single person hacks a grave here now—
        but by community the thing is done:
six hundred sixty common graves throughout
the city: in trenches twenty thousand yards
sappered with dynamite. Turpentine stench:
dead drenched in. Water's death taste:
                corpses dropped into ice holes.

      Petropolis
an *idée fixe* for Hitler: Teutonic Baltic's
glory; pride of the Hanseatic League.

    Early, he'll drive the Baltic fleet to
quit Tallin. Russia's Dunkirk: 155 mines per
mile for many miles back up to Leningrad:
losses are catastrophic in ships and men. The
fleet would have been better off sailing into
the sea—but feared the Nazi submarines. In
fact, they were a lesser menace than the mines.
Later in the blockade, Hitler demands, but does
not get, complete annihilation of the Baltic fleet.

            And then Directive 1a, 1601/41.
            "The Führer
                    has decided
            to raze the City of St. Petersburg
            from the earth's face. After defeat
    of Russia there won't be slightest need
        of any future life for this large city.
                    Blockade the city closely
            is the proposal:
by means of guns of every caliber
and ceaseless bombing from the air
                        to raze it to the ground.
Should this create a city situation
which conjures up an offer to surrender
            the offer is refused."
Later, however, the Baltic Fleet itself
from Leningrad trains its huge guns
    on German lines and
                helps to break their teeth.
Petropolis, rather than surrender,
            swears it will blow itself sky-high.
        "I went to the Front
        through the days of my childhood
        I ran to school along those streets.
    There stood the fence around our home
        and here the rustling maple:
        Going to war was like a dream

>   along familiar streets remembered
>   like a dream..."
>   Olga Berggolts, poet.

8.9.42: Throw One of Shostakovich Seventh.

Same day, escapee Budy Penal Colony, Wiese,
Frieda (8.6.42) taken, sent into Auschwitz.
Search operation off. 1069 *Judaic* with 16th
transport, from Pithiviers, Beaune–La Rolande,
in *douce France*, adults & children. 794 into
the gas chambers. Subtraction due to death.
Male: 57720–57782; Female: 15961–16171
                        admitted into camp.

14th July, One Nine Four Three. Only the day
six hundred eighty third of the Blockade. Kursk
in full progress: almost over. 7.24.43: heaviest
bombing of Leningrad in the whole war.
                        That is one take
on what the city suffered. The final Liberation
not till Month One Nineteen Four Four—and then
political obliteration of the whole story.

> *How beautiful the sky looked,*
> *how blue, how calm, how deep!*
> *How brilliant and triumphant that setting sun!*
> *How sweetly shimmering the waters of the distant*
> *river! And finer still far, far blue mountains*
> *beyond the river, mysterious ravines,*
> *pine forests wreathed up to their tops*
> *in mist... there all was peaceful, happy...*
>   *I could wish nothing, nothing...*
>   *if only I were there...*

II: *TARAN AND SUCH*

              ... but if it's that I want—
glory and fame through men and love from them,
I can't be blamed for wanting that, for wanting
nothing ... if not that ... cannot be blamed alive
for that alone. Yes, and for that alone! Never
tell anyone, but, God, what can I do if I care
nought—but for the glory and men's love?
    And dear and precious as many are to me—
why I would sacrifice them all,
        dreadful, unnatural as that may seem,
for a moment's glory, of triumph over men,
                for love of men I do not know,
shall never know,
                 for the love of these men here.

    [From the Records of the *V.V.S.* for just one month out of this war]: 7.6.43: Gorovets, Alexei, Lieutenant, Flight Deputy Commander, 88th Guards, Second Air Army, Communist, flying Yak-9, Voronezh Front, returning from an op.: solo attacks a bunch of twenty *Stukas* and brings down nine: *tarans* the last and dies. Posthumous HSU. This month, the spike of *taran* combat hits the ceiling. From July 5th to the 13th thirteen times *taran*—plus many more before Kursk's over. Fifth: Gusarov, Nikolai, Captain, 486th Fighter Regt., 16th Air Army, Communist, brings down two fighters, one of them rammed. Same day: Polyakov, Vitaly, Junior Lieutenant, 54th Guards, same Army, *Komsomol, tarans* a bomber and lands by parachute. Again, Sidorov, Ivan, Capt., 92nd, Communist, downs bomber and two fighters, ramming a third. Clothing and parachute catch fire and end him. Seventh June: Gorovets (see above). Same day: Flight Comdr. Kuptev, 30th Guards, still 16th Army, brings down a *Focke-Wulf 190* in a nose attack and lands his aircraft. Again: Polyansky, Rostislav, Flight Cmdr., 581st, of the 10th Army, Communist: also a *Focke-Wulf* and parachutes to safety. Again: Sevrikov, Vladimir, Sergeant-Pilot, 581st, Communist, in the same action destroys another *Focke-Wulf*. 7.7.43: Vizhunov, Mikhail, Senior Lieutenant, Squadron Cmdr.: 517th, 16th Air Army, Communist, *tarans*, dies. Again: Dierdik, Aleksandr, Junior Lieut., 438th, 2nd Air Army, near Prokhorovka, flying *Yak-1*, bags couple *Stukas* and rams a fighter and does not make it down. Next day, the 8th: Kolbassa, Vasily, Junior Lieutenant, 176th, 16th Air Army, brings down a bomber, dies. Ninth: Kubyshkin, Mikhail, Junior Lieutenant, 193rd, 2nd Air Army, *Komsomol*, Voronezh Front, while saving his Commander, *tarans*, explodes, parachutes out. On 12th: Alekseef, Nikolai, Junior Lieut., 64th Guards, First Aviation Corps, *Stavka* Reserve, Communist: breaks up two planes, runs out of ammunition, rams a third and dies. 13th: Samonov, Aleksandr, 171st, saving his leader Vichnyakova, rams a fighter and comes down safely. Greatest exponent: Kovzan, Boris Ivanovich, survives four *tarans*: '41, '42, '43. Left eye destroyed during his fourth, yet goes on fighting, adding some ten more to his victories. Total of *tarans* for the whole war in Soviet records: six hundred thirty five. Two hundred thirty three of these reported landing in their planes; one hundred seven seven come down by 'chute. The rest are killed or missing.

III: THE WHITE RED ROSE
OF STALINGRAD, 1941–43

> *She had one thought alone:*
> *can it be really possible*
> *that not one of those men will notice me—*
> *those men who either do not see me,*
>
>   *or, if they do,*
> *look like they're saying "she's not the one,*
> *no, she is not the one—so it's no use*
>
>   *looking at her!"*
> *No, it can't be, she thought,*
> *they must know how I long to dance*
>   *how splendidly I dance,*
> *how much they would enjoy dancing with me!*

Raskova, Marina, Major, H.S.U., non-stop
Moscow to Komsomolsk–Amur *"Rodina"*
flight, 6,000 km., One Nine Three Eight, the
navigator. "Idol of Soviet Youth." In 10.41,
summons all women flyer persons;
      selects 2,000 for interview.

Three Regiments of women formed: 586th
Fighter; 587th Bomber (on *Petliakov Pe-
2*s); 588th Night Bomber (on *Polikarpov
Po-2*s). The whole is 122 Aviation Group.
Treated as any regiment, until '43 no special uniforms. Training begins at Engels on
the Volga 10.15.41. Three years of flight
experience crammed into some few months.
Lidiya Litvyak (Lilya for short), born 1921,
father a railway worker tortured and killed
Purges of Nineteen Thirties; brother name-
changed to save himself; lives Moscow city,

Nova Slobodskaya Ulitsa, Moscow—and is an early joiner. Teenage (16) instructor at an Aeroclub. (After only 4 hours of dual flying, had soloed on *Po-2*, an old pop-pop *U-2* bi-plane trainer upgrade.)

All want to fly on fighters—Lilya especially. Distinguished for outwitting her instructor in a mock dog-fight, performs the first of her resplendent victory rolls. 5.18.42: the 586th sent to the front at Saratov on new *Yakovlev Yak-1*s, a quantum leap in speed and strength. L distinguished here for working all one night to transfer boot-lining furs to flight-suit collar. Told by Raskova to put it back again. Noted for splendid flying. 9.42: sent out to a variety of *macho* groups, last being 296 at Stalingrad. C.O. N.I. Baranov swears he won't have *girls*! Men pilots purloin L's *"Troika"* no.3, & other insults. One pilot will not fly *"Troika 3"* after L's mechanic, Inna Pasportnikova has worked on it. (Poetic justice: he's killed soon after). Alexei Solomatin, Baranov's dearest friend & number two, a Kaluga man, takes Lilya's part and she will be his wingwoman. Tests her abruptly and finds her formidable.

Now on *Yak-9*s, faster than *1*s, swift climb at a steep angle, 37 mm. cannon and 2 machine guns with high explosive ammo., almost as good, for all in all, as the *190*. L & AS out on free hunt above their Stalingrad. Spot *He111*s below through clouds, trio of *109*s perching above them. But AS wants to catch the *Heinkels* changing route after their bombing run and off-load.

L some 600 ft. behind and right of A.
Long dive straight at lead bomber. A
fires and through; L same, zooms up,
half-rolls and back toward the Nazis.
Where's Leader? *"Troika! Behind U!
Break to Right!"* 109 after her, cork
in her slipstream. L breaks to right &
rolls over and over. Then ball of flame
behind her: Alex has killed him. Zooms
up and rejoins Leader 600 ft. from him.
Pick on a straggler on the way back &
put it down. Go home at 50 above the
runway. One left, one right, and soar
into their victory rolls. A.S., on landing,
                      prophecies an ace.

Lilya, a 5ft., fully-figured beauty,
and Alex ("Losha") very soon in love.
Sit holding hands at evening in the
women's bunker; from time to time
a walk into the freezing weather. No
"conduct unbecoming" at any time but
greatest tenderness at take off and
on landing—where A will lift L from
her cockpit like a doll & whisper to
her at face level. L bleaches hair
white with hydrogen peroxide; sews
bits of multi-painted parachute silk
into a neck-scarf, washes her hair
under *Yak* radiator with hot from it
and snow admixture. As for her No.3,
Inna adjusts the pedals each time she
flies it after another pilot. A love of
flowers known above all: always small
bouquets on her panel and photographs
of roses. Said to love red ones mostly—
yet, on her fuselage, both sides, a

white rose painted large and wee ones
for her kills along the nose. Some say
not roses but white lilies. By Xmas
'42, she has three fighters and three
transports, is known both sides from
Sov. publicity and German pilots are
heard to shout on inter-coms *"Achtung,*
               Litvyak is flying!"

In 5 '43, L's in the Donbass, going ten
months. Getting her 9th a/c, a *111*,
she is shot down with a substantial leg
wound. Losha visits in the field hospital:
a poem book; a small dagger he's carved.
He leaves. She thinks "if he turns back
at door and speaks, we shall be married
someday." Turns and says something she
cannot hear or lip-read. Sent back to
Moscow on convalescent leave and sees
Ulanova (the Bolshoi). Returns after
less than two weeks to a new airfield:
Rostov on Don. Baranov killed the day
she's back. L volunteers to bag a
troublesome and heavily protected spy
balloon; flies way behind the German
lines to come up right behind it and
is successful. She goes on fighting
with Alexei. In May '43, Losha is up
with a new young man arrival, teaching
him all the tricks. A drives the new
kid far, far down. They reach an air-
speed dangerously low. A pushes it
to tighter, tighter turns to get the
kid to lose his piss and break. A goes
into tight turn to tail his pupil; he
loses height; his wing drops as he
turns and hits the ground. General

rush. No smoke, no fire. One wing
sheered off; one crumpled. A's face
untouched but body cramped into a
fraction of its normal size. Wrapped
in his chute. L kisses him and puts
his dagger in with him. 7.18.43, the
other ace from 586, with eleven kills,
Katya Budanova, fights off a group of
Focke-Wulfs, gets two before she dies
                              in flames.

Lilya exhausts herself in flight. Tenth
kill: a German ace. Brought in, he asks
to see his captor. He will not believe it.
L. stands him up, retells the scrabble to
him in such detail he can't deny her, is
sitting down again & utterly deflated. In
three weeks following, L is downed twice,
the second time on fire. 8.1.43: L is at
Krasnyi Luch, in Donetsk Region. Three
sorties on that day and shares a *109*. Fourth
sortie, out for bombers, finds Nazis ten miles
from the front. Fails to see escort or disre-
gards them. Attacked by pair of *109*s and
turns to them—near village Marinovka. All
fade in cloud. One pilot sees no less than
eight ganged up on the White Rose. She
crashed? She brought her fighter down?
All hope she'd seen her panel flowers as
she died. Buried under her wing—by Sovs.
or Germans no one knows. A monument.
Blank space for H.S.U. C.O. had done the
papers 8.43—but medal stopped for lack of
evidence. Inna & mate find three buried a/c
with mine detector—but not Lilya's. Body
found finally fifteen years later by boys out
for a snake hole. 3km. from Dimitrovka

village. Buried in common grave 19 at D.
Memorial put up to her in Krasnyi Luch. In
May of '90, Gorbachev, Mikhail signs her
                              Hero's decree.

                    That day, 8.1.43:
"Quarantine Camp" set up Camp B-IIa at
Birkenau for new arrivals Male. (From 9.
43 to 11.44, deaths 1,902, gassed 6,717.)
Chief of police of Sosnowitz requests of
Governor of Kattowitz 690 rations for his
SS to wipe the last Silesian ghettos out.
Approx. 10,000 *Judaic* adult & infant come
from Sosnowitz & Bendin. Approx. 7,600
gassed, the others given numbers. 11 *corpse*
to the main camp morgue.
                Subtraction due to death.

          Back there at Stalingrad, Jan.'43,
Some planes of 587th Regiment delayed
to front by trouble with the engines. Stuck
at Kirzach. Raskova, then in Moscow, opts
to go collect and guide them on to Stalingrad.
Jan. 4th: from Lopatino, start for the Front
in lousy weather. R, navigator trained, had
taught herself to fly the unforgiving *Pe-2*.
R won't hack any other place but Engels
on the Volga banks. One bank right there is
50 meters higher than the other. The zero
visibility . . . Raskova's plane is lost in mist.
All three kites crash and all survive that—
except Raskova and two crew. As R flats
out, her head's split open by the gunsight.
Surgeon sews her together for her open
                              casket.

    And though, just one moment earlier
he had been galloping ahead to reach these men
                                             and cut them down,
their nearness now seemed so godawful to him
that he could not believe his eyes.
                                   Who are they? Who?
Why are they running? Is this a run to me?
Really coming at me? And why? To kill but me?
                         Me whom all love?

IV: THE KUBAN, FEB–JUN, 1943

In giving and accepting the great battle,
the commanders acted irrationally & contra
                              their best intentions.
But, later, to fit the accomplished facts,
historians advanced craftily devised proofs
of foresight and genius in the commanders—
who of all the involuntary agents of events
              are the most slavish and unwitting.
The ancients have left examples of epic poems
in which the heroes provide the whole interest
              and yet we are still unable to grasp
                        the fact that for our epoch
history of that sort is strictly meaningless.

Tide rolls on down from strangled Leningrad
and the mass captures of the Steel City
to where it turns, close to the sea, across
the Kuban Bridgehead. High Caucasus, glory of
Russian Letters, land where the "lemon blooms,"
or would bloom for them were the quote theirs,
where mountains reach their climax for this
continent, and all romance shines in black
tribal eyes. Their *South* in brief which raises
sun, light, heat, grape, rose and pomegranate
                              in their imaginations.

Mineral Kuban squeezed in between oil fields.
Very hot summer on the Kuban steppes. Wind,
troublesome wind along the rivers, rustle
of tall grass everywhere. That and the
                              music of the rivers.

The two month air war here, the most important—
for now the tide turns for the Soviet airmen.
No big deal ground-wise—but the Air Force passes
to the offensive. Fierce business. Many times:
up to a hundred clashes in a day. Germans deploy
Fourth *Flotte*—includes *Mölders, Grünhertz, Udet*,
other star units, with *109G2/G4s, FW190s* and all
the panoply of bombers; *JU87Gs*; *88Ps* as well as
HS129s. But: bilked by Med. and Home demands,
must turn to the defensive fast. Sovs, meanwhile,
keep up the constant reinforcements from beyond
the Urals—that far *Sibir* which shadows Rus into
the untamed Asia of her oldest fears. Improve 4th
Army (Air) with newer types and Lend-Lease a/c
adapted ever more to Nazi tactics—as in all Arms
of warfare at this time.

Massive defeat of Nazis at freezing Stalingrad.
Only two days after the end of Paulus, Sovs.
land by Novorossiysk, then take Myskhako
bridgehead (2.4.43). 4.17: look at Novorossiysk
itself and right extension of the Kuban Bridge.
Huge fight on 20th: a thousand German sorties
(four fifty bomber; two hundred fighter planes)
against five hundred Russian craft, many brought
from a distance. Assault stretches four days
and Nazis on the ground (17th Army) swallow
big loss. The name "Myskhako" to equal sacrifice
in Russian minds. By April 20th, Nazi advance
is stalled. Soviets harry the opposition ever back
into Crimea. On 4.21, Rykhlin, N.V. and gunner
Yefremenko, I.S., defending Novikov's Command
Post on *Il-2*, ambushed by four *Luftwaffe* men.
Ilyusha amazingly gets two. Wounded, Rykhlin
brings back his *Shturmovik*. Immediate field pro-
motions for the pair, later made H.S.U.

At the skin factory, fat factory, smoke
factory: same date, 4.5.43: one of one
thousand, & eight hundred, & five two
fine days in this perfecting world—
Irena Janosh, *Gypsy* Camp-born, Z6663.
Transport of *Gypsy* (Austria): 44 Male,
Z5957-600-0; 34 Female: Z6664-6698.
Group transport, Male: 112641-112691;
Female: 40222-40241. 10 *German* Female
in this lot transferred ex Ravensbrück for
smuggling scripts via experimental farms *SS*.
Commandant's Office receives Directive
(Branch D) to move 2 *Polish* medical
to Neuengamme Camp: Tadeusz Kowalski
(93197) & Janusz Okla (41698). Branch
D orders 10 Female prisoner personnel
from Ravensbrück to Auschwitz. *Polish*
politico Kazimierz Brenner (3551) outs
from his camp. 36 *corpse* delivered to the
main camp morgue. Dachau transfers 3
shepherd; 1 blacksmith and 1 gardener;
Gross-Rosen 3 blacksmith; 2 surveyor
to *SS* Major Caesar, Agric. Department,
                                        Auschwitz.

Mid-February '43: the 588th (46th Guards
since 1/43) sent to the Kuban for eight long
months, under Bershanskaya. Extraordinary
feats in snail-slow *Po-2*. April 22: night-long
bombing of enemy Novorossiysk, squadron
post squadron all night long. Upon return,
one a/c tries to land . . . . . . goes round again.
No one's aware the pilot's dead. The plane
has duplicate controls—the navigator Ira
Kasherina has never piloted since her club
days. But controls heavy: pilot is slumped

against them. Ira stands up, reaches for
pilot's head, gropes in her brains. Takes
hold of collar and yanks the body back,
head lolling in the slipstream. Controls
in back seat now rather more responsive.
No question of inverting aircraft to tip
the body out: this friend has to return.
So close to landing, Ira loses her grip—
hence the go-round. Eventually lands
with both her sleeves crimson and shiny
      up to the elbows.

      Same date, 4.23.43:
Male: 117884-117943; Female: 42699-42707,
(Group Transport). *Gestapo* Prague sends
117944-118289. Female: 42708-42811 (GT).
GT *Austrian Gypsy*, Male: Z7040-7096;
Fale: 7751-7799. Rosenberg, Manfred, born
Gypsy Camp gets Z7097. Franz, Bruno, idem:
Z7098. Adler, Marie, idem: Z7800. Horwath,
Hermann, idem: Z7104. Gutenberger, Ursula,
idem: Z7806. Also 34 *corpse* to the main *lager*
    morgue. Subtraction due to death.

    Meantime the German
sorties shrink, down by the 24th to some two
eighty from a twelve forty start. The Soviet bear
      begins to know his bite.

      April 27,'43:
Pilecki, Witold (alias Serafinski, Tomasz);
Redzej, Jan (Retko, Jan); Ciesielski, Edwd.
escape from bakery at 02.00 hrs while the
bread is baking. Pilecki had had himself

arrested Sept.1940, inserted into camp
to organize resistance. [. . .] Branch D in-
forms Commdt. that *SS* boss decides op.
14f-13 only applies in future to the *men-
tal ill*. Phenol injections &/or poison gas
stop for a while: even bedridden inmate
can work in bed [. . .] Labor Deployment re-
quests 30 "Bible Searcher" (Yahweh Witness)
Female from Ravensbrück to Auschwitz
where needed for the care of *SS* children.
Political Department moves out 8 prisoner to
Dachau "for a cooking course." [. . .] 3070
Judaic out of Ghetto Salonika arrive in A.
Selection: 2529 *Judaic* into the gas chambers.
180 Male: 118888-119067; Female: 43123-
43483 admitted into camp. [. . .] 1238 *Greek*
Female *Jüdinnen*, selected Doctor Clauberg,
allotted for experimental purposes. Klein,
Heinrich, *Gyp*. (Z5353) runs, retaken, 5.25
shot. *37 corpse* to main camp morgue. Sub-
traction due to death.

4.29: at Krimskaya (NW Novorossiysk)
Sov 56th launches big offensive. Among the
warm-ups, 46th "Darkness" (Guards) on *Po-2*s.
07.00 hrs.: 144 bombers; 82 ground attack; 265
fighters pound the *Fascheests*. Dmitri Glinka,
War's 7th air ace—makes a dramatic debut on
the field. Leading six fighters, attacks *Ju88*s,
downs lead a/c, and kills two more. The Glinka
Bros.: Boris, Dmitri, both teen-age miners at
coalfields Krivoy-Rog. Join aero-club. B sent
to school Odessa; D to Kacha. B instructor;
D fighter pilot. D joins the 16th Fighter Regt.
At one point, D runs into brother Boris during
Stalingrad in some backwater of the Caucasus &

the 16th "kidnaps" this brother to fight with D.
One day, the Kuban, *JG53 Udet* sets trap for D
in a group of six. Top: Berestnev and wingman.
Three thou. ft. below, D and his "shadow" Babak.
On down: Mikitiansky and his wingman. *Udet* ups
couple *109*s as decoy. On line with Sovs but much,
much lower. D sends Mikitiansky down. They get
one enemy—but do not chase the second. *Udet*
much puzzled. Germans send out two pairs against
the Soviet *paras*, frontal attack. Berestnev and
Dmitri each down one a/c. D then zooms up, sees
four attacking Berestnev. *Udet,* not then expecting
D, sheer off every which way. The final eight *Mes*,
kept hidden by the Germans in reserve for finals,
come in for kill and find an unexpected situation:
Glinka and six in tidy group and echelon formation.
Yet *Udet* scraps again, loses two more. Six Sovs vs
eighteen *Udet* of which five downed with no loss to
themselves. April 24: Dmitri's first HSU. His 2nd,
to the day, later on August 24.

Pokryshkin, Aleksandr, born Leskov Street,
Novosibirsk, Siberia. Inspired, aged 17,
like many others, by Chkalov, V., famed
intercontinental flyer. Works in a factory.
Sent to a Flight Mechanics' school. Joins
Krasnodar Avclub to train on gliders and
on parachutes. October '37: first flight in
U-2 trainer. Packed off to flying school,
Kacha, reads French World War Ace René
Fonck's *"My aviation combat."* After some
reccy. work at Rostov and a dive-bomber
squadron, joins fighters: pilots look down
on him with his mechanic's badge. Trains
with Sokolof whose fierce modes of attack
impress him. Spring '41: first victory riding

MiG-3 over Romanian Jassy. Serves in the
Kuban in 16th Guards with Cossack Dmitri
Glinka "he from Zaporozhe," G. Rechkalov
and others. He's good at propaganda: his men
put out on German frequencies "Take care!
Take care! the Ace Pokryshkin's in the air!"
Totes Gorky's "Story of the Falcon" poem
    to combat sandwiched in his map case.

That same April 29, '43, on *Kobri*, no.100,
out on patrol. Front line approach at speed
and at high altitude with undulations for
reconnaissance and slight descents for hold
on speed. During one of descents, makes out
three Sov *LaGG-3*s holding ten *109*s at bay.
A "falcon strike," *sokolnyi udar*—P's single
burst, point-blank, fires one up. Sharp pull
up to avoid collision: black out. Dzusov,
Ibrahim M., Lieut-Col., C.O. of the 16th, is
well delighted with the combat. Pokryshkin
trains Golubev, Klubov, Trofimov, Zherdev,
Chistov to "uniformity of style:" concerted
action of a set of partners throughout a
battle. Trains some, like Aleksandr Klubov
he sees as leaders. Selects his wingmen with
great care—e.g. Golubev, a Siberian. For
Soviets, he develops "roving mission" (the
German *Freijagd*)—acme of fighter pilot
enterprise: no group support; no voice of
combat master from the ground, no Russian
land is visible . . . lurking in ambush inside the
                      German holdings . . .

                Same date: 4.29.43:
Arrest-cause for *"re-education"* prisoner (female)
changed to *"politico:"* 43122. From Kattowitz:

119068-119111; 119112-22; 119123-26. From
Warsaw: Male: 119127-119526; Female: 43488-
43593. 119339 tagged to a Zygmunt Lempicki,
Prof. Dr. (*German*), Warsaw Varsity; his wife
Wanda Lempicka tagged 43530 and film director
Wanda Jakubowska gets 43513. 119527: man
from Kattowitz. Armanda Braun, *Gypsy* Camp-
born: Z7816. 18 *Corpse* to Main Camp morgue.
                    Subtraction due to death.

The flying's ceaseless: some four to seven sorties
daily; dog fights, arising out of "nothing," no rea-
son visible or planned, drawing in every plane fr.
different heights; "impenetrable" tracer; ack-ack
curtains through which all penetrate nevertheless.
April 29th to 10th of May, Soviet 4th Air Army
flies some 12,000 sorties. But Sovs fail in their
break-through to Anapa & JG52 has a great part
in this. Area slim: over four days, 4th Army con-
centrates near all their sorties on twenty miles out
of a front five times as long. May 4th, Sovs back
in Krimskaya but advances shallow. Loss on each
side may mean 10 bombers and twice as many ff.
in one day. By May 9-10, Germans take back the
air at Krimskaya. The *Luftwaffe* remains too strong.

Two weeks go by. On 5.26: Doroshenkov, A.A.,
Major, 43rd, flying *Yak-7b*, attacks JG52 right on its
fields. He comes up from the sea instead of from the
East, their dawn patrol just up, and smithereens nine
planes: a loss felt many days until new fighters in.
6.2: Sen. Lieutenant Dedov, N., counters *Luftwaffe* &
ack-ack with a defensive circle at the target from wch.
each kite of 36 can dive onto the enemy, bank out, &
back into the circle. Fighters cover the outer ring, in
opposite direction. *VVS* also tries penetration raids on

bridges, ports, water traffic, naval bases in the South Crimea. The Nazis on their part, try out new tactics. A major one: Rudel, Hans Ulrich's anti-tank *Stukas*, the *Ju87Gs*, toting their high-speed ammo (tungsten-cored) first ordered to Crimea in Spring '43 v. new Soviet tanks (T-34s) and operatic Katyusha rockets.

The "Kuban Heroes:" the Glinka Bros., Dmitri & Boris with records of ten kills in fifteen combats; the handsome Rechkalov, Grigori. A. (later HSU twice & War's fourth ranking ace, reputed to care more for his own tally than for a group's success); Semenishin, Vadim G.; Fadeyev, Vadim I.; Koval, D.I.; Lavitskyi, N.E.; Prukozchikov, A.L.; Naumchik, N.K.; Berestnev, P.M.; Fedorenko, V.I. . . . each with a decad, maybe more, in two months over Kuban. "*Kobri's*" arrival (P39, a.k.a. *Britchik*, "L'tl Shaver"): high tide for this lend-leaser, with engine back of pilot great for ground attack: far better than a *Spit* the Russians think. Soviets mimic the *Rotte* w. the *Para, Schwarm* w. the *Zveno*. Pokryshkin mainly codified all this—his war-time drawing books still visible: "Altitude / speed / maneuver / fire" his formula, evolved in parallel with other distant pilots' by this ace practician, with altitude as primal, shifting the Russian *istrys* to tiered formations & vertical maneuvers. And N. Platonov (249th Regt.) adds head-on strikes out of altitude. The threat of *taran* makes the attacker swerve away, whereat he is more open to attack. Tactical meets in scores, endless palavers, analysis and study.

"The Kuban Escalator" comes out of this: fighters deployed in altitude: each group apart by two / three thousand feet— with lower flights protruding forward = plus visibility and range of motion. Thus, more & more, the Sovs co-ordinate command posts,

fighter formations and anti-aircraft fire—pry
out the bombers; then shepherd them into the
ack-ack zones, also luring the fighters to feed
the guns. And, too, develop to the highest the
escort patterns for their own *Ilyushas*.

Deeper we delve in search of combat's causes,
  the more we might discover,
and each one cause, series of causes,
  appears to us equally valid in itself,
equally false through insignificance
  beside the magnitude of the event
and by its impotence (unless conjoined
  with all concurring causes)
    to bring the thing about.
Accordingly all of these myriad causes
joined up to bring about no more
  than merely what took place.
And so there was no single cause for war:
  it happened simply because it had to.
Millions of men, renouncing human feelings
  as well as reason,
had to move east to slay their fellows,
just as some centuries before thousands of
  men had to move west slaying their
    fellows. History, the
  occult, common, swarm life of mankind,
uses each moment of the lives of leaders
  as instrument for working its own ends.

The Kuban air war
calms down by June 7th. One month more
to the day the Russians claim an ousting of
the *Luftwaffe* and all attention swivels . . . to
focus on the North. Perhaps three thousand

Soviet aircraft lost in order to achieve this: the Soviets give few figures.

V: ZITADELLE: KURSK, JULY 1943

Though the condition and numerical strength
of the enemy army were unknown to us,
  this change had no sooner occurred
than the need for attacking made itself clear
in countless signs. And above all, in dim
awareness dawning in every soldier's mind
that the relative strengths had changed
and that advantage now settled on our side.
And all at once, as clocks begin to chime
and strike the hour
    when minute hands have gone
  through a whole cycle,
this change was seen in increased business
    among the higher spheres . . .

  Kursk, the Ukraine,
    West of Don river,
heart of a goldening bread-basket.
Hitler's prestige is down because
of Stalingrad. Kharkov recapture by
the Soviets (though lost again): no
help. *Afrika Korps* dead in Tunisia.
Hitler requires a brilliant victory:
something a little like a German
Stalingrad. After many delays, Kursk
Salient (Orel North, Belgorod South)
is picked for one last great assault—all
the more so since Russians have been
fortifying it *en masse* and thus could
be encircled. In less than ninety days,
Soviets have sent in 500,000 railway
wagons stuffed with equipment. Into
the bulge, they cram 1.3 million men;

guns/mortars: 20,000; tanks/self-prop.
guns: 3,600—and near 3,000 aircraft.
Nazis engage huge *Panzer* armies with
their new tanks, *Tigers & Panthers,* for
very little gain. On July 5th, Soviets
claim 586 tanks. Next day 433; next day
520; & next day 304. *"Tigers* are burning"
goes the refrain: carnage among both
armies scarcely seen before.

July 5,'43:
Two woman sent from Kattowitz, given
48234 & 48301. Group transport. Male:
127680-127710; Female: 48302-48320.
Theresie Steinbach, *Gypsy* Camp born,
gets Z8914. 8 *corpse* to the camp morgue.
Subtraction due to death.

German ambitions less bloat than ever
yet: but seventy per cent of *Luftwaffe*
flies over the East Front. Sixth Air
Flotte (Orel) and Fourth (Belgorod-
Kharkov) with some 1,800 kites face
Sixteenth (Front Central, Orel–Kursk);
Second (Voronezh Front near Prokho-
rovka); Fifth, Seventeenth at Steppe
and Southwest Fronts (nr. Kharkov)—
total: near on 3,000 planes and rich
back-ups. But Nazis weak: *lack*
of reserves; over-extended far too
much—trying for air-control *and*
giving *Wehrmacht* ground support.
Bugged too by partisan offensives
versus their "secret" preparations.

Inside the bulge, the Sovs well set
to strike and parry both at the
clock's say—with a fierce flow of
reinforcements back of the Urals
which would eventually drown
the Germans out. Add Novikov's
bright management of these back
troops. For the entire campaign,
with First, Fifth & Fifteenth Air
Armies held in reserve, *Stavka H.Q.*
aims to deploy some 5,400 aircraft.
Sovs also field improvements: two
seater ground-attack planes; new
cannons and new rockets; hollow-
charge anti-tank bombs; radio and
radar use toward co-ordination of
a host of units; new tactics from
the Kuban; new training for all air-
men; subtler intelligence; extended
use of air reconnaissance; sharper
detection of Nazi concentrations;
increased number of airfields (154
for Central Front alone). New planes
(e.g. *Lavochkin5FN* [later *La-7*] in
some ways better than *Fw190*)—only
in day bombers did Nazi *Luftwaffe*
hold on to any clear advantage. Night
bombing with antique *Po-2s* inflicts
much harm. Free-hunters, the *Okhotniki*,
first used at Stalingrad, are now not
only fighters, like Vorozheikin, but
also ground-attackers against the Nazi
air and ack-ack forces. One major hitch
both sides: the Kursk Anomaly (magnetic)
making a compass virtually useless. Both
sides train pilots to memorize terrain—
more than a few distressing episodes

                (though comic also) of pilots in the air,
                frantic, asking directions from the troops
                                            along the ground.

                        One step beyond that line
            which calls to mind
the boundary divides the living from the dead
and—here's uncertainty, pain, misery and death.
And what is out there? Who is out there? Beyond
that field, that tree, that roof lit by the sun?
None knows, yet longs to know; one dreads crossing
                    that line, yet longs to cross it.
You know sooner or later you'll have to cross it
and find out what there is on the other side,
just as you'll surely have to learn what lies
                                        beyond the death.
                But you are strong,
macho and vigorous, your blood is boiling and
you're ringed around by just as vigorous and
                            nervously exhilarated men.
So thinks, or feels at any rate, each man who
            comes in sight of enemies—that feeling gives
a special luster and joyous zest to everything
                        takes place at just that moment.

The start is murky. Kharkov debacle on July 5th
is not well known in Soviet sources. Sovs launch
field pre-dawn air-raid in the vicinity of Kharkov:
aiming to bristle German bombers just as they lift
for Kursk. Radar detects over 400 Soviet aircraft,
raising *JG Udet* and *JG Mölders*. Fighters above
10,000 feet; ack-ack at lower levels take a disast-
rous toll: over 120 Russians down & bombs fail to
descend onto the fascist fields. A 2nd raid on city
by the southern Armies completely fails to hamper

the first Nazi strikes. Post this, the Soviet Air boys do not do well on the first day. But by the second, July 6th, organization begins to tell. The *Luftwaffe* puts up 4,300 sorties on July 5th—but only half that number on the next. By July 9th, in the Orel sector, the *Luftwaffe* puts up only 350 sorties. By contrast Sovs had flown 7,600 by July 12th—end of defensive stage of the Kursk fighting.

On 6th July, Kozhedub, Ivan N., 16th Army, flying an *La-5*, makes his star debut on the field of Kursk with the first kill of sixty-two will bring him up to the first place in Soviet Acedom. Ukrainian, peasant-born, long time instructor, held back from all the fighting, K., on a dawn combat sortie north Kursk, begins most modestly. Starts by mislaying leader in a swoop on over 20 *Stukas* with a fighter escort. Tails one and fires away. Again. Again. K. thinks of *taran* but, finally, the target smokes. Two *109*s now nose his tail. Abrupt collapse to tree-tops height on basis of a let-me-out-of-here!—where own crowd, misreading him *190*, shoot off a wing-tip. By July 9th, he bags two *Stukas* & couple *109*s—well on the way to his own squadron.

But still no cause—winner does not take all—to lose sight of achievements much more modest. Maresyev, Alexei (feet had been crushed in a crash landing one year before: crawled nineteen days in snow feeding on ants, berries and hedgehogs to lose both legs in surgery) was back and flying Kursk on *La-5*, destroying five

out of the enemy in just two days. Later
an HSU. One day, during the build-up,
the woman pilot Tamara Pamyetnich,
Ria, bales out with bruises. Peasants
attack her, pitchfork & scythes; then see
the red stars on the aircraft and hug and kiss
her. She takes off helmet; hair cascades
down—peasants step back amazed and
                              disconcerted.

                    July 8, '43:
Judaic, 750 Male, 750 Female, rejects fr.
Majdanek, checked out for wherefores.
49 Male: significant exhaustion; severe
skin & connective tissue inflammations;
hernias. 277 to Auschwitz camp: slight
case exhaustion; 424 can go to Farben
rubber plant after four weeks of quaran-
tine. Of Female: 5 out post income; 2 show
trace gun shot wounds; 2 emphysema; 5
gangrened legs; 44 wounds on arms plus
legs; 1 flare-up of connective tissues; 80
are work disabled; all rest have scabies.
Established further that the transfer ge-
neral conditions do not permit their la-
bor to be fully used in Auschwitz Con-
centration Camp [. . .] *SS* Corporal
Josef Koch, 1st Company, *SS* Death's
Head: a commendation + three days
leave (exemplary conduct during *Gyp-
sy* flight.) 9 *corpse* delivered over to
the morgue. Subtraction due to death.

Fifth of July, day *Zitadelle* begins, *Normandie-
Niemen*, Free French Air Force, serving with

Russia at de Gaulle's insistence, given a dozen mint *Yak-9*s. C.O. Tulasne, Jean. Two squadrons: first led by Pouyade, Pierre; second by Littolf, Albert. Total: 22 pilots (with 2 in hospital and 5 still below grade in training comes out 15). July 13th: Littolf, Durand and Castelain each get a *110* while shepherding *Il-2*s. The *110*s from lot 2 / ZG1 who lose their *Kommodore* Joachim Blechschmidt, also his gunner Worl.

On the 14th, both French and Russians form a square inside a forest clearing: the *tricolore* flies on this corner of the Russian icelands "that is forever France." 14.00 hrs. Pouyade & seven *Yaks* go out for Bolchov protecting *Shturmoviks*. Four *110*s they run into are set upon and two go down. Albert, Marcel (had flown in France, escaping to Gibraltar, some 50 missions in U.K. with Free French forces before going to *Normandie*) is credited with one (later made HSU, 12/44). *NN* loses a man, de Tedesco. Again the ZG1 admits two down. At 17.50 hrs.: nine *Yaks* under Tulasne go w. the *Il-2*s on top of Kirekovo. Tulasne, Béguin attack a pair *FW190*s: no joy. Castelain fires on yet another while it is at the tail of a sister *Yak*. The plane explodes. C goes for *Ju87*s— without a wow, & lands at night on a neighbor field. Much other scrapping up to that month's 19th in course of which 19 kills recorded—but 7 pilots are broken, Tulasne included. General Zakharov critiques the corps for individualism— there are communication glitches also with the Russian ground crews. All French mechanics in the end sent back, replaced by Sovs. Because of Vichy and Free French conflicts, *Normandie* no way as well rewarded as it should have been. But fights (with growing reputation) to the end.

By 7.10th, Germans deep stalled in the north
sector. The action now is Prokhorovka, south
of Kursk. 7.12.43: the monster tank encounter
of all time involves over twelve hundred tanks—
as in a zoo mad with rhinoceros and elephants
snarling over each other, farting black oil soot,
smoke and dust into the upper skies. Burdina,
Galia now reports: thick oily smoke seeps in-
to cockpit during dog fighting. Colonel Rudel
brings in experimental *Stukas* with heavy anti-
tank potential. Inside a day, Rudel eliminates
total twelve Russian tanks. Soviets move
up ack-ack guns among first row of tanks.
Also use smoke to make the *Stukas* think
they have success but tanks truly on fire are ex-
tremely bright. Best target is the stern of tank
with engine site and thinner armor to keep the
engine cool. Sign from above when a tank's run-
ning: blue flames of exhaust.

Star of the battle and the Soviet Air Force—
tank of the air *Shturmovik Il-2M3*: created
for the object number one of Soviet flying:
support of Army on the ground. Easy build;
operation easy; maintenance easy and *most*
forgiving in unforgiving air or unforgiving
fields: "You can begin to taxi our *Ilyusha*
at fifty meters altitude" goes a pilot's joke.
Classic German description: Col. Hrabak,
Dieter, flying a *schwarm*, sets his four men
to kill an *Il-2*. All fire at point-blank range.
Hrabak, astounded at zero reaction, asks on
the radio what is going on. "You cannot bite
a porcupine, *Herr Oberst*, in the ass." Touted
Sov methods close to the deck—sometimes
as close as fifteen feet—going for infantry, mo-
torized columns, tanks, airfields and ack-ack.

The plane can "stuka" into pinpoint targets,
with *shallow* dives however, from 2,600 ft.
"Circle of Death" set up by the *peleng* forma-
tion with planes abreast in staggered line or
by approach in line astern diving sequentially
in a closed loop—with good maneuverability
within the circle against the ack-ack fire. The
bronekorpus (armored shell) gives the flight
leader a special feel of sweet invincibility
as he must incarnate disastrous walls of fire.
The *S* becomes the major Soviet power-icon
in the Great War—much as the *Spit* for Brits;
Zero for Nippon or *Mustang* for our folks.
Correctly named "sky infantry."

                        July 19, 1943:
Mieczkowki, Tadeusz, ex Zuromin, escapes
from camp. Female from Potsdam, Breslau,
Oppeln, Ravensbrück, Kattowitz coming in.
Large, 12-noose, gallows set up on square
in front of kitchen. Reprisals for the survey
camp escapes in January '43 on those too
much informed of the escape. 12 Male, all
Pole, in overalls and handcuffed, hauled up,
put into nooses while Comdt. Höss reads
sentence. He's not allowed to finish. In pro-
test, Skrzetuski, Janusz (253) kicks out the
stool on which he's standing. *SS* runs up to
the others, yanks out the stools . . . finishes off.
Subtraction due to death. 8 prisoner of Special
Squad shifted from Main to Birkenau to run 4th
Crematorium. First Crematorium
                        from now no longer used.

VI: LUFTWAFFE: OSTFRONT

At the moment the Horse Guards passed him
and disappeared into the smoke, he
was uncertain whether to gallop after them
or go where he was sent. This was
the brilliant Horse Guards charge
that had left thunderstruck even the enemy.
He was appalled to hear after the fact
that from that mass of huge & handsome men;
of all those splendid, rich young officers
and bright cadets who'd darted past
on horses worth uncounted rubles,
only eighteen in all survived
                    this far-famed charge.

At start of *Zitadelle*, a hot reshuffling among the German Squadrons. At that beginning, *Geschwaderstab* and III / *JG52* at Ugrim in Ukraine. On 7.4., I *Gruppe* raked out of Kuban and sent to Besenovka, near Belgorod. On 7.6., Rall, Gunther, C.O. of 8 / *JG52*, named *Gruppn.-Komdeur.* of III / *JG52* after Von Bonin, Hubert. (II / *JG52* stayed within Kuban, moved several days to Yepatoria in the Crimea and then back to Anapa, 7.14—not seeing Kursk *Oblast* till August 8th nearby Stalino. On August 24th, all of *JG52* at long last re-unites near Makeyevka, east of Stalino.)

The early action is mainly in the north. On July 5th, von Bonin, H. becomes

the *Kommodore* of *JG54*, succeeding
Hannes Trautloft, welder of *Grünhertz*,
named from the Green Heart badge of
his Thuringia province. *JG54* & *JG51*
(I, III & IV) assume the fighter role of
Luftflotte Six. Same day, *JG51* escort
the bombers and the *Stukas*, first meet

    Sov fighters in the afternoon.
With *190A4s* & *5*s just now provided,
JG51 grabs air superiority from Sovs
for the first few days. All *Experten* add
to their scores. At *JG54*, a record never
matched again is Gunther Scheel's, who
downs 71 planes in 70 sorties. On 17th,
though, luck runs out: rams a *Yak-9* in
Orel neighborhood, falls
        from 700ft, explodes on impact.

  JG52. On July 5th, Wiese, Johannes,
2 / *JG52*, brings down twelve Sovs near
Belgorod. (On July 10th, he scores his
magic hundredth.) On the same day, the
"Bubi," Hartmann, Erich, a very junior
pilot who will after a while become the
"top" Ace of the war, up four missions,
brings down three *Kobrys* and one *La-5*.
Same day, his friend Krupinsky, Walter,
an ace whose capability for getting into
scrapes is legendary and worries "Bubi,"
loses rudder control after some rumbles
over the 7th sqdr.'s field, ground-loops
to miss another bunch, skull breaks and:
six weeks off. Five other pilots lost on
same day: now a substantial third of the
whole squadron. On 7.7, EH breaks up
four more *La-5*s plus three fat *Ilyushins*.

8th: adds another couple pairs of *La-5*s.
At Ugrim until 7.17, gets 7 more *La-5s*,
the last his 223rd sortie & 39th destroy.
E on his way to his war's Everest: 352
victories on mission number 1405 and
combat count at 825.

At school with Rossman, Paule, Bubi
learns to avoid the dogfight. A careful
man, he does not lunge at anything in
sight as many hot shots instinctually do.
Takes stock of picture: 1] "See." Then
2] "Decide" best tactic. 3] "Attack" in
close, with previous study of vulnerable
points on each Sov type (e.g. oil cooler
on *IL-2* for which you have to climb up
underneath the plane) and break-off fast.
In case seen by the prey—then choose a
"Coffee Break:" let go and don't engage.
Such tactics studied by Pokryshkin and
most of his accomplished foes.

Clear sky: come in high/fast. With over-
cast: low/fast. After attack, roll over,
dive 2,000 ft. if space allows to come up
from behind for a second lunge. Should
this one fail to terminate, H would be up
again for a third try. On the defence, H,
above all, waits for opponent to commit
and show what he will do: fire from too
far away (a novice) or slam in very close
as he would do (an ace, maybe a Guard).
From a behind/above attack, H goes at
a hardy climbing turn into opponent fire.
From a behind/below, H moves hard left
or right, then down—again into the fire,
adds ultimate bepuzzlement: negative Gs

for the most desperate escapes. Such sets
of careful tactics earn the highest praise
                      and diamond reputation.

                A tale of Gerhard Barkhorn, 2nd
ranking ace of the whole war and Bubi's
most respected friend. GB and EH, flying
together, East Front. GB fires up the lower
section of a Soviet fighter. Flies alongside
his enemy, opens his canopy & gestures to
the Russian to bale out. Asked why GB did
not kill off the falling fighter, B said to say:
"Remember that this man was son to some
fine Russian mother. He has his right to life
and love as much as we do." GB known all
             through *Luftwaffe* as a "gentleman."

VII: SOUTH KURSK: EIGHTH SOVIET FIGHTER DIVISION

Eighth Guards Fighter Division, after the Caucasus, rested in European Russia and granted *La-5*s in March '43. Triad of regiments: 40th, 41st, and 88th. Early in April, go to Oboyan; three fields around the township, one for each regiment; H.Q. a half ruined church, village Kazatskoye, part of Second Air Army *sub* Krasovsky.

7.6.43: the 88th distinguishes itself on this 2nd day. Fights three engagements, brings down 17 kites, mauls bad one *Ju88*. Now here's the epic of Gorovets, Aleksandr, *Gv.*, Snr. Ltn., Posthumous HSU, Dpty. Sqdrn. Leader. As such, he leaves a skirmish last, covers hurt planes after his men had gotten seven enemy. G sends pair of his fighters off, follows his boys, &, over Yakovlevna, sees 9 *Stukas* below him on way to bomb Sov soldiers. None know if G orders his men to fight: maybe his radio fails; maybe too much loud noise drowns out his signal. Gorovets left fatally alone all by himself. Attacks the Germans from behind & brings down two while two others collide. Remainder, rid of bombs, circle formate to cogitate a while on this horrid disaster. Picked off by Gorovets. Leader is last & dives to try escape under the ground-smoke. G ends him almost on the deck. Now out of ammo. Set on by 4 *FW190*s. Prop stops: his engine hit. G tries a brilliant spiral. Thousand feet up, on fire, his nose dips, rams to earth. Arsenyi Vorozheikin:

>   "Undoubtedly one of the most astonishing big
>   hits of the big war."

The Nazis rest up to a point July 8 to 11.
On 12, the great tank battle, Prokhorovka.
The smell of smoke reaches to pilots up to
9,000 feet. So many fighters up in the sky,
there might be dogfights going on between
your plane and your opponent: risks of colli-
                        sion way beyond the normal.

He heard the speaker of these words
addressed as 'Sire.' But heard the words
as he might well have heard
the buzzing of a fly. Not only were they
of no interest to him; he took
no note of them and instantly forgot them.
His head was burning; he felt
that he was losing blood, and
saw above those far, eternal heavens.
He knew at sight it was the Emperor
(his hero) but, at that moment, the man
appeared to him so small and insignificant
a thing compared with what was happening
between his soul
and that infinite sky with all those
clouds sideslipping over it. Just then,
it meant no single jot to him who it might be
was standing over him—
or what they might be saying over him:
he was glad only that there were people there,
wished only they would
help him back to life—which seemed
to him so beautiful now he could
understand it differently.
He made a supreme effort to stir & utter sound.

*He feebly moved his leg, produced
a faint & sickly moan thus rousing his
own pity. 'Ah! so he is alive!' the Emperor said.
'Now pick up this young man
and carry him back gently to the*
                                      dressing stations.'

VIII: AN INTERLUDE. PERSONAL, VOROZHEIKIN, ARSENY

Vorozheikin, Arseny: Captain, 728th
Fighter Regiment, 256th Fighter Division,
5th Aviation Corps, 2nd Air Army
on 1st Ukrainian Front. 240 Missions;
over 90 Combats; 52 Victories. Twice
H.S.U: 2.4.44, 8.19.44. Later with
32nd Guards Fighter Regiment; 3rd
Guards Aviation Division; 1st Guards
Aviation Corps; 3rd Air Army on 1st
Prib. Front. [Which is why Military
    documents are full of acronyms.]

Kursk Region, July 14th, 1943, flying *Yak-7*.
There are five of us. Would we
be able to execute the mission? *Yak-7*'s
a tenacious plane. We are dead set on
inflicting damage. I look toward the Group.
We're flying wing to wing. Timonov,
edging from his own Flight Leader Sachkov,
moves up, formates on me. Experienced
wrangler Melashenko, Arjip, also moves
to me. We have a real good airspace overview,
in shape to help each other
if the need arises. Vibornov, Timonov
fly compact. I call them on the radio:
              "Break off; fly open order!"

    Approaching the front lines,
we run across six *109*s. They move aside,
gain altitude: there's little point in
mixing with them: job is to wipe out bombers,
cover our troops. Vibornov
and Timonov, sensing danger, move in close.

Below, quite suddenly, a spotter-reccy—
the *Henschel 126*. And explosion flashes
down there as well: the Germans
gun our troops. This lousy spotter bird
points out their targets. Our chief job
manifest right now is: get *that* wretched plane.
And the *109*s? And if the fats appear?
All accusations possible flash through my mind:
Shit! why did I try so hard
                    to get the rank of Captain?

                Henschel continues circling.
I order Melashenko to go for it.
He only manages to damage it a little.
Then the *109*s fall down upon us. Frontal attack!
Nothing to be afraid of. But Nazis
mostly do not like frontal attack: perhaps
they try it now to help their spotter.
We rush toward each other. It seems no go to
turn aside. And yet, let's not accept their rush.
Let's let them go for now. Let's risk
a little for a greater aim. We'll fake a weakness.
The *109*s will read us cowards, attack
as we veer off. My pilots . . . will they comply
with what I'm doing? Another brainwave of a sudden.
Is this complex maneuver really worthwhile?
What if it turned against us? No:
this is simple! Only, *must* be precise.
You can't make war without these risks! Abruptly,
we break left, at the exact, the crucial moment.
Like meteors the *109*s rush by. Now usually
we Sovs will not turn off from a frontal attack—
but here we do. The *109*s don't understand
and chase our tails, continue turning.
We shall forestall these turns, the *109*s, never
divining this, continue round: they don't yet
know the *Yak*!

And suddenly I have a *109* right up my nose!
He devils on to break away. Steeply
he rolls his plane but finds turns now impossible
and using one among their well-known tricks,
sharply he zooms upsky.
My *Yak*, named *"Prisosatsya,"* ("Sticking to it,")
follows him up. The *109*'s slim fuselage
filling my gunsight—
distinctly, yes, below the slender wings,
two cannon there: must be a *109G-2*.
My 20mm. cannon and
two large caliber machine guns
at such short range go through his armor-plating.
Tracers like flashing daggers slam into him.
He staggers,
rocks, freezes for seconds, starts to smoke
and shivers earthward.
Right under me, the Melashenko *para*.
They also turn and, from
the tangle, isolate a German. Bursts into fire
and from the wreckage flowers a parachute.
Plus, in all this, our man the Melashenko contrives
                              to get the *Henschel*!

        Now three *paras* of *Focke-Wulf 190*s,
fresh out of Kursk, come to our stage.
And, obviously, will help the *109*s.
At the same time, a worried voice calls out
"I see the bombers!"
Of course, the new guys
won't tolerate our getting near the bombers.
And we aren't able to penetrate that screen.
Impetuous combat is given up because fuel is low.
The *Stukas* go on dumping on our troops
but we must break away. We desperately fight
to break off contact with the *Focke*s.
We cannot see the *Stukas*. Where *are* the *Stukas*?

Not evident. Have they already bombed and
gotten out? We rush for home. The *Fockes*
                       fail at voiding German losses.

       Well, combat proved not bad.
But this our mission was not fulfilled:
                       we failed to stop the bombers.

Same day. Off as a group, losing
ourselves in haze, pilots squinting &
eyes screwed up. Considerable cloud
thickens. Beyond that though, great visibility.
Bombers will no doubt come
a'growling out of that and unexpected!
Attempts to get some guidance from the
ground don't work out. Smoke fouls
efficient observation of approaching planes:
we aim to skulk back of the clouds.
Ah boundless blue aflood with sunlight:
airscape at once will slide apart and
we are breathing free!

                    But what is there
below us? Spring floods across the land,
stretches of ice-free water glimpsed so fleetingly
through cloud. And thus, one question.
Can bombers suddenly sneak up below
these clouds? I leave Fl. Lt. Koslovsky, Ivan,
way inside the shining transparent ocean
and I, with four, go plunging down
from out the smoke. Get hit immediately by
ack-ack groups. One plane brought down,
hidden in turbid gloom, now leaves a trio:
Vibornov on my right, Timonov on my left.
Fly out the ack-ack zone, our birds cross
sharply to the right.

    Fronting "our" *Junkers*, some
twenty more. And further out, in distance,
still one more flight? Dark to the eyes. Smoke? . . .
or E/A suddenly in sight? Need
for a quick decision. Delay out of the question.
First group already over front.
The fighters *where*? The Fascists don't
dispatch their *Stukas* all alone!

    "*One-O-Nines* attacking!" up
at Koslovsky's altitude! I see them now!
They dart around us like fierce angry pike.
Against cloud background we see them clear,
pinning from height Koslovsky's boys. Hope
I can reach the bombers before they do:
got to make use of these advantages! "Timonov:
Beat it back to port! Vibornov: Cover us!"
ordered by radio, forgetting data
    and all consideration of Nazi fighters.

    An alarming thought cannot be
shaken off: what if the *109*s rush and outstrip us?
I pin most hope on Vibornov. He has the
power to hold them—if only a few seconds. "Sanya!
Don't stand there gaping!" my mind
shouting at him. I look out at the *109*s
and the first group of bombers. What shall it be?
Can Koslovsky get out here? *Junkers* in front
loom larger in my sights. Their Number One flies
close, wing/wing with his companions
and there are more of them and always in close order.
Formation sticks together like
one huge machine, a perfect unity. Take aim.
Feel my hands tremble. I'd like to be backed up some
to make better approach—no way, impossible!
Lose time! Aim at the engine of
the clumsy, ink-jet *Junkers*. Non-retracting

undercarriage sticking out, like a rapacious
bird's—the fairing rather like strange footwear:
no wonder we call 87s "old bast shoemakers"! Press
trigger. Hold back. He tumbles down.
One black-crossed wing, mashed,
falling past. Only have seconds to pull back
from the wreckage and soar well out of range.

    But where's Vibornov? He also
hits the "ancient shoemakers." Not witnessing
any fighter attack, he'd reckoned cover now
excessive for us and thrown himself into the scrap.
I rush once more toward the bombers:
hellish temptation those darned unfinished pests!
Then, *109* steals up to Timonov. A
sudden shatter and I drive him off . . . Right
with the same manoeuvre, T. gets *him* off
my case. Friend rescues friend! But where's Vibornov . . .
Damn it! Again where *is* the man!
He almost falls to a *109*. And where was *that*
one out of? Again, in stealth, approaching
from behind. In the same move, struck by
          Timonov, that *109* is driven off.

    Vibornov gets much lead inside them
Stukas! They lose their strong compactness.
Without the time to dive, they drop their bombs
from level flight. Three or four pairs
of *109*s attack us. Koslovsky, obviously held,
can't come to help us. The forward group of
bombers . . . already started to open wide
          their bomb bays for the dive.

    The *109*s will not allow us near
that first darned group of bombers.
Whirling around and round like dervishes,
they force us into combat.

Timonov close to me: I save him from a *109* . . .
and order him into the bombers.
A flash—he executes the order. Covering him,
I see he gets into the *Stukas* and strikes and
strikes and strikes. His victim flames. And all
the bombers begin to leave their target, still
in formation. Now I no longer have the will
to look around for T: too many *109*s are at us.
Close by me: troika of *109*s. Can't close in to
the fats. "Do not allow a single bomb to fall!"
rings in my mind—our orders from the Regiment
H.Q. But now we need to cast off from the Nazis.
        Why? They're swallowed up by cloud!

        My dear old *Yak* soars upward. A snow-white
shroud descends; coolness pours down. At once
the world proves gentle, friendly. No fire
                      and no alarm.

                Same day, July 13:
All *Jude* prisoner, excepting *Pole* & *Greek*,
to write some letters home requesting mail &
packages. And must be stated: they're well
& healthy. Return address: Birkenau Labor
Camp, Neu-Berun Post Office. Ex Kattowitz,
Male: 129745; Female: 49791–49803. From a
Group Transport: 129746–129777. Two *Gypsy*
in Group transport: Z8277–8278. Six *corpse*
into the morgue of the main camp. "Like rat they
die yet will not disappear. Like louse they live
forever in our hair." Subtraction due to death.

                One near Orel, July:
Vladimir Lavrinenkov, 9th Guards (The
"Regiment of Aces") a double HSU with

five and thirty kills. Brings down a *109*,
watches the German land, scramble out
of his cockpit, dashing for cover among
some trees and bushes. L lands & finds
his Nazi, and wrecks his neck with his
bare hands. L dashes for his plane to take
off back to battle, leaving some Russian
                infantry more than astounded.

IX: CODA

Coda: July two five. Kilometers about two five East of Orel. Scion of von Sayn-Wittgenstein, *Graf* Pyotr Khristyanovich (Ludwig Adolf), C.O. a Hussar Regt. against Napoleon at Austerlitz. Tolstoy's "brilliant defender of St. Petersburg." Made Rus & Prussian *Prinz* same time in 1834. Heinrich, *Prinz* zu Sayn-Wittgenstein, cosmopolite, seduced by Hitler Youth in childhood, *Hauptmann* and one of Germany's great nightfighters. Rumored to be in love with a Russian princess, Marie Vassiltchikov, stranded in Berlin. Passing over the front, a giant light-worm made of flashing guns, brings down a septet of Russian planes in that one night. And in the bowl of this, amid the giant nightmare shadows looming ahead or overhead, an army radio station caps the R/T frequency offering Mozart's *Kleine Nachtmusik*. The contrast is atrocious, the prince begs for a switch-off, the radio operator Herbert Kumnitz, wholely bemused, knows not if he is glad or sad he cannot. Heinrich slain over Magdeburg, 1.'44, allegedly by lucky R.A.F. *Mosquito* protecting *Lancasters*. By this time probably in sympathy with the idea of killing *"liebling"* Adolf—July twenty, One Nine Four Four. (The plot involves 100 to 200 souls. The Nazis wrack & massacre some eleven thousand—the leaders hung with piano wire from butchers' hooks—films of their agonies gloated upon by Adolf—who knows . . . perhaps to Mozart).

"Es lebe unser geheimes Deutschland!"

7.12.43:
Russians strike back against Orel—
two days after the Allies disembark
on Sicily. Evening July 13th: Hitler
halts *Kursk*—the first great Soviet
summer has begun. The salient now
a hellish desert with not a tree or
bush left standing. Perhaps 150,000
half-buried corpses set up a stench
nosed many miles beyond the area.
Wrecks of some six thousand tanks,
three thousand planes, ten thousand
motor vehicles, two thousand guns
create the mightiest scrap-dealer's
dream in all war's history. The first
of some three hundred salvoes fired
from Moscow Center honors the men
& cities: Orel, Belgorod. Orel retaken
7.19. By August 8th, the sector's clear:
no alien bodies. By August 3rd, attacks
will move against the Kharkov sector
via Belgorod. Late August drive toward
the Dnieper River. Last month of year:
Kiev liberated; Nazis sealed off in the
Crimea; in the late apple season here at
Kursk, Soviets restore control over three
hundred eighty six thousand sq. miles of
Russian territory.

Opening his eyes, he hoped to witness
how the struggle ended between the
enemy and the gunner soldier. But
he saw nothing. Above him there was
nothing but the sky, the lofty sky,
not clear, and yet immeasurably high,
with grey cloud drifting slowly over
it. 'How quiet, solemn and serene,

not as it was at all when I was running, shouting, fighting—not as the gunner and the other with their fierce, distraught, infuriated faces fighting over the rod . . . these clouds how differently they float on high, infinite heaven: how come I never saw this sky before? How happy now to have discovered it at last! Yes! all is empty, vain, all's vanity, delusion, but not those distant, interminable skies. Nothing but that. And even that does not exist: nothing but stillness, naught but peace.
    Thank God. Thank God . . ."

  The Russians evidently won this war. With millions upon millions decimated. However, war pop. of Gulag Archipelago, the penal colonies for politicos *et al*, gigantic landmass—with Kolyma alone four times the size of France—some 20 million souls worked to the bone, tortured or executed. One price among the many paid by the Russian nation for its
         own triumph.

6. RETURN TO EUROPE:

BOMBERS & FRIENDS

1944: There had been from June 1942 on down, the immense build-up of the USAF in Europe: 8th, 9th & 15th AFs. The German *Luftwaffe* is low on fuel, parts, a/c and men—shorter and shorter. Galland thinks up a mass of trickery: *"Sturmjäger"* groups with massive armoring on *FW190s*; *Ju88s* fitted with rockets thrown at the U.S. bombers; *"Mistels:" Ju88s* loaded with high explosives, mounted by *109s* & thrown as well; fighters with bombs attached to long steel cables, blown off by activators in the drag-plane's cockpit; night fighters used by day, especially the *"Wilde Sau"* units. Even thinks up sending some captured U.S. ships among the genuine ones to do their damage.

"Big Week" the cap for Doolittle, C.O. the 8th AF in Britain and the 15th in Italy. Aware that the D-day fate depends on weakening the German fighter forces, their factories. Major series of raids: precision bombing as much as weather will allow, and with escort protection maximal. Waiting for cloud break On 2.19.44, a wide high pressure area makes for the air space of the *Reich* and prophecies clear skies. The 8th has some one thousand thirty a/c on the books: big buggers these: the *Forts* and *Libs*. With them, of fighters, some ninety-four *P38s*, seventy-three *P51s* and six six eight fat *Thunderbolt P47s+*. In Italy, 15th AF has smaller forces. Germans marshal one thousand interceptors in *Reich* and Italy. The R.A.F. had gone against the Junkers factory at Leipzig on the night before: the Brits bomb nightly, the Yanks by day.

2.20.44: four seventeen *B17*s, two seven two
*B24*s follow the R.A.F. route in a long single
strand with all available long-range ff. Twenty-
eight *Liberators*, one seventeen fat *Fortresses*
have to abort to base for a variety of reasons.
So five four four set out. First Div. *B17*s,
white triangles on tail, sends three two zero
versus the plants for *109*s and *88*s at Leipzig,
Abtnaundorf and Hesterblink, Bernberg and
Oschersleben (*190* plants) with some thirteen
*B24*s. Second Division (white circles) move
two five one *Lib*s to Gotha, Brunswick (*110*s)
and Helmsted areas plus hits on opportunities.
The Third Division (white squares) fly, minus
escort, on a North diversion: Tutow (*190*s) and
Rostock (*111*s) with three one nine *B17*s. The
Luftwaffe picks concentration on the unescorted,
taking down six, so main group lost just seven
*B17*s and eight *B24*s. The force bore two four
two a/c hurt as a whole, five of them write-offs.

Among the fighter groups, the far-famed "Wolf Pack."
Zemke, Hub, had gotten back from home detachment,
took over highest scoring bunch again, 56FG. Would
have acquired the *Mustang* had he remained, but his
replacement stuck with the *Thunderbolt*—now much
improved, including broad, paddle-shaped props raise
climb rate 650ft. a minute at low altitude. With drop
tanks, endurance pushed to just over three hours—
as long as minus combat. A major change in tactic:
from escort-&-return of bombers the priority to going
after Germans at whatever level. Except on escort,
ff. can bounce the *Luftwaffe* ff. before they attack
their bombers. Toughness of flight reforming after
break or bounce eased by return to squadron cowling
colors: 61 sqdr.: red; 62: yellow; 63: blue. As leading
fighter group in England, the 56th now has two forces:

A and B groups, squadrons flying twelve planes and not sixteen.

The Sixty First squadron meets up with bombers, flies on their left at angels twenty-two, break escort thirty miles west of Hannover. Formation of two seaters down below are bounced. Gabresky, Francis, a major ace to be, thunders on one in the rear formation. Target blows with one wing and tail breaking apart from the dying machine going on down. Gabby continues down to the front bunch and gets another (500/50 yards) seeing the shattered pieces floating deep as if the movie's running in slow motion. Ending, the sky is full of planes on fire and parachutes. Three victories by Schreiber, Leroy. Two by Bob Johnson, Fred Christensen, Don Smith. Gabby acquires two *Me410*s "Hornissen" (Hornets), planes not unlike the *Me110* in looks. Much suffering for *III / ZG.26*. Further on down, *352FG* claims five; "Pioneer *Mustangs*" of *354FG* (9AF) break up sixteen and Donald Blakeslee's second early *Mustang* bunch, the *357FG*, attacks Max Ibel's *109*s and rules out two. Inside of this, Anderson, Bud, a triple ace in waiting, eager for wins, tries to download a *Focke-Wulf 190* by hurling to 11,,000 ft. in danger of his canopy falling apart. He finally sees reason and gives up the chase, thus choosing brilliant futures over the death warrant.

Same scale attack on 02.21 but in bad weather. Icing on wings and carburetors discountenance both sides on taking off. Same choice for both: either go down to warmer levels or continue climbing until a change of temperature and humidity—and the sun's aid—break off the problem. *Luftwaffe* fighters have it much easier than 8AF bombers with t.o. of innumerable aircraft, milling at lower levels trying to rise in spirals, with agreed on speed and intervals, to altitude of rendez-vous around their splasher beacon.

Fighters still: finding themselves at leisure before more calls to service in the R.A.F.—not very fond of it, a set of Poles had been recruited into 56FG to fill the gap left by Americans with finished tours of duty. B group56 intercept-dive a bunch of times, claim 12 to 13 kills, mostly *109s*, with two falling to the "One Man Polish Air Force," name of Mike Gladych. Pioneer *Mustangs* chalk up ten victories with two to Don MacDowell. Zemke swears to less German experts in the air (the *Luftwaffe*'s abridgement by the 8AF), too many Germans now diving off & away although the *Thunderbolts* can overtake them. Also the pilots often refuel at another base than theirs and join another unit for a second go—in that risking a loss of concerted action. Outstanding record on their side however: Major Hans Bar (*II JG 1*). Claims two B17s, one *Thunderbolt*, one *Mustang*.

02.22: Happy good-looking weather forecast on this day but not encountered. 8AF off to Schweinfurt area; 15th to Regensburg. The 8th's Division Three forced to abort because of fog collisions; Division Two recalled because boxing of bombers thwarted by the Third. But not, alas, before mistaken bombing of Dutch Nijmegen by Division Two with some two hundred non-combatants killed. Weather obliges First Division breakup. Only ninety-nine heavies manage to hit primary targets; only two hundred twenty-five a/c hit anything at all. Forty-one bombers lost while the 15AF from Italy pays with fourteen.

Among the fighters, Jim Stewart led B group 56 on ramrod mission into West central *Reich*. By now this part of Germany has been nicknamed "Happy Hunting Ground." Total of 15 victories. Gabresky led A group, happy at gaining a *190* near Arnhem and, homing, tried his hand at strafing a new field sporting a sitting *Dornier*. Best of all, no doubt, the 61*FG* becomes the first in Europe to reach the 100th bull's-eye.

On 02.23 bad weather slices "Big Week" down: five days to four. 02.24: both 8AF and 15th up & doing. But 8th's *Libs* fly into a miserable fortune: (Second Wing, 389th Bomber Group). Leader a/c's man loses his oxygen, creeps his ship off course; bombardier also, collapses on his bombsight, and accidentally trips its release. Bombs fall wild, also the other aircraft (389*BG*) follow the leader pilot. Some sixty bombers plus are lost in all. In this the final blow on 02.24, total (8 & 15) some thirteen hundred bombers "befriended" by one thousand ff. take off for Regensburg, Augsburg, Stuttgart and Fürth. The famous episode of the "mad bomber," who had been killing with friendly fire, discovered and pinned down in a *B17* of Third Division, 95th *BG*. The man in a ball-turret slung underneath the a/c in the most dangerous position: a courageous flyer stressed out who goes insane in combat. Pilot finds out by noise of shooting when there's no danger near, the gunner taking friendly bombers for enemies. No one can haul the man out of his turret: he keeps it spinning at high speed and there's no way to interrupt the flow of juice—the electricity the plane depends on. Plane taken out of stream, attacked by two *190*s. Pilot orders a bailout while gunner hits an attacker and makes him crash into a compere. The crew is now able to drop & end as P.O.Ws. Pilot tries to get gunner to depart, but realizing he is the mystery that all are looking for, he will not jump. Pilot bails out, is rescued from the Channel.

This day, Agroup gathers five victories, Bgroup snatches three. One flyer loses his plane and life, proving how bad and dangerous strafing can be. Zemke is leading 56FG supporting bombers toward Schweinfurt, when the lead *B17* under attack calls out for help. Hub rushes on and finds four *FW190s* down below—in line and flying wide. Roll over, dive. Hub sees a German wingman much to the rear of target, discovers cannon shells exploding round his mount. Hub's wingman disposes of this guy. H continues on but finds his gunsight out of use and has to switch to an old-fashioned post and ring back-up. Round & down they go till close to treetop finally but H is minus a single hit: let's live to fight another day. At home, cannon shell holes are found in flaps and elevator. Gabby: a hole like that in one more wing as well and you'd have never homed!

In those five days, the 8AF performs three thousand three hundred sorties, dropping six thousand tons. Some sixty to seventy per cent of Nazi a/c plants destroyed or hurt, also the vital ball-bearing enterprise. Dispersion of the factories had begun however so that the German industry was back on soon. But Doolittle had proved superiority which then held up until invasion day. In all he'd sent out nearly 4,000 heavies against its factories and depots. The total loss, some 6% of force. But this translates to some twenty-six hundred men killed, missing, maimed, hurt bad. Men wiped out far too often, on over-drive—from sleep-lack, pill-pops, weather fuck-ups, and accidents in mists before they even start, *(vide* the big fiasco, Feb.22nd: two out of three divisions must abort) sent out over five days on the most massive show-biz operation of the war.

Bomber or fighter pilot: which is the happier? In the lay mind's eye, the bomber's paralyzed, ploughing his ship through thick and thin, almost incapable of deviating while enemies come fast, incessantly, sometimes averted by his crew and sometimes not. Many a case of craziness and nervous breakdown in mid-air has to be parried by the crewmen—until decision's reached among the medics not to send out again men who had behaved insane prior to treatment. Except on escort, and even then, the sense is that the fighter moves, maneuvers, changes positions, he being his own armorer (unlike the bomber who needs a bombardier—is but a taxi driver without the bombardier).

Dealing with sanity alone, how can it sound—in a couple of famous stories? Try: Lawley, William R., (Lieutenant), Alabama-raised: 305th Bomber Group atop day one, Feb. Twenty, Nineteen Forty Four. Coming off target on *B17* with his load still on board (all the racks frozen), set on by twenty fighters, shot out of his formation, his aircraft severely riddled. Co-pilot killed by 20 mm; + seven crew hit badly. Lawley himself painfully slashed about the face. One engine is on fire. Controls are shot away. L moves his buddy's body with his right hand, brings bomber out of a steep dive with the left hand only. Blood over windshield and the instruments: vision impossible. "Bail out!" shouts Lawley. But two of crew so badly hurt: bail out's not possible for them. The fire is spreading, with danger of explosion. Lawley decides to stay with ship, gives others option. Zero takers. Fighters come in again. Bye! Engine on fire again: put out by skillful flying. Lawley collapses. Revived by bombardier, Mason, Harry J., First Lieutenant, who'd freed the racks and let go of the load. Over England, one engine loses fuel, has to be feathered. Another one begins to burn, continues burning—until a crash-land on Redfield's little fighter drome. Lawley's Medal of Honor.

Now story two: *B17* named *"Mizpah,"* 351st Bomber Group in a lead wave for Leipzig. Shell kills co-pilot, gravely wounding main pilot. Plane's cavorting crazy in a Nazi propwash, then slides down five full miles in empty air. Bombardier jumps while others hesitate. Matthies, Archy, Staff-Sergeant turret-gunner and the engineer (coal miner once in Pennsylvania), with navigator Truemper, Walter (2nd Lt.), take turns at flying, crouched between pilot seats, with ailerons and elevator only & *very* limited flying experience. Matthies does most of flying: often so numb with cold, he has to be relieved. Ferocious cold up there not mentioned here as yet. Have to radio tower re stupid little problem: the question how to land. C.O. takes off to try radio advice: radio won't work and wounded a/c's erratic course will not allow for visuals. C.O. orders the a/c to head for coast & then let go. Pilot, M says, is still alive. Matthies & Truemper go on for land. First pass too high. Second as well. Third time, which has to be the time—M is exhausted. The a/c stalls, M & T killed. Pilot is rescued, dies a trifle later. Medals of Honor for M and T—the only 8th AF date on which this big one's laid on more than one man flying out of Britain. Another version has it that C.O. tower-talks and manages orders to take ship higher. Five parachutes fall out while plane is muddling over Polebrook. The boss orders the pair to bail out—they refuse. Reaching that point, C.O. goes up but wind increases and it's too dangerous. C.O. flies down to talk again from tower. After the second pass, M: "I'm too tired, cannot do any better." Line-up is v. erratic. Because high speed, he bounces back to air, wing drops, then one colossal cartwheel and a mass of flames. Even today, see, narrations do not jell into a final version: confusion lasts as in those days of myth.

As down upon a shore of echoing surf
big waves may run under a freshening wind,
looming first on the open sea, and riding
shoreward to fall on sand in foam and roar,
around all promontaries crested surges
making a living spume inshore—so now
formations of the allies *rose and moved*
     relentlessly to combat . . .

June 6th, 1944.
Doolittle, Jim, C.O. the "Mighty Eighth."
Up before dawn on *Lightning* over the D-Day beaches. No opposition. On the way home, spies cloud-hole, takes a look down. Five thousand ships blacken the wine-dark sea, pound beaches, huge flashes breaking on the eyes, then the explosions far inland. The glare hiding the little navigation lights of other planes in the formations. A myriad ships are heading back to England, another heading out to France. J.D. takes his report to Eisenhower some hours before the boss
                hears from his own intelligence.

Gabreski, Gabby, 56th Fighter Group, is out there also around 03.30 hours. And Gladych, Bolesław Michal, a legendary Pole, detached to 56th, gets him a *109* near Croisy. Rankin, Schilling, Lanowski, Christensen . . . all aces, flying among *famosos* on this day. Zemke, Hub, 56th C.O. stays home: commanders not allowed to fly in early sorties: they know too much. Gets out on seventh sortie of this day and downs a *Focke-Wulf* without a shot: his man tightens his turn, loses control and spins into the ground. Also a mercy: one German baling, with clothes and hair on fire, with no way clear to reach the ground, is pacified by Zemke. Donald Blakeslee, 4th *FG*'s C.O. from Debden: Rouen evening patrol, sees fifteen *109s*, mixed in with *190s*, bring down some seven *Mustangs* quick succession. Whereas, luck of the draw, our Mistress Fortune, the 355th meets up with *Stukas:* they swear they down 15. Among the aces with one kill: list Minchew, Les; Bert Marshall; Bud Fortier:

their break to torch slow *Stukas* near their ground. 357th's Anderson, Bud, on *P51B*, also up there at dawn, leaves open radiator door. A black mistake, owing to darkness, costs him much anguish. Fear of the loss of coolant. Abort or not? He's flown some 50 missions and now risks this one. Long, long flight: six hours and minutes fifty-five from take off. No enemy in sight—some of Bud's colleagues get lost as far as Spain. Yeager, Chuck, Anderson's room-mate, also aloft. As well, old Eagle Squadron boys in there: Dunn, Bill of 406th *FG*, of the 9thAF there, McColpin Carroll, 404th *F.G.*, also Ninth Air Force. They'd flown from mid '41 up till this day. Gentile, Don, of *336 FS*, wld. have been with them, except he went on furlough in April '44.

As for the *Luftwaffe*, its honor is upheld by *JG26 190s*: Priller, Pips, with Wodaczyk, Heinz, (wingman), careening over Sword at 400 per hour, 50 ft. up, firing m.gs. and cannon. Barrage from every tracking gun survived, they claw for cloud and whiten. And Johnson, Johnnie, the great RAF ace is in the air as well with his Canadians: he had inherited, short while before, Beurling of Malta. His men meet with a wing of U.S. *Thunderbolt P47s*: they circle round each other warily, then break away. Patrol path lies just between our naval gunner and his target—so that J keeps his wing well sub-2,000. Space under cloud is over-saturated with every kind of aircraft—mediums and lights; the fighter-bombers; reconnaissance; the naval planes; spotters and fighter-jocks

themselves—all in great danger of head-on
collisions. After nocturnal lions roaring all
through the dark, out of the morning mist:
forty-five mile procession of towing planes
and giant gliders. Cast off and spiral down
to land their Trojan horses on French fields.
For most attackers in four patrols or so no
                                  sign of enemy.

Among those present, surely or probably—
our scope not near as well-informed as we
would wish it—Accart, Jean, 345th. French
Sqdr . . . *Groupe de Chasse Berry*, flies with
the ghost of great Mouchotte ex Shoreham.
Clostermann, Pierre, another famous French,
602nd *City of Glasgow* Sqdr. out from Ford—
(also Charney of Malta, Ken, with that 602).
And, on that day, many of France's children
                         returned with tears to her.

150 Wing's Beamont, Roland with *Tempests*,
ex Castle Camps. 198th's Belgian Lallemant,
Raymond, *Typhoons*, up from Thorney Island.
Brothers, Peter, leading the Culmhead Wing.
Zumbach, Jean, 133 Polish Wing ex Coltishall.
132nd *City of Bombay* Sqdr.'s Page, Geoffrey,
patrolling Omaha, Utah both from Gravesend.
New Zealand's Spurdle, Robert, 80th Sqdr. es-
corting gliders out from Manston. Australia's
Smith, Donald, 453rd Sqdr., R.A.A.F. Hibbert,
Walter, of 124th *Baroda* Sqdr. from Bradwell
Bay. Lindsay, Jim, 403rd *Wolf* Sqdr. R.C.A.F.
out from Tangmere &, perhaps, Jack Charles,
commanding in those parts. The very senior
Malan, "Sailor," won't miss a show, takes off
on the fourth sortie with 145th. French Wing,
                     C.O. Deere, Al, ex Selsey.

How many more were there, unknown to us,
no one, or few, can say—such was the vastness
of that battle both in its size and spirit. All men
had steeled themselves for a black killer day and
not an ounce of mayhem anywhere! Deep, angry
disappointment. On this momentous day, perhaps
the most momentous of the war, a quiet time in
the high air is had by almost all—and, once again,
the warfare on the ground is the location of . . . all
                                          of the savagery.

7: PACIFIC: SETTING SUN

*With intrusions from the ritual indigenous poetry
of Hawaii, Arnhem Land, Fiji, New Caledonia & Hokkaido*

I: LINDBERGH, PACIFIC

Seventeen years from now—this day June
7th, one nine four four, patrol over Rabaul,
New Guinea with Marine Fighter Squadron
VMF 218. Also the day the Allies, back in
France, finish their first day's fighting. Who
tells me this from my left shoulder? I have
long ceased to recognize a single voice out
                        of this choir of voices . . .

My growing opposition to a war, hearing all
I have heard, bursts into fire as I reach home
between this flight from Paris and the slow kill
of a long peace after the "war to end all wars."
This opposition to having our free country be
maelstromed into a mortal conflict not its own
earns me the hatred of the higher bigwigs. Now,
Pearl Harbor broken, I find it very hard to be
accepted in the Army and waste away my time
consulting on the ground. Vought pulls me out:
"Go look at *Corsair* ff. in the Pacific, our gull-
winged beauties, see if you can improve any
on their performance." Arrive Hawaii, 4.25.44
as a "Tech.Rep." in uniform but without rank
tabs. Midway, 04.30—first dawn patrol flying.
Boy! have the aircraft changed in all this time . . . !
Thinking of Transportation crates right now.
So much change to come: in size, in crew load,
radios and instruments, freight, passengers and
every kind of comfort: the change so magnified
since these beginnings: will I get used to it?

                    On to Palmyra, Funafuti,
       Espiritu, Guadalcanal and Bougainville. I
       visit my first battle site: seventeen hundred

Japanese dead for but a few of ours—the
body parts scattered over the whole inferno.
I'll see much more of this—the suicides and
murdered, not taken prisoner—before I'm
through. 5.21: Marine Air Group 14, Green
Island. From the next day, 5.22, until this
anniversary, up with near everyday patrols:
Rabaul, Kavieng and Emirau, Rabaul again.
After 5.22, Carleson, C.O.14, worries about
my firing guns as a civilian, informs me the
Japanese would slice my head off if I were
ever taken. One of his men: "but it would be
O.K. if L were to engage in target practice
on the way home? . . ." No fuss after this one.

5.24: I spot a man at sea, standing alone
and moving steady toward the beach. His
life is in my trigger finger: I give it back
to him, unable to do more. Native or foe
I'll never know and, for all that, I'll never
care. At least I *saw* him. The problem with
this air war is that you never prove what
you destroy below the palms: is it a foe
you've killed or someone harmless? The
trouble with *all* air war: we are too high
above responsibility, coming to grips with
our results. And this will always be, there
is no remedy. Will life grow ever more in
distance from itself: is this what my flight
prophecies? Last days of May, first days
of June, bombing of Kavieng with 115 &
                                      222, Marines.

There is the Sailing Island,
the swiftly fleeing land,
no man has seen before:

poised to begin long voyage
to the far shores' horizon,
great land of birth, of light,
great land of death, of dark,
where food & drink abound,
where souls fly in to roost,
(waters for gods to lap up
in their mouths.) The Island
like a flock of birds, dreams
flocking, wheeling around the
clouds, the fleeting shadows
floating along the land. The
Sailing Island is like a travel
bird flashing in silver flight,
now launched upon the wind.

6.9: four hour escort Rabaul with *VMF 212*. O beauty!!! Six thousand high over New Ireland we see beyond the peaks to a volcanic harbor at Rabaul. Clouds at each level everywhere. A lone squall by itself without impinging on the rest of sky—as squalls do in our Western *patria*. Palest blues, deep blues: ocean, jungle, volcano— tropic colors: indigos, emeralds and royal purples. Over all this, our *Corsairs* four, hanging like falcons along the air, move a little in their dance, the only sign of life. And yet death lies in wait below us, guns pointing upward out of all that beauty— thousands of enemy waiting to end us, us poised to pounce on them. Death, subtle snake, is all around us: we play unheeding, critters in a clearing, trapped in the unbelief
                            of our own passing.

More travel. On 6.15, arrive at Nazdab. Next day, try out the twin-boom *Lightning P38*, anxious to measure two-engined fighters against the single-engined. It's pretty and it's handsome and it's strange to sit as in a nest between two roaring beasts. At least I so imagine, never having had more than this *one* at my nose. 6.26: join up with "Satan's Angels" A.F. Fighter Group (475th) who'd reached Hollandia on 5.15 under high ranking ace C.H. MacDonald. (He, at chess, pays scant attention until the name dawns on him. A deputy: "My God! *When* did he fly to Paris? He's much too old for this!") On the next day, a 6hr.20 flight, then others also, shooting up barges. MacD flying *"Putt Putt Maru,"* a silver *Lightning*, Blue Hundred. One of the flyers, one more high ranker, T.B. McGuire, C.O. of 431st (the *"Hades"* squadron) future Medal of Honor holder, flying a silver *"Pudgy III"* Red 131.

6.30: first bombing from a *Lightning*. All the while, I'm working on persuading pilots to drive at lower r.p.ms. and higher manifolds. The aim's a radius of 700 miles, a vast improvement on the actual. And, all the while as well, a stream of messages I should not fight: civilians don't fly combat is the rule. "If the Japs get you, you'll lose your head and we will never hear the end of it!"

Apart from this, I study scuba diving and get to love the jewels of the sea and visit simple tribes to trade with them, perhaps as ancient pirates did. I fly more missions than ever are expected of the regulars for ninety hours of combat time. I'm even summoned to Australia by the Mighty One (7.10.) and wise him up to this big radius business—which spurs his interest much more than ever I had hoped.

By 7.20, back in *P-38*s again, still in MacDonald's gang and two days later I get to Biak and its coral caves. Nightmare of corrugated bodies, many skulls broken apart to excavate gold teeth, corpses thrown into craters, covered with garbage, men tied to posts with heads cut off, stench of flamed, decomposing flesh ravaged by ants: How to be proud of our lot for
all this horror?

7.27: escort bombers to Halmahera. McGuire gets an *"Oscar."* And 28th to Ceram with 433 Squadron: get one kill. I'd wondered much if that would ever happen. Starting return, we hear of enemy and struggle to define locations. At last, on Elpaputih Bay: two Japs. The air over Amahai strip puckered by AA bursts: black, heavy caliber. Lose drop tanks, switch on guns & nose down to attack. Of two, one banks in to Amahai and the AA protection. Second shoots into cloud. MacD smoking the first: he's pushed into reversing bank. Another pilot follow-fires—to no effect. The Jap fulfills his turn towards me, I start to fire—with some success. He comes straight at me. We ram toward each other at something like five hundred. Pull back. He also, with stallion-rearing sharpness. A hit? His ship's grown from a toy to lifesize-huge: I see the finning on engine's cylinders. A jolt as he's behind me. By how much did we miss? Perhaps ten feet or less. Climb steep and bank to left. No!!! Amahai AA! Reverse to right. My kill dives down, picking up speed: sea blossoming with spray—the flower of a moment. Ah! MacDonald hit a *Sonia.* After much care looking around, I rendezvous w. "Possum" flight & back to Biak. Rest. *P-38*

a famous fighting aircraft for Pacific. Strong
landing gear for jungle strips. Twin engines'
safety factor over water. Outstanding range.
Impressive fire power. Climbing spectacular
right up from brakes-off—the torque is neu-
        tralized by props counter-rotating.

> *The guardian spirit world,*
> *the Aumakua world, is a wide*
> *level world of many habitations.*
> *There are the manifold, the mul-*
> *titude of heavens, sky levels &*
> *cloud levels; higher and lower.*
> *There are the adamantine walls*
> *of the high spirit; a serpentine*
> *horizon line around the surface*
> *of the earth; there are fathom-*
> *less depths of ocean, beauty of*
> *sun, glory of stars, bright moon*
> *and other places too numerous*
> *to call: these are denominated*
> *the aumakua world. Many they*
> *are the gates of aumakua world.*
> *If any man or his descendants*
> *is parent to the spirits, then they*
> *can entertain the aumakua world.*
> *If they belong to floating cloud,*
> *then there they fly to the floating*
> *cloudland. And if to ocean depth,*
> *then there they sink to ocean depth.*
> *If to volcanic fire, then there they*
> *walk into volcanic fire. If to high*
> *spirit's walls, then they are taken*
> *to those walls. And those of them*
> *who go to cloud or heavens, have*
> *wings and rainbows at their feet*

*and they are seen flying on the
wind's wings. And those to ocean
gather in the deep purple sea of
the high spirit. But the deep dark-
ness, the everlasting darkness, the
stratum of deep cleft, stratum of
bitterness, stratum of misery, that
world has many names: the evil,
friendless, fearful world—world
without family, of dread, of pain,
of trouble, world to be patiently
endured, a tearful world, a cruel
world in which the dead are dancing
their fearsome dances among the shadows . . .*

On August 1ˢᵗ, combat again. The weather's bad except over Palau. But there are one five o enemy fighters there so caution is advised. We strafe a ship & make to strafe a second but go for couple seabirds in their stead. We get them both. Meantime, too close to strip: how many fighters up by now? We are too low and head out toward sea. *Zero* above us at six o'clock. Goes for my wingman, then for me. I cannot climb to him, wld. stall before I reached him. Bank right & let my folks cut in my direction. Push to the fire wall but he is gaining on me. Too low to dive. Can't out-turn a *Zero*. I do the best I can, hunch down, wait for the hits. Eternal clarity. But nothing. MacDonald & my wingman get him off my back & start the *Zero* down. And out of there real asap. Boss gets a *"Rufe"* and a *"Val"* also.

A few days later, told to desist from flying combat. Leaving for home in any case. We move

ahead in France while London suffers rocket Vs.
Start back on the 16th, flying over the jungle. What
will become of it after the war? Will our cuts and
gashes ever heal? Will Natives be abandoned to
their simple lives or force-fed into servitude? Will
archeologists explore the coral caves, finding the
thousands dead? Will foes go native and survive?
Surrender now we're taking prisoners again, seize
that chance? Or fight to the one conclusion, left in
the mud to rot? Again, as pilot, I bless our deaths
in air, quick, clean as knives, sheathed in by clouds
and sky. Except of course for fire . . . except for fire . . .

> "Now listen up, ye Gods of Flying-Sand,
> now hear Forehead-of-Metal speaking:
> Now listen well people of Flying-Sand:
> the sacrifice stands tip-top on the tree!
> A girl, Slag-of-Gold-Ore, atop the tree!
> Let us, the Gods of the Beginning, fly
> to that tall tree and collect our tribute!"
> Forehead-of-Metal now flies upwards,
> flies up towards a second sky, butts up
> to strike the forehead of white cloud,
> a blinding sheen upon his metal brow,
> and swoops now to the sacrificial tree.
> His rival hurls his weapon at the skull,
> the god is cut between the eye-brows,
> his brain splattered over the tree trunk,
> falls lifeless at the tribute's feet. Then
> fly the Gods of the Beginning upwards
> to the tribute tree. Then they are clean
> mown down and heaped there dead at
>   the tree's foot.

I go on testing bombs from *Corsairs* (*MAG-31.*) September 2, 1,000 lb. bomb on wrecked Taroa. September 3, three bombs striking at Wotje. This plane is now a genuine fighter-bomber. 9.20: home.

II: WIND OF THE GODS

And viewing this now—from the other side:
exactly one month later, 10.20.44, *Shimpu*—
a Divine Wind, much later baptized *Kamikaze*.
Sun's forces overwhelmed, so turn to suicide—
ultimate paradox of war: to save your country
by dying for it, but this time with no concrete
purpose: merely point of high honor now: that
the Sun's spirit, if not this incarnation, might
survive. Before that: "body-smashing;" "self-
blasting;" "flesh-ammunition": i.e some kind
of *taran*—but only personal, not systematic.
U.S. destroys half Fighter Grp. over Davao
and Cebu, Legapi, Tacloban, Manila, 9.44.
On 10.15 Admiral Arima crash dives into a
carrier. And there'd been other suicides in
                              all the services.

> *Born is rough weather,*
> *born the booming sea,*
> *the foam breaking born,*
> *the waves roaring born,*
> *born the receding waves,*
> *the rumbling sound,*
> *the soughing sound,*
> *the earthquake,*
> *born is the stormy night,*
> *the sea rises above the beach,*
> *little by little drowns the land,*
> *to the inhabited places,*
> *dead is the tide sweeping in*
> *from the earth's navel*
> *it's a warrior wave:*
> *many who came there vanished*

> *born from the night of plenty,*
> *lost in the roaring sea,*
> *lost in the passing night.*

Item: three months before official start, first *Shimpu* mission ordered, 7.8, ex Iwo Jima against the U.S.N. (its Task Force 58) which had, June onward, for something like a month, kept up the war against Ozawa's Mobile Fleet of carriers (nine altogether) with battle line support. Mission included aces Kaneyoshi Muto and Saburo Sakai of *Yokosuka kokutai* who both survived. (Sakai the hero, in 8.42, of the astounding flight, 560 miles, after a long trip to the fighting, the fight itself—all of it grueling, now all alone— with one eye blind, the other shard-full, wounds in left leg & arm, metal in back & chest, fragments of bullets in his skull, hurt plane, making it home into Rabaul.)

        The order is: avoid air combat. No way one can survive endless attrition. Dive into carriers together. Sakai is furious. This order! A samurai must be prepared to die in combat—but . . . suicide . . . another matter. Eight bombers leave, nine *Zeros*. The planes enveloped in a storm of *Hellcats* all jostling each other overmuch, too inexperienced, yet seven bombers fall. Sakai cuts through another storm, a thunderhead, sucking his flock relentlessly into the sea. No chance of reaching ships. If they *were* reached . . . no chance of doing damage

with three wrecked fighters. Sakai's in
agony. Goes back. Return interminable
back into darkness. Muto sits weeping
on the ground, agony too: he'd done
idem but lost his wingmen. Learn after-
wards one heavy bomber out of eight
    survives, lands back, South Iwo.

    The fruit a sun hanging above,
    the fruit a moon hanging above,
    the fruit a star hanging above,
    the fruit a cloud hanging above,
    the fruit a wind hanging above,
    the fruit a light hanging above,
    up, up, above the flying clouds
                and above that!
    Here here / here here / here
    hangs a great wind cloud,
    the south winds blowing,
    the wind traveling rough,
    beating the leaves of trees,
    pushing against the trunks
    making them fall to earth,
    these trunks, these branches,
    the leaves, flowers & fruit,
    till they lie bruised below.
    Trees bearing fruit above
    struck by a southern wind.
    Fall down, fall way, way
    down. Fall way, way down
                    below.

          The "Shoot," that is
the "Marianas Turkey Shoot," Eleven
June—Eight August, brought flaming

down in combat about 600 of Admiral
Ozawa's birds against a U.S. loss of 65.
Many a famous episode had featured in
this Shoot—e.g. Adm. Mitscher's turning
on the lights in total violation of security
when his planes homed in utter darkness
from the 6.20 strike against the Japanese
at the enormous range of miles 560 to
combat out and back. Many a famous ace
as well: like Vraciu, Alex & McCampbell,
David, a one time Malta man on the ship
Wasp in late One Nine Four Two—(top
Navy fighter of the war, with score of
thirty-eight and record for one sortie of
9 victories.)

10.17: U.S. invasion force appears
at mouth of Leyte Gulf. 10.18: *Sho*
operation launched by the Sun and
Philippines declared "decisive battle
theater." Enemy carriers must now
be neutralized at least one week. This
is the time that Admiral Onishi pro-
poses his solution to the problem.

On 10.24: *Shikishima* (Sun land), *Yamato*
(Old Japan), *Asahi* (Morning sun), *Yama-
zakura* (Mountain cherry blossom) planned
and now organized out of the weakness of
201 Fighter Group: 30 a/c are operational.
Various sorties—without success because
no sightings—plus ship-protecting squalls.
Ships of the Sun's three striking forces are
decimated. Within three days, from various
lots, 3 battleships, 4 a/c carriers, 9 cruisers,
10 destroyers (half plus of total vessels in
the engagement) are lost at sea. On 10.25:

reports at Cebu of the first major *Shimpu* triumph: *Shikishima*, C.O. Yukio Seki, 5 suicide, 4 escort, sink carrier "St. Lo," & hit both the escort carriers "Kalinin Bay" and "Kitkun Bay." Escort led by a great ace Hiroyoshi Nishizawa—recalled from hated training job—downing two *Hellcats* to protect his suicides. (Next day, killed in a transport a/c at northern tip Mindoro —two *Cats* from VMF-14. 12.47. Official burial, given the Zen posthumous name *Bukai-in Kōhan Gikō Kiyoshi*). *Yamato*, on that day, 10.26, hits U.S.S. Santee, & the Suwanee—but do not sink them.

What is that song? Must be Black Cockatoo. Why is it calling out, from the sacred tree with such a feeble cry? The sun is hidden: a bird saw the red sunset, the red reflections on the clouds; it saw the glare of the sun's glow; saw sinking sun, a spreading sunset. Cloud shadows falling cross it, making it cold. Grasps the tree with claws, rasping and pecking just like the magic water-stick stabs at the ground. It cocks its head from side to side, up in the leaves of the topmost branches, hearing the sea-roar. That cry? The bird looks back at us as we prod ground with a Water-Stick. It has seen clouds arising on the sea, has seen the clouds there in the Place of Stars. Giving its long-

> *drawn cry it watches as we make
> new country with the Water-Stick.
> It saw the water; heard roar of ri-
> sing tides, the spreading foam; it
> cried from the top branches. Cry-
> ing its long-drawn cry, calling the
> sacred names of the new land.*

Standard sortie is tiny and high to bilk
each interception (3 suicide, 2 escort):
more than one plane needed to waste
a carrier. Escorts protect the suicides
always with severe limitations on their
action. Escorts need to be major pilots—
their own desire to die must be inhibited.
Attack: boost speed; ready the bombs
(sometimes forgotten in the excitement);
steep dive to carrier if possible; go for a
flight deck into elevator, right through
the intercepts and the ship's own guns.
Alternative: to fly some 10 to 15 meters
above the sea, avoiding radar and visual
detection, after which climb 500 high to
dive from there. And then the "Splendid
Death" (*rippa na shi*), the "Blaze of Glory"—
& then the mopping up by our own men,
       portions of pilots littering the decks.

Never a shortage of volunteers. Morale
high. Many reports of sleeping soundly
before the missions. Not much belief in
a post-death survival—despite the gags
re meeting up at Yasukuni Shrine. No
loathing of the enemy or racial hatreds
(unlike many examples among our boys).
To die a part of duty: debt of gratitude

to emperor & parents. One maintenance
scours his a/cs' cockpits clean as jewels:
   these the coffins of his beloved pilots.

Little belief that sacrifice will help the war
—but it might have some repercussions on
the country's spirit. Indeed it may be better
for the Sun to fail—so that it may arise into
a better future. Meanwhile Japanese Spirit,
Yamato damashii, cld. overwhelm Greater
America's material force. The only ones to
feel abandoned, lost & homeless are those
forced to turn back without success. Note:
these were *not* fanatics, country-mad, but
mostly college students (humanities & law)
without great measures of military training—
(indeed the *Navy's* flyers were frequently
held back, in fact more frequently rejected
by regular non-coms who felt such godlike
hero officers, promoted automatically upon
their deaths, were privileged . . . while they
               stagnated in the ranks.)

           "You arc alrcady gods, without human
           desires . . ." "And you will never know
           whether success is ripe or not, for we
                         can never tell you . . ."

                    "If only we might fall
           like cherry blossoms in the Spring
                    so pure and radiant!"

           "Die every morning in your mind
                    and then you won't fear death"

           "May our deaths be as sudden and as clean
                    as crystal shattering"

> "I shall in quiet become nonexistent
> like a nameless star fading away at dawn"

There is even a Christian among these boys:

> "We fly now in the spirit of J. Christ, and die within that spirit . . . My only search is for an enemy on which to dive . . . I will precede you now, dear mother, in the approach to Heaven. Please pray for my admittance."

> "And let your eyes be open till the very last so that you never fail to strike your ship."

She walked for days in search of a new home, arriving Koné as the sun went down. Stood at the heading of a path. The master of that place is at his chieftain's house, sweeping the ground (according as the grasses grow——light or dark) with no secret aim in mind. He sees the woman leaning against a tree, shimmering fresh, the light declining, a sun-breeze rivering her hair, bringing the curls down on her forehead so that her busy hands work ceaselessly to liberate her eyes & the snow bracelets round those wrists exhibit firm and lovely skin. Chief anchored, speechless. "Where is one from?" man

*asks. She tells her story. He
takes her to his mother; she
lives there several days. The
tribe's brought in to build a
house, lay out some fields &
gardens. These given her, &
more. Now an adoption, then
a marriage.*

At various times, closer the end is coming,
some other toys are used: manned rockets
and torpedoes. These immolations may well
have caused in our own wits (American)—
one of a bunch of factors—the sense that no-
thing but a single huge disaster would cause
the Sun's surrender. To then go on into the
greatest suicide: our own & last penultimate.
8.6 one nine four five: Hiroshima. 8.9: . . . &
$\qquad\qquad\qquad\qquad$ Nagasaki.

*Just then, west of the land of
Chirinnai, black mists rose up.
And, before long, fell over us.
Like being thrust into a black,
somber abyss. Then, bird-like,
dreaded* kuruise, *fantasmago-
ric monster insects, we heard
flying all round and over us—
a whirring, whistling sound.
Wounds, shallow into deep,
were gouged into our bodies.
Excruciating pains shot thru
our innards. Nor could one
tell when it was daytime or
when night. Roared, raging*

*everyplace, in blackest mist.
Top of their blades, beneath
that sky, we flew around like
birds with hands, like a light
breeze atop their blades, we
fled and fluttered, triumphing
through. We reached a point
with ribs alone still clinging
to our robes. Only our spines
they had failed to reach. We
went on thus until those mists
faded into the sky. Just then,
a spirit blew her puffs of air
into our bodies. Big wounds
and small would bring their
rims together, to seem whole.
The robes we wore, after the
battle, made our prime robes
              look insignificant.*

8: SPACE LAIR, GERMANY

So there had been the last disaster:
oblivion looming for the *Luftwaffe*.
Terminal squabbles between their
Nazi brass, the generals, the flyers.
Galland's attempts to save his lot
against the Allied bombs frustrated
by Hitler's yen for ground support.
The cost of Operation *Bodenplatte*
on the West Front: four hours kill
one hundred fifty pilots including
valuable leaders—the whole Arden-
nes that winter eventually will cost
$\qquad$ some seven hundred.

And then that "Mutiny of Aces," 1.22,
against the Fat One, with Galland cast
into the cold. Lützow, Rödel, Steinhoff,
Von Meltzahn, Graf, Trautloft: ignored,
insulted. Finals:—one Hajo, Hermann's
plan to risk one catastrophic blow with
tiny assets now that was all in stock: a
Rammkomando Elbe made up mostly
of babies (as to flying)—using by now
old-fashioned fighters stripped & bare,
for a mass strike on one last occasion.
The boys are told to fire &, if no luck,
to ram or tail or wing. Told now they
have a 10% survival chance. Loss rate
of the committed (40) is "only" 33%.
This try erases nine *Flying Fortresses*.

One tale of many. Zell, Werner, an
Unteroffizier. From some 26,500 ft.
dives on the *17*s thousands of feet be-
low. Prop grinds like saw into his
tail, his plane then thrown against the
bomber. Z out of it. (At least he keeps

his wing—unlike a case where wing is
smashed, hitting waist-gun's position,
as plane then tears along the fuselage
against ball-turret's gun, to drag itself
under the bomber's wing before falling
away—no longer aircraft). *109* drops,
Zell wakes but oil covers his canopy.
Cuts the ignition but can't open cage.
A *Mustang* closes in, shatters the cage
and frees him. The *Mustang* fires at Z
while falling—the probability: to film
Herr Z, thus clinch his kill. Then *109*
collapses on a barn, killing a bunch of
ten Russian POWs. Werner survives.

    And, final symbol, we dare say,
the torching of some fifty *262*s of *JG44*
on their home ground around May 3rd
after frustrated efforts by Galland to set
    some favoring conditions for delivery.

CAL again.
Only four days after German surrender,
a rep again (United) to study Germany's
development in planes & missiles. New-
foundland, those Azores—a boring ride,
planes getting ever more like subways—
wake over St.-Michel (O Illiec!)—then,
that early dream: the dream within this
dream—Paris miraculous! Look for old
friends, buildings and people . . . the city
not too wounded, but people yes, some
broken: Carrel, Détroyat . . . Ann's St. Ex:
that one is rid now of all insinuations . . .
    about his opposition to de Gaulle.

Then, over Germany: the cities wrecked
mile after mile, the farms still up in many
cases. Our Allied troops compete in mis-
behavior: rape, theft, looting everywhere.
Is this what we amount to? We mix with
Huns, Brits, Frogs, &—most of all—
the Sovs. to seize technology, grab men
involved. Among ourselves, the service
rivalries continue, Army & Navy trying
to clap a hand on every toy. Meet with
all those, including Willi Messerschmitt
(a broken man I think but others say not
so), who could talk planes with us. Visit
a bunch of factories & airfields, hunting
machinery which may not have been fired
                              or bashed or battered.

Nordhausen. Canary-full Harz forests.
We move to the sub-terra factory via
Camp Dora. I will write one day "the
inmates told, when they walked in the
tunnels, the only way they would come
out would be as *smoke*." Mousy smell
of excrement, urine, garbage. Quarters
the likes of which one could not ever
dream: tail sections of giant rockets,
fins flying back, with sleeping shelves
built in. In/out the tunnels, we among
these people: the first to fly in space!

To Dora barracks. Men from all over
Europe. Dozens of stretchers, soiled
by blood: cadaver outlines stain them
like acid. Bodies, some now coffined,
some laid on floors like planks. Talk
of the furnaces which are too short
to take a complete body: so, cut off

arms, legs & stuff them in just so.
A skeleton occurs: a boy, of seven-
teen. Points to the furnaces. "Twen-
ty-five thou. in eighteen months . . ."
Shows us a friend: the friend is *tot*
but kid looks *tot* as well—there is no
contrast. Outside, big pit some eight
feet long and six feet wide, filled up
beyond the brim with ash and bone.
        And two more, covered over.

Mind distorted by a strange disturbance:
where've I seen such things before? The
Biak caves, of course! One day I'll write
"What German's done to Jew in Europe,
we've done to Jap in the Pacific." And
doubtless they will say of me I smothered
holocaust—elided it—by dwelling on our
own horror of Japs, our own mistreatment
of the conquered Germans. Death, death
is all around, only in sky is hope, only in
that which man has never touched, which
God forbid, he ever will. All death. Death
flowered in the cherry blossoms falling on
the ocean; death fruited in the mushroom
cloud over Hiroshima. This war, whoever
"wins," will sow the death of earth and we
will not survive unless we move to space.
Yet space was why this buried world was
planned: we'll rise out of this planet on the
                      death of millions.

        Triumph of our machines bought with
        the death of millions. I'd hoped much
        more for this frail *Spirit*. I'd dreamed
        of it flying over all earth, carrying men
        into fraternity. Alas! we used it as we

have used cars, trains, ships and all of
transportation. Well, our antique gods,
undead, need sacrifice. The butchered
victims become a smoke rising into sky
we pilots believed safe. *Luftmenschen* . . .
When all's attained in my oncoming life,
I'll try to save an earth for us terrestrials.
Aliens may vanish into smoke: we must
not have too *many* home *mit uns*. They
may bring chaos when so numerous. Let
them become extraterrestrial to resurrect
among the planets. As we must send each
communist, perverted hater of community,
to those outer Siberias they know so well.
America, our only holy land, *that* must be
preserved: I'll see to it. So done, expand
activity over the globe—save animals and
birds, the early people who have survived
with us despite our travails (those Papuan
"savages" I traded with). Now Greenland
passed . . . my Newfoundland . . . now we're
within the gates of home at last . . .

     I'll wake at Washington.

9: POSTMORTEM DEBRIEF

"For me, the experiences of the battle have paved the way toward an enquiry into the conditions which await us after physical death."

Air Chief Marshall Sir Hugh Dowding, R.A.F., 1951

"This soldier-husband," (Richard Aldington) *"magician-lover"* (D.H. Lawrence) *"theme runs through all this writing. I dream of Lord D.,"* (Lord Dowding) *"its last physical and psychic manifestation, last night. Was he an instrument or medium of the 'Secret' . . . 'the secret Christ?'"*

H.D. (Hilda Doolittle) 'Thorn Thicket,' 1960, p.36.

"Gentlemen,
If you wish to broadcast Lindbergh's Flight *as part of a historical survey, I must ask you to add a prologue and to make a few slight changes in the text . . . The title of my radio play must therefore be changed to* The Ocean Flight, *the prologue must be spoken and the name of Lindbergh expunged.*

Bertolt Brecht, *"To the South German Radio, Stuttgart",* 2 Jan., 1950
From Bertolt Brecht: *Collected Plays*: vol.3.
Edited & introduced by John Willett, Methuen, London, 1997, pp.320–321.

Beloved, here I am, white—as it were a
		ghost. I am surrounded by my friends:
we have a corner; we meet from time
		to time; live over ancient exploits. As
you expect, great crowds: we few,
		in my own prime, now legion. Here,
our Paradigmatics: the Wrights, Ader,
		Chanute, Santos-Dumont (a suicide
depressed at use of planes for war)
		& Lillienthal. The Seminals: Farman
& Blériot, Levavasseur, Vuia, Cody,
		Voisin. Our "Age of Heroes" gang:
Alcock & Brown; the 91 who flew
		Atlantic prior '27—one of my models,
Portugal's old Coutinho made it south
		over to *Sur* America before Mermoz
and all that group. Great many ladies:
		Deroche, Beese, Quimby, Dutrieux,
Coleman & Scott, Hewlett, Zvereva.
		Some rivals (now I know their graves)
Costes & Bellonte, Spinder & Kohl,
		and Nungesser and Coli, who were un-
fortunate during my days of youth off
		Newfoundland. Then Cobham and de
Havilland, and Roe, Curtiss, and Grahame-
		White, Paulhan, Chavez, Garros, Ulm,
Focker, Le Brix, Chkalov, Kingsford-
		Smith, Hughes, Chichester (I cite them
all pell-mell: elsewhere you'll check
		the dates). Again: many fair women—
Earhart, Johnson, and Markham (not
		to omit my own Anne Morrow—but
she's not here as yet). Plus Amundsen,
		Italo Balbo, Jim Doolittle, Anne's own
de Saint-Exupéry (I now know where
		he lost his *Lightning* and his life.) All
would tell story, maybe they will one

   day: I know a few who still hang on
to drafts of what they'd like to write.
   Then those who flew in all our wars:
Bishop & Richthofen, Ball & Fonck,
   Boelcke, Guynemer, Mannock & Im-
melman, Nesterov, Rickenbacker . . .
   and the innumerable of our own war—
many you've met in books of mine,
   many are featured in this dream-story.
Are we embarrassed running across
   the *60 million* dead of that last war
(I'm leaving out Korea, Nam *et al*)—
   many of whom we killed, when they
were so invisible and destitute, from
   the high air? . . . But just as we and many
Axis men became fast friends before
   we reached this place (a pilot is a pi-
lot is a pilot)—no such embarrassment.
   The color has drained out of us, with
it the passions: an only distance 'twixt
   us and you folk is that we can inhabit,
whenever we should please, all other
   minds—obsessing them as we did not
in life—the travel in and out, as if trans-
   gressing, keeps us forever entertained.
But: 60 m. *is* a figure yes—I cannot ever
   quite forget—hope, in my charitable
way, that no one else will. Specially big,
   late massacres: like Hamburg, Dresden,
Hiroshima and such (greater by far than
   Warsaw, Rotterdam, Coventry, London
or Berlin . . .) in which more than 100,000
   died every fire-storm—storms so fierce,
hell-fires (we used to hear of) could not
   have matched them. Ah, all the bombers,
ploughing their miles for mission after
   mission, far braver than we were, come

to think of it, so much like sitting targets
        compared to fighters: how many aircraft
falling . . . . . . collapsed like broken eagles,
        pieces of fractured wing and fuselage
scattered throughout the air and boys
        in fragments colliding with the wings?
Yes, "fortresses" perhaps—but not impregnable.
        Alas, another day will come
when empires send out planes empty of pilots
        and all the lore of chivalry
will disappear and change to meaningless. I
        fear then for our country left
supreme among the powers to create inferno.

        There is another corner I must visit,
        from time to time, where those dear
        tribes I tried to aid or save still meet
        in concourse. I had, like many for so
        long, become disgusted at our human
        "progress" which appeared to spoil
        the sphere, the very air we breathed,
        and taint whatever spirit we might be
        said to possess, divine . . . or human. I
        who'd loved science with fanaticism
        grew to distrust it with all my heart.
        This went not just for men, but for
        the beasts, our co-inheritors on this
        fair star—I tried to help, wherever
        some
                might tend to disappearance.

I a Romantic then, the same romance
        drove some my age to views others
would hate: need of authority, power,
        discipline, love of the nation above all,
faith in elites versus the rule of mobs,
        contempt for chaos. I still believe that

war most favored was a monstrosity
        and that the leading lands were much
corrupted by it, their leaderships in
        tatters by the end: certain it is huge
changes came around: my world has
        died, it's gone into new phases I'm
glad I do not see, though I must fear
        for children. No, never yet repented
of opinion—nor spoke against myself
        retracting and denying: I still declare
all cruelty is one and *all* were cruel
        in that history. They'll hold I was a
simpleton, a hick you may decide:
        it is a fate many of us have shared,
we of this great republic—but we
        built finest—and must believe it
or grow pale, even if that republic must one
        day also perish. You cannot be
another than you are, at least be true unto
        yourself and then t'will follow as
        the night the day—well, you must
                know that tune.

        There is a pilot I'm distressed for: Lt.
        Frankl, Will, Old Eagle & Blue Max,
        pupil of buxom Melli Beese, first of the
        German female flyers, at Johannisthal.
        Chief *Jasta* 4 in February '17. High
        flying ace. Good looking fellow too.
        And there were more, I know, there
        must have been. I hear he was extra-
        terrestrial. We could perhaps admit
        him to our corner; he and a few. As
        long as there are few, all is o.k.: I've
        always figured, it's when one club is
        swamped with them chaos ensues . . .
        (And, after all, there's one right here,

buried w. me in the same graveyard,
albeit at the far end near the church,
Kipahulu, the other side of Hana on
the Isle of Maui: a place in which to
lie dead as a bone is a real pleasure,
perhaps the loveliest in the universe.)
That crowd of dead I named—those
who had died in the great fires—be-
yond them is another cloud, made
up of smoke? a *larger* cloud, we're
told belongs to other realms. It is
the place of the extra-terrestrials.
Thousands of years they've never
been seen clear, or recognized, or
understood, or ever been accepted,
though they initiated much we call
our own. So many light years away
from us! Yet space is being won I
hear: maybe that story will also be
recounted in a book like this—but
then some day for others' eyes and
ears. I guess I can suppose, that we
may find ETs not quite so startling
some time as we had thought they
were. Great deal to be revivified in
life if we do not destroy the planet
altogether. I rest my case, content
to let it rest, so must not
      either choose or else recant.

A ghost now talks here as you see
but yet an active one—who could
not rest in any life—and finds it
hard to rest in this. Forgive his
trespasses as he does yours: for-
giveness is impossible yet we are
bound to find its mercy at the last.

A stillness here. Right in the middle
	of our world, these tropics, emeralds
on a fierce sea (there was in England
	once a hint of this). Nature miraculous,
an honest ancient culture, wounded by
	us and yet still tangible. The vegetation
rich beyond images in a dryer setting;
	red birds on land and the great gliders
of the ocean in / out the cliffs. Fantasy
	sunsets: how know whether you dream
or wake? Sea's everlasting murmur—or
	else its pounding under charcoal skies,
as if all the world's whales each butted
	bone against our islands simultaneously.
Soft air, heavenly food and spirit balms,
	this "liquid sunshine" of mist and rain:
to early vessels promise of paradise. If
	any Eden were American, t'was seated
here. Well I a hero of the movies now—
	all of our culture fated to end this way.
But not right here, not in this silence.
	Here I'm not overseen at last, cameras
off, mikes off. No houndings. Perhaps
	I rest now: grave well designed (by me)
shipshape and water tight. I'm out now.
	Perhaps I rest. No traveling more. No
flying. Maybe long rest now. Long rest
					I trust.

APPENDICES

1) ABBREVIATIONS

17: *Do17*, the *Dornier 17* bomber of the *Luftwaffe*.

88: *Ju88*, the *Junkers 88* bomber of the *Luftwaffe*.

109: *Bf109* or *Me109*, the *Messerschmitt 109* fighter of the *Luftwaffe*.

110: *Me110*, the *Messerschmitt 110*, a twin engine fighter of the *Luftwaffe*.

111: *He111*, the *Heinkel 111* bomber of the *Luftwaffe*.

215: *Do215*, the *Dornier 215*, German seaplane.

262: *Me262*, the *Messerschmitt 262*, first active jet fighter of the *Luftwaffe*.

A.A.F.: Auxiliary Air Force of the R.A.F.

A/C, a/c: aircraft

ack-ack: British term for Anti-Aircraft fire.

A.F.: Air Force.

Alex.: Alexandria, Egypt.

A.O.C.: Air Officer Commanding in the R.A.F.

A.R.P.: British Air Raid Protection Force.

Aut.: Italian *autonomo*.

B17: *Boeing B17*, the heavy bomber par excellence of the U.S.A.A.F.

Bb: Bombers.

B.of B.: Battle of Britain.

Beau: R.A.F. *Bristol Beaufighter* a/c.

Bentley: Bentley Priory, Headquarters of Air Chief Marshall Hugh Dowding's Fighter Command in Middlesex.

Bf109: Messerschmitt 109, German fighter.

Blenheim: the *Bristol Blenheim*, a light bomber of the R.A.F.

C.O.: Commanding Officer.

C.T.: Italian *Caccia Terrestre*, Land fighter force.

Defiant: Boulton Paul Defiant, two-seater R.A.F. fighter.

D.F.C.: Distinguished Flying Cross: Both the R.A.F. and U.S.A.A.F. have a decoration thus named.

D.H.4: A British De Havilland single-engined biplane also used by the U.S.Army Observation Corps in W.W.1.

Do.: *Dornier*, usually *17*, German bomber or *215*, seaplane.

E/A, e/a: Enemy aircraft.

Erp: Erprobungsgruppe. Aviation Test Group of the *Luftwaffe* used for working out new tactics.

F.C: Fighter Command, the fighter branch of the R.A.F.

Ff, ff: Fighters

Ffbb, ffbb: Fighter bombers

F.L.: Flight Leader, often of Flight Lieutenant rank in the R.A.F.

Ft.: feet, usually of altitude.

G: unit of measurement of gravity-induced stress in flying.

Gib.: Gibraltar.

G.C.: the George Cross, the highest civilian British decoration for bravery. Held to be the civilian equivalent of the Victoria Cross.

GIAP: Guards' Fighter Regiment of the Soviet Air Force.

Gö: Hermann Göring, Head of the *Luftwaffe*.

Group or Gr.: Group Captain rank in the R.A.F.

Gr.: *Gruppe*, the basic flying unit of the *Luftwaffe*, initially composed of three *Staffeln* each with nine a/c, and a *Stab*, Staff H.Q. unit of three a/c led by a *Kommandeur*.

G.T.: General Transport units to German Concentration Camps.

Gv.: *Gvardeyskyi*, a Soviet Guards unit.

He.: *Heinkel*, usually *111*, German bomber.

HQ, hq: Headquarters.

Hs: *Henschel*, usually *129*, German ground attack, armor-destroying, a/c.

H.S.U.: Hero of the Soviet Union: Soviet Russia's highest decoration.

Hurri: *Hawker Hurricane* fighter of the R.A.F.

IAP: *Istrebitel'nyy Aviatsionyy Polk:* Fighter Air Regiment in the Soviet Air Force.

Il: *Ilyushin*, usually the *Il-2 Shturmovik*, ground attack aircraft of the Soviet Air Force. nicknamed *Ilyusha*.

Jafu: short form of *Jagdführer,* a leading administrative and oversight office in the *Luftwaffe*.

JG: *Jagdgeschwader*, a Fighter Unit of the *Luftwaffe*.

Ju77: The *Junkers 77* dive bomber of the *Luftwaffe* which created havoc during the early *Blitzkrieg* of WW2. Known as the *Stuka*.

K.C.: The *Ritterkreuz*, Knight's Cross of the Iron Cross, German Decoration.

KG: *Kampfgeschwader*, a bomber unit of the *Luftwaffe*, usually composed of three *Gruppen* of bombers and a *Stab*.

KGr: *Kampfgruppe*.

Kia: Killed in Action.

K.G.C.B.: Knight Commander of the Bath, a rank in a high British Order.

Komma.: *Kommandeur* C.O. of a *Luftwaffe Gruppe*. (also *Kom.*)

Kommo.: *Kommodore* C.O. of a *Luftwaffe Geschwader.* (also *Kom.*)

La.: Lavochkin, S.A. Russian aircraft designer of the *La-3; La-5, La-7* fighters etc.

LaGG: initials of Lavochkin, S.A.; Gorbunov, V.; Gudnov, M.: designers of the *LaGG3* fighter.

LXVI: Louis XVIth, a King of France.

L: *Luftwaffe*, the German Air Force.

L.a.: Line Astern, an R.A.F. flying formation.

Lightning: *Lockheed Lightning P-38*, an American twin-boomed fighter.

M.A.G.:   U.S. Marine Air Group

Mia: Missing in Action.

MiG: Design firm of Mikoyan, A.E. & Gurevich, M.I., creators of the *MiG3* fighter and many other a/c down to present times.

mk.: mark, a numbering system of successive models of an aircraft in the R.A.F.

M.N.: British Merchant Navy.

m.p.h.: miles per hour, sometimes mph, sometime mh.

Musso: Benito Mussolini, Fascist Italian Head of State during WW2.

N.C.4: The Navy-Curtiss Flying Boat, an American seaplane, an early Atlantic record holder (May 31,1919).

N.C.O: Noncommissioned Officer; also Non-com. Corporals, Sergeants and the like.

Ops.: Operations.

Pe-2: Russian trainer-bomber designed by Petliakov, V.M.

P.O.: Pilot Officer rank in the R.A.F.

Po-2: Russian trainer a/c designed by Polikarpov, N.N.

P.R.U.: Photographic Reconnaissance Unit in the R.A.F. High-altitude Spitfire PRX1s painted blue and low-altitude FR1Xs painted pink.

Prib. Front: One of the Russian Army Fronts in WW2

R.A.A.F.: The Royal Australian Air Force.

R.A.F.: The Royal Air Force of Great Britain.

R.A.F.V.R.: The Royal Air Force Volunteer Reserve.

Reccy.: Reconnaissance

Regt.: Regiment, usually of the British Army.

R.N.Z.F.: The Royal New Zealand Air Force

r.p.m.: engine revolutions per minute.

RS.HA.: *Reichssicherheitzentralstelle:* Transport organized by Adolf Eichmann's office to German Concentration camps.

S.A.A.F.: The South African Air Force.

SD: *Sicherheitsdienst:* Security police within the German S.S.

SIPO: *Sicherheistpolizei*: German Security Police combining *KRIPO* (Criminal Police) & *Gestapo* (Political Police).

Sqdrn., Sqdr.: Squadron, usually of the R.A.F.

Spit: *Supermarine Spitfire* fighter of the R.A.F.

Stuka: *Junkers 77* dive bomber of the *Luftwaffe*.

T.O.: an aircraft's take off.

U: *Uchebnyy*: Russian: Training, as in *U-2*, antiquated training a/c.

United: American United Aircraft Company

u/c: under-carriage.

U.S.A.A.F.: The United States Army Air Force.

U.S.N.: United States Navy

V.C.: Victoria Cross, the highest British gallantry decoration.

vis.: visibility.

V.M.F.: U.S Marine Fighter Squadron

V.V.S.: *Voyenno-Vozdushnyye Sily*, the Soviet Russian Air Force.

Wellie: R.A.F. *Vickers Wellington* bomber

Wingco.: Wing Commander rank in the R.A.F.

WW1: World War One, 1914–1918.

WW2: World War Two, 1939–1945.

Whitley: *Armstrong Whitworth Whitley*, an early World War 2 R.A.F. Bomber.

Yak: A/c by Yakovlev, A.S. Designer of *Yak 1, 7b, 9D, 3* Russian fighters.

2) GLOSSARY

Angels: a term used to denote altitude in units of 1,000 feet.

Adlerangriff: the Luftwaffe attack against Britain on Eagle Day.

Adlertag: Luftwaffe Air Force term for Eagle Day, August 13th, 1940.

Aufklärungsgruppe: Luftwaffe Reconnaissance unit.

Autonomo: Italian a/c units not operating under *Gruppo* or *Squadriglia* command.

Balbo: R.A.F. term for a very large group of aircraft, named after Italian Air Force's Marshall Italo Balbo's mass flights to the U.S. and South America in the 1930s.

bandit(s): an R.A.F. term for e/a.

bar(s): British, to a decoration: second or third award of the same decoration. Indicated by a rosette worn on the first medal's breast ribbon.

Beau: *Bristol Beaufighter*, a twin-engined a/c of the R.A.F.

Bodenplatte: Operation B. Final blow of the German Ff. on 1.1.45: low level attack on fifteen Allied airfields with 800 a/c destroyed at a cost of 150 German.

Bordmechaniker: Luftwaffe flight engineer.

bunt: to dive straight down in half an inverted loop, often entailing Negative G.

Caccia Terrestre: Land based Fighters in the Italian Air Force.

Cant: Italian Air Force twin-engined bomber, usually the *Z1007bis*.

Caproni-Fiat: an Italian a/c firm of the WW2 period.

Condor: German bomber unit's name refering to the German's Condor Legion fighting on Franco's side in the Spanish Civil War.

Corsair: *Chance Vought F4U*, a gull-winged American fighter favored by the U.S.N., the U.S.Marines and the R.A.A.N. in the Pacific theater of World War Two.

Crispin: Reference to a famous battle fought on St.Crispin's Day in Shakespeare's "Henry Vth," Act.IV, Scene III.

"Darkness": a nickname of the 46th Guards Fighter Regiment of the Soviet Air Force.

Deckungsrotte: Lowest flying *rotte*, lit. on the deck.

Ditch: the Ditch, H.Q. Fighter Command, R.A.F., Malta.

Echelon Starboard: a flying formation of the R.A.F.

Erprobungsgruppe: an elite Test formation of the *Luftwaffe*.

Experten: *Luftwaffe* designation for highly experienced pilots.

Franco-Roumaine: *Compagnie d'Aviation Franco-Roumaine*, a French Aviation Company formed in 1920.

Glass House: R.A.F. term for the cockpit canopy.

Guinea Pig Club: an association of badly burned R.A.F. flyers treated by the great surgeon Dr. Archibald McIndoe.

Graf: German: Count.

Grünhertz: "Greenheart," the crest of the state of Thuringia used as the unit name of the renowned *JG54* of the *Luftwaffe*.

Gruppo: Basic Operating Unit of the Italian Air Force, roughly corresponding to a German *Gruppe*, though normally smaller, usually comprised of two *squadriglie* of multi-engined a/c and three of single engine a/c.

Hauptmann: Rank of Captain in German Armed Forces.

Hellcat: *Grumman F6F* fighter of the U.S.Navy in WW2.

Herm: an island in the Guernsey group of the Channel Islands, United Kingdom.

Holzhammer: *Luftwaffe* unit name.

"Hun": British derogatory nickname for the Germans. Used mainly in WW1.

Hurri: *Hawker Hurricane* British WW2 fighter.

Ilyusha: Russian Air Force nickname for the *Il-2 Shturmovik*.

Illiec: location in Brittany, France, where Lindbergh built a pre-war house.

istry: (Russian): slang word for fighter aircraft.

Kanalkampf: Lit.: Channel Battle, the German term for the Battle of Britain.

Kamikaze: (Japanese): "Divine Wind." See *Shimpu*. Name eventually given to the mostly Japanese Navy suicide-attack pilots of the Pacific Theater, WW2.

Karinhalle: Hermann Göring's hunting lodge.

Kobri: Russian name for the U.S. Lend-Lease *Airocobra P-39* fighter.

Kokutai: Japanese Air Group traditionally composed of a number of different a/c types.

Komsomol: Soviet Russian Youth Organization.

Knight's Cross: the first rank of the major German gallantry decoration, the *Ritterkreuz*, followed by promotions to "with swords;" "with oak leaves;" "with diamonds."

Krieg: German: war.

Kriegsmarine: the German Navy.

Jasta: World War 1 German Air Group.

Jerry: British nickname for the Germans.

L.G.: *Lehrgeschwader*, *Luftwaffe* unit usually composed of former instructors.

Lager: German name for a camp; a concentration camp.

Liebling: German: loved one; darling.

Luftwaffe: the German Air Force.

Manifold presure: Absolute pressure in the induction manifold of a reciprocating aero-engine used together with r.p.m. settings to control engine power output & fuel consumption.

Major: Rank in the *Luftwaffe* equivalent to the R.A.F's Squadron Leader and U.S.A.A.F's Major.

Mare Nostrum: Latin "Our Sea" often used by Mussolini of the Mediterranean.

Messerschmitt 262: first active fighter jet of the *Luftwaffe*.

Mistel: A composite German a/c first used on June 24–25, 1944 composed of an *Me109F-4* mounted above a *Ju88A-4* carrying a warhead with 3,803lb. of high explosives.

Oberst: German Armed forces rank of colonel.

oblast: Russian geographical administrative unit, roughly: province.

Oscar: Allied code name for the *Nakajima Ki-43* Japanese fighter.

para: Two aircraft flying formation of the Soviet Air Force.

peleng: Staggered Line Abreast flight formation in the Soviet Air Force.

Pik As: "Ace of Spades", the unit term for *JG53* of the German Air Force.

Ponyal!: (Russian): Roger! Let's Go!

Prinz: German: Prince.

Ramrod: Fighter escort operation in support of a bomber sortie.

Readiness: a flight status availability term used in the R.A.F.

Reggia Aeronautica: The Italian Air Force in World War Two.

Reichsmarschall: Supreme rank created for Herman Göring as Head of the *Luftwaffe*.

Release: a flight status availability term used in the R.A.F.

Rilke's insect: See the German Poet Rainer Maria Rilke's 8th Duino Elegy: *"O Seligkeit der kleinen kreatur, / die immer bleibt im Schooße, der sie austrug . . ."*

Rodina: "Motherland:" name of an *Antonov ANT-37* a/c flown in a Russian women's record attempt in 1938.

Rotte: name of a two a/c formation in the *Luftwaffe*.

Rotteführer: lead pilot of a *Rotte*.

Rottehund: Lit. *Rotte* dog; the *Rotteführer's Katchmarek:* a wingman or protector pilot.

Rufe: Allied code-name for the *Nakajima A6M2-N* Japanese Navy fighter.

Savoia: *Savoia Marchetti*, usually the *SM81* or *"Pipistrello,"* a twin-engined Italian bomber.

Schlageter: the unit name of the *JG26* fighter unit of the *Luftwaffe*.

schwarm: a two *Rotten* formation in the *Luftwaffe*.

Shimpu: One way of reading the Japanese characters for *"Kamikaze"* the "Divine Wind" and its Navy and Air Force pilots against the U.S. in the Pacific War.

SHO: (Japanese): an offensive/defensive operation to counter the main U.S.Navy thrust from whatever direction, here: the Leyte Gulf, Philippines.

Shturmovik: the *Ilyushin Il-2* ground-attack plane of the Russian Air Force.

Sibir: (Russian) Siberia.

Sonia: Allied code-name for the *Mitsubishi Ki-51* Japanese Army assault aircraft.

Splasher beacon: a single radio beam sent vertically into the air around which a/c would circle at defined speed and climb-rate until clear of cloud.

Squadriglia: Italian Air Force unit comparable to an R.A.F. "Flight" more than to an R.A.F. "squadron."

Stab: Flying Formation of a *Luftwaffe* squadron's staff officers.

Staffel: a three *Schwarme* unit of the *Luftwaffe*.

Stavka: (Russian) H.Q. of the Soviet Armed Forces' Staff.

Stormo: Unit of the Italian Air Force usually comprised of two *Gruppi*.

Tally Ho!: Verbal signal for Attack! given by an R.A.F. fighter flight commander.

Taran: (Russian): Ramming of one aircraft by another.

torque: that which produces or tends to produce tension or rotation. The rolling force imposed on an a/c by the engine in turning the propeller.

U: Russian *Uchebnyy*. As in *U-2*, an antiquated Russian training a/c.

Ultra: Very complex and ultra-secret systems of deciphering German and other enemy codes such as "Enigma." Thanks to Polish sources, used from January 1940 in B.of B. and B.of the Atlantic and on throughout the war.

Val: Allied code-name for the *Aichi D3A* Japanese Navy carrier bomber.

Vic: an R.A.F. term for a letter V-like flying formation, usually of three a/c.

Wehrmacht: The German Third Reich's Armed Forces.

Wellie: Nickname for the R.A.F. *Vickers Wellington* bomber.

Wilde Sau: Wild Boar (*lit*. wild sow), a tactic devised by *Major* Hajo Herrmann using small forces of fighters against lit-up Allied bombers without the use of radar, late in WW2.

Y: Y-Service: Allied system of organized groups of listeners to enemy brodcasts at recording stations. Messages deciphered and sent on to appropriate commanders.

Yasukuni: Shinto shrine in Tokyo, Japan, built to receive and honor the spirits of dead Japanese military "heroes."

Z.G.: *Zerstörergeschwader, Luftwaffe* long-range fighter unit equipped with *Me110*s.

Zero: the legendary *Mitsubishi A6M Reisen* Japanese fighter which bore the brunt of the war from Pearl Harbor until the end.

Zerstörer: "destroyer," a term used of certain German weapons like the *Me110*.

Zveno: Four aircraft flying formation of the Soviet Air Force.

3) PRINCIPAL INDIVIDUALS

(The information does not include World War Two combat pilots)

Ader, Clément: (1841–1925) Considered by the French as the father of aviation, pre-Wright Bros.

Alcock, John: (1892–1919) British, first non-stop Transatlantic flight, June 14, 1919. With Arthur Brown.

Amundsen, Roald: (1872–1928) Major Norwegian polar explorer.

d'Annunzio, Gabriele: (1863–1938) Italian poet, politician, dare-devil and WW1 ace, famous for a dozen feats, later friendly to Fascism.

Apollinaire, Guillaume: (1880–1918) Major XXth century French poet.

Balbo, Italo: (1896–1940). Leading Italian pilot and member of the Fascist party. Great Atlantic "raids" in the 1930s. Minister for Air 1925–35. Governor of Libya 1939.

Ball, Albert: (1896–1917) Leading British air ace of WW1. Holder of the Victoria Cross.

Batten, Jean: (1909–1982) New Zealand pilot. Breaks Amy Johnson's record by five days in 1934. First woman's round-the-world flight.

Beese, Melli: (1886–1925): First German woman pilot licensed in 1910 despite male sabotage. Ran a small but famous flying school.

Bellonte, Maurice: (1896–1984). French. First Paris–New York flight with Costes, 1930, conceived of as a return visit after Lindbergh's.

Bishop, William: (1894–1956) Major Canadian WW1 air ace, holder of the Victoria Cross.

Blériot, Louis: (1872–1936) French pilot & designer. First France–U.K. Channel flight July 25, 1909.

Boelcke, Oswald: (1891–1916). Leading German air ace of WW1, head of *Jasta2* squadron.

Brown, Arthur: (1886–1948) British. First transatlantic flight with John Alcock.

Camm, Sydney: (1893–1966): British aircraft designer, creator, *inter alia*, of the WW2 *Hurricane* fighter.

Carell, Paul: (1911–1987) Nazi official during WW2, successful war historian afterwards.

Carrel, Dr. Alexis: (1873–1944) French medical scientist, friend and colleague of Charles Lindbergh.

Chanute, Oscar: (1832–1910) Franco-American pioneer. Important information source for Wright Bros.

Chavez, Georges: (1887–1910) Peruvian. Record flight over the Alps ends in a crash, 27 September 1910.

Chichester, Francis: (1901–1972) British record setting aviator, sailor, author.

Chkalov, Valery: (1904–1938). Russian pioneer aviator famous for his June 19–20, 1937 Moscow–North Pole–New York flight in an *Ant25*; exalted as a national hero by Stalin.

Cobham, Alan: (1894–1973) British pioneer air route-explorer 1910s–1930s.

Cody, Samuel F.: (1862–1913) American-British flier, first to fly in the U.K.

Coleman, Bessie: (1893–1926) World's first African-American licensed pilot. Had to be earned in France.

Coli, François: (1881–1927). French. Died with Charles Nungesser crossing the Atlantic East–West just before Lindbergh's flight, 1927.

Costes, Dieudonné: (1892–1973) French. First Paris–New York flight with Maurice Bellonte, 1930.

Coutinho, Gago: (1869–1959) Portuguese Admiral, flew with Arturo Cabral (1881–1924) from Lisbon to Brazil in four laps on May 31, 1922.

Curtiss, Glen: (1878–1930) American major early aircraft designer: *JN4* ("Jenny"); Navy Flying Boats, including the *NC4* (1914–18).

De Havilland, Geoffrey: (1882–1965) Major British aircraft designer. *Tiger Moth* (1930); *Mosquito* (1941); *Comet* (1952).

Deroche, Elise: (1886–1919) French artist, actress, car racer, world's first woman's pilot license.

Détroyat, Michel (1905–1956): French military pilot and air racer. Rescued Lindbergh from massive crowds on his Le Bourget landing, 1927.

Doolittle, Jim: (1896–1993) U.S. General. WW1 air ace; champion racing pilot, Medal of Honor for the Tokyo Raid, April 1942.

Dowding, Sir, later Lord, Hugh: (1882–1970). Air Chief Marshall, R.A.F., C.O. of Fighter Command during the Battle of Britain. Knight Commander, Most Distinguished Order of St.Michael & St.George (KCMG).

Dutrieu, Hélène: (1877–1961): Belgian winner of the *Copa del Re* in Florence, 1911. Reccy. pilot for France in World War One.

Earhart, Amelia: (1898–1937) Legendary American flyer, first woman to cross the Atlantic, June 17, 1928 and holder of several other records. Disappeared on a Trans-Pacific flight in 1937.

Farman, Henry: (1874–1958) Anglo-French aviation pioneer. First town to town flight, 1908.

Focker, Anton: (1890–1939) Dutch. Major designer and builder of classic World War One German fighters and many post war planes.

Fonck, René: (1894–1953) Leading French air ace of WW1. A rival of Charles Lindbergh.

Frankl, Wilhelm: (1893–1917). World War One aviation ace, holder of the "Blue Max," (*Pour le Mérite*), one of a few Jews in the German Air Force. A squadron was named after him post WW2.

Garros, Roland: (1888–1919) French. First crossing of the Mediterranean, 1913.

Göring, Hermann: (1893–1946). German WW1 ace ("Blue Max"), prominent ally of Adolf Hitler, Commander-in-Chief of the new *Luftwaffe* from 1935. Committed suicide at the Nuremberg trials.

Grahame-White, Claude: (1879–1959) British pilot, and historian, holder of the first U.K. License, founded Hendon airfield.

Guynemer, Georges: (1894–1917) Legendary French air ace of WW1. Subject of a great many propaganda books. Massively decorated.

Hewlett, Hilda: (1864–1943) First British woman licensed, at Brooklands, 1911. Ran a flying school near London. Instructed Ff. pilots in WW1.

Hughes, Howard: (1905–1976) American. Millionaire oil-man, film-maker, aircraft designer and racing record breaker.

Immelman, Max: (1890–1916) German WW1 ace and tactical expert, known as the "Eagle of Lille"; invented the half loop / half roll "Immelman turn."

Johnson, Amy: (1903–1941) British woman pilot. First U.K.–Australia flight, 1920, and several other records.

Kerr, Deborah: (1921–2007) Well known British movie actress of the WW2 period. Married RAF pilot Anthony Bentley in 1945.

Kesselring, Albert: (1895–1960) German *General der Flieger*, C.O. of the *Luftwaffe's* 2nd Air Fleet during the Battle of Britain. December 1941: C.O. of the same fleet in the Mediterranean during the Battle of Malta.

Kingsford-Smith, Charles: (1897–1935) Australian. Famous pioneer of Pacific flying with Charles Ulm. First global flight 1929–30.

Köhl, Hermann: (1888–1938) German pilot of the *Junkers W33* "Bremen" on the first East-West Atlantic crossing from Ireland to Labrador, April 12/13, 1928. With Baron von Hünefeld & Irish Capt. J. Fitzmaurice.

Le Brix, Joseph: (1899–1931) French pilot. World tour with Costes, 1927–8; eight world records, 1931.

Lee-Mallory, Sir Trafford: (1892–1944) Air Chief Marshall, R.A.F., C.O., 12 Group of Fighter Command during the battle of Britain. Rival of Sir Keith Park of 11 Group. Later a C.O. in S.E. Asia and killed there.

Levavasseur, Léon: (1863–1922) French designer of, *inter alia*, the beautiful, classic *Antoinette* aircraft.

Lilienthal, Otto: (1848–1896) Major German aviation pioneer, famous for glider experiments: his last one killed him.

Lindbergh, Anne Morrow: (1907–1999). American pilot wife of Charles Lindbergh and prolific author.

Lindbergh, Charles, Augustus (CAL): (1902–1974). American pioneer flyer, famous for his solo Atlantic New York–Paris flight of May 27, 1927. Later an airline executive; research person; WW2 flyer and ecologist. Buried on Maui, Hawaii.

Mannock, Edward: (1887–1918). Top-ranking British ace of WW1. Victoria Cross.

Markham, Beryl: (1902–1986). British bush pilot and author in Africa. First woman to fly Atlantic from East to West.

Mermoz, Jean: (1901–1936). Legendary French pilot. First France–South America liaison, 1930. Prominent member of the *Croix de Feu* French Fascist party.

Messerchmitt, Willi: (1898–1978). Major German aircraft designer: *Me109; Me110; Me 232*.

Milch, Erhard: (1892–1972). German WW1 pilot. Though Jewish, *Generalfeldmarschall* in the WW2 *Luftwaffe*, built up the Third Reich aircraft industry.

Mitchell, Reginald: (1895–1937) Legendary British aircraft designer, creator of many flying boats, the Schneider Cup winners in the 1930s and the immortal WW2 *Supermarine Spitfire* fighter.

Nesterov, Pyotr: (1887–1914). First Russian pilot to loop the loop (punished); first Imperial Russian Air Force *taran* (ramming) action on September 8th, 1914.

Nungesser, Charles: (1892–1927) French World War One ace. Died with Coli crossing Atlantic East-West, 1927.

Paulhan, Louis: (1883–1963) French. Daily Mail prize for London–Manchester flight, 1910. First U.S. Air meet, Los Angeles, 1910.

Paulus, Friedrich von: (1890–1957) *Feldmarschall*, German Army, surrenders at Stalingrad.

Park, Sir Keith : (1892–1975) Air Chief Marshall, R.A.F. C.O. of 11 Group Fighter Command during the Battle of Britain, widely considered to be the man who won it. Later C.O., R.A.F. Malta.

Pinedo, Francesco de: (1890–1933) Italian multi-record holder. Tokyo–Rome flight in 21 days, 1925.

Post, Wiley: (1900–1935) American. Round the world record with Harold Gatty, 1931.

Pound, Ezra: (1885–1972) The pre-eminent XXth Century American poet. Imprisoned for Fascist activities in Italy during the WW2.

Quimby, Harriet: (1884–1912) First American woman to obtain a license. Flies Dover–Calais, 16 April, 1912. Killed in an air accident.

Richthofen, Manfred von: (1892–1918) Legendary German air ace of WW1 (Blue Max). The immortal "Red Baron" due to the color of some of his aircraft.

Rickenbacker, Edward: (1890–1973) U.S. General, WW1 and WW2 air ace and racing driver. Medal of Honor.

Rilke, Rainer Maria: (1875–1926) The most influential major Austrian-German poet of his time.

Roe, Edwin: (1877–1958) Founder of British aircraft *Avro* design team: *Lancaster, Vulcan,* Flying Boats.

Saint-Exupéry, Antoine de: (1900–1940) Renowned French author and early pilot of the French mails. WW2 war pilot and fatality. Friend of the Lindberghs.

Santos-Dumont, Alberto: (1873–1932) Brazilian leading figure in early French aviation.

Scott, Blanche: (c.1890–1970) American pre-license flyer working for Glenn Curtiss.

Sperrle, Hugo: (1885–1953) German C.O. of the *Legion Kondor* in Spain, 1936. *General der Flieger* C.O. of the *Luftwaffe's* 3rd Air Fleet during the Battle of Britain.

Udet, Ernst: (1896–1941): German WW1 ace ("Blue Max"), test, sports and aerobatic pilot. *Generaloberst* of the WW2 *Luftwaffe*. Committed suicide after serious production failures.

Ulanova, Galina (1910–1998) Prima Ballerina of the Russian Bolshoi Ballet.

Ulm, Charles: (1898–1934) Australian pilot. Set many records in the Pacific with Charles Kingsford-Smith.

Voisin, Gabriel: (1880–1973) Builder of first industrial aircraft in France.

Vuia, Trajan: (1872–1950) Hungarian-Romanian pioneer aviator, claimed firsts in France 1906, but capped by Santos-Dumont.

Zvereva, Lidia: (1890–1916) Russian woman pilot, soloed in 1911.

Afterword

ONE

The story of *Avia* is simple. Charles Augustus Lindbergh has been ordered back by his President after his historic flight from New York to Paris on May 21–22, 1927. The *Spirit of St. Louis* is to be crated up and plane and pilot are to return on the U.S.S. Memphis. CAL had looked forward to continuing on round the world or, at the very least, to flying back over the Atlantic. During his effort to try to obey orders, he begins a lengthy dream which will take him back over the ocean. As occurred during his initial flight, he hears voices in his cockpit. The voices are those of later pilots who tell him many episodes of the future World War Two: Battles of Britain, of Malta, of Kuban–Stalingrad–Kursk, of the Pacific, etc. Eventually, the dream shades into waking life. CAL sees combat for the United States in the Pacific, visits Germany in 1945 and dies on Hawaii. Throughout all this and, after his death, CAL may be thought to change some but not all of his views about human life and values as well as the outcome of a Second World War. It looks to me as if he predicted our present environmental crisis.

I started from two considerations.

First: I was interested in seeing if it were possible to get back to a poetry of fact and thing. "No ideas but in things" said the American poet William Carlos Williams. But what *thing* did he come up with: a wheelbarrow!!! In what was, at any moment, to become the age of jets, the age of space!

Of fact and thing: Despite all the contemporary talk of keeping out the author's ego or even killing off the author, the author always creeps back in one form or another. Including here—but minimally, that is mainly in terms of choosing which campaigns to cover since there were too many to cover all. I wanted a subject which would involve things primarily and men's use of them secondarily so that the human would not interfere overmuch with the thing. Objectivism in many senses.

Second: I had been fascinated from childhood by flight and this grew into a passion when a child during WW2 in places where there were definite interfaces with the air war—mainly but not only the British. Now, virtually all the poetry written about this subject is sentimental and basically "Georgian." What about getting back to some combination of epic and the American multidimensional long poem? The reader will find echoes of epic throughout the work.

That's it. A huge amount of research has gone into the work—just over fifteen years—but, despite the innumerable challenges, I believe it is readable in both poetic and technical terms.

TWO

In this text the last *knights*, the last *chevaliers*, demonstrate a matter-of-fact "heroism" which, with its ultimate vestiges of ideology—basically "us boys together . . . and country if you insist!"—borders on, and arrives very quickly at, the *absurd*. I guess that it is one more of my "beautiful contradictions": on the one hand, the admirable circus of courage played out in the abstraction of the sky ("abstraction" is important: as Lindbergh insisted, you cannot see much damage from the air); on the other hand, far below this, the horror of a devastated world now seemingly devoid of any possibility of spiritual salvation whatsoever.

I bear in mind the famous Adorno injunction, reading it—not as "Do not write poetry after Auschwitz," but as "It is impossible for poetry to be written after Auschwitz." Yet, the longer it takes for our world to perish, the more frenetically, alas, we have to try to keep it alive.

There is something else. I have been able to do little here to mitigate the relentlessness and, let us face it, the monotony of day-after-day combat—though I *have* worked hard linguistically to make the *texture* of the story vary. The inventiveness of this writing has to be looked for in the way in which actions, often seemingly similar, are varied in description. Note also that the technical nature of the subject matter acted as a severe constraint on anything too close to what is usually considered as "the poetic."

While aviation has inspired a fair amount of prose literature, it has led to the production of very little distinguished poetry. One can name Yeats's poem on an Irish Airman; Apollinaire's *L'avion*, Blaise

Cendrars's *Le lotissement du ciel*; Huidobro's *Altazor*; (though I hold this to be a poem about sailing rather than flying); Blok's *The Aviator*; and there are references in Rilke, Perse, Valéry, Brecht, Claudel, Cocteau, Jouve, Marinetti, and many Americans, among others—but the list is not extensive. On the other hand, it has to be recognized, alas, that the average amateur flight poem, usually connected to this century's wars, is formally sloppy, ruled by obsolete conventions of rhyme and meter and, for the most part, dismally sentimental. There are exceptions as always.

Since it has always been extremely hard for me to give up the musical element in verse, rhythm and meter can be recognized throughout this piece. Very often, they can best be sensed by reading aloud. Sometimes they have to be looked for. A simple example. A date will be given at times as normally read, but at others it will have to be read differently to keep within the rhythm. The date "1923," for instance, can be read as "nine/teen/twen/ty/three" but it can also be read as "nine/teen/two/three" or "one/nine/two/three" depending on the line's or rhythm's requirement at the time. Another instance: the same applies to the marks of particular aircraft—such as, let us say, the *Thunderbolt P47*, or *Spitfire Mark 1* or *Messerschmitt Bf 109*, or *MiG-3* and *Yak-9* as well as to a number of other items or bits of information. We could also adduce U.S.A.A.F. for United States Army Air Force or R.A.F., for Royal Air Force, pronounced separately or run together as "RAF" or U/SAAF" and marked as such in the text.

There are other manifestations of this principle. The prose "intrusion" passages from Coleridge in "Malta" or Tolstoy in "Russia" are versified in this book. This occasionally requires the changing of a word or expression to suit the rhythm. Thus, we are *not* dealing with exact quotations. Finally: a small "reality check" here: the use of Spanish expressions sometimes simply marks the fact that *Avia* has been composed in New Mexico.

THREE

The history of World War II is so immense and so massively full of details, the record so unbelievably extensive, the quantity of memoirs so innumerable, that, even by concentrating on the war in the air alone, it is almost impossible to offer more than a minute portion of the whole picture. What is normally called "poet's license" has had to be given its freedom to roam among campaigns as the spirit willed, acquaintances inspired, or dates determined. There is a pattern of dates chosen here to serve as a limiting or boundary factor in the information provided. My own biography, astride a number of nations, periods, disciplines and interests has, of course, played a part in the process. A wartime childhood in Britain, for instance, led to strong emotional associations with the deeds of the R.A.F.

The frame of the work is American, dominated by the difficult, for some unpleasant, figure of Charles Lindbergh. Inside the frame, the picture itself covers the Phony War; the Battle of Britain; the Battle of Malta; the Battles of Leningrad, the Kuban and Kursk and, finally, the American Pacific War pitting us against Japan, especially in its latter phases with the advent of the Imperial *Kamikazes*. I wish it were not so but there is much less, or virtually nothing, on, for instance, the war in the Arctic or the African Desert or in the South East Asian jungles, or in the final invasions of Europe. It should be added that I chose fighter over bomber warfare as another limiting factor—though bombers are present very often. One thing is certain: even within these self-imposed limits, there was no possible end to this process. Information is still coming out; much of it has not been read or researched by me and there are other matters demanding attention. An end has had to be declared, period.

Originally *Avia* was to be much larger. The 'Cal's Dream' section was at least twice as long. This, the work's original name, was to be framed in its turn, by the story of the American Wright Brothers and that of the Transatlantic Pioneers from many nations coming before it—and the American-Russian race to the moon coming after it. Parts of all this were written but remained unrevised and dormant. In fact, much, or all of this, was lost in a computer crash. This writer's life is not long enough for more to be done at this time than what is found here. As it is, the work was cut down in 2005–06 from well over 500 single pages to 400 or so (thus a book of some 350 pages) and cutting continued.

I cannot say that I have felt, or even now feel, "comfortable" with Lindbergh's character. He figures here mainly as a great founding pilot though it is hard to keep out other aspects of his life and views. While I know that it is difficult for someone at this time to fully understand the workings of another mind living in the 20s and 30s of the last century and while I think that some of what Lindbergh said and did may have been misinterpreted, I have to stress that I dislike his record—as I do that of other founding pilots—Balbo, Mermoz and many more seduced by futuristic or, frankly, fascist "action"—and that my own politics are at the antipodes of Lindbergh's. While obscene genocide is as old as history, Lindbergh's attempt to equate Nazi elimination and what some American soldiers did to some Japanese soldiers is absurd: Japanese torture and outrage on the Bataan Death March, for instance, appears to have preceded such American actions. Something of Lindbergh's problematic character as husband, father and public figure finally comes through in his daughter Reeve's book (she is a better writer than her mother). CAL's great achievement of 1927 and many subsequent ones remain as a matter of record and his life-long battle to remain true to himself, whatever the value of his views, attitudes and opinions, continues to be worthy of some appreciation.

There are other famous post-pioneer founding pilots in our history who have awoken the interest of writers: *inter alia* Amelia Earhardt, Antoine de Saint-Exupéry, Manfred von Richthofen, not to mention those known mainly to the aviation community: Eddie Rickenbacker, Jimmy Doolittle, Albert Ball, Charles Kingsford-Smith, Alan Cobham, Jean Batten, Francis Chichester, Alex Henshaw, Francesco de Pinedo, Dieudonné Costes, Valery Chkalov, Beryl Markham, William Mitchell, Wiley Post—a very few names, very much at random, in an extremely long list. Somehow, Lindbergh, seems to remain *primus inter pares*. Needless to say, too, hundreds of wartime and peacetime pilots remain outside the purview of this work. Here again, the choice of names recorded has depended on many circumstances. Many great figures are never mentioned; many smaller ones glide through the skyscapes. No hierarchical value judgements should ever be thought to be implied. Ultimately, each individual mentioned stands for a hundred others. The section 'First Move: An Entry' affords some sense of this. Fortunately there is a truly vast bibliographical repository of records that anyone fascinated can consult. One could spend several lifetimes on the archives of WW2 alone.

What I hope will be perceived here is something that Lindbergh eventually discovered for himself: whatever the beauty of flight and whatever the astonishing chivalry of many pilots in war, nothing can mask the implicit deadliness of the technology which so many in his time had had such majestic hopes for. It may well be that the airplane has turned into a plague for the planet both in war and in peace. I refer to bombing in the former, mass tourism and pollution in the latter.

To elaborate a little on ground already covered, consider. First: the sense that so many pilots expressed in the founding years to the effect that flight placed them not only physically but also emotionally above human suffering serves as a demonstration of how dangerous our unconscious behavior can be—not only in action but in the consequences of action. Second: the fact that modern industrial technology led in too many places to the development of murder-inflicting systems whether in fighting traditional war or in perpetrating the atrocious elimination of whole populations. In the very *last* resort, there is no ultimate difference between the beauty of a fighter aircraft and the hideousness of a gas oven. Third: the distancing from human suffering experienced by so many pilots and the "tumult in the clouds" characteristic of fighter war seem to me to be metaphors of a disassociation between heart and head, between pity and unconcern that is more and more characteristic of a "bottom-line" finance-capitalist society. Fourth, this theme of abstraction from suffering meshes with my sense that a great deal of "writing" today, usually misnamed as "poetry," overwhelmingly derives its momentum from current versions of abstract philosophical thought and that it is time—if there is still time—for some semblance of a *"retour à l'ordre."* By "writing," (the great majority of stuff produced in today's creative writing schools), I mean work done mostly with the intellect. By "poetry," I mean work that is done by intellect and the emotions—by head and heart together. If this work is given its due as social and cultural critique it will not have failed entirely in its aim, even though, often as "writing" rather than as "poetry," it may be forced to mimic some of the attitudes it ultimately opposes.

I have to thank a great number of historians and record keepers as well as pilots from all the nations concerned who at various times have become interviewees, good acquaintances and/or friends. There is no point in naming them here since they and their exploits are recognized in the piece. In the nature of the subject, textual distillations of various kinds are to be found throughout the work. I do not believe that they constitute plagiarism since they are re-worked into "writing" on every occasion in the interest of a worthy aim. In a sense, I see this particular kind of reworking as a form of *translation*: not from one language into another—but from one *genre* into another. Should any author or authority feel badly about this, I would beg his or her indulgence in the common cause of recording an atrocious period in human history while, at the same time, picking out along the way some flowers of courage toward maintaining a particle of hope in faltering humanity.

The list of sources is extremely long and risks overloading an already long text. I propose to deposit such a list with the rest of the work's archive for public consultation among my papers at Stanford University and trust that I shall be forgiven this rather unusual procedure. However, there are factual appendices in the text.

Ombligo de Tesuque,
New Mexico,
June 30th, 2007

Nathaniel Tarn, born in Paris, was educated at Clifton College; Cambridge; the Sorbonne; Yale; Chicago; the London School of Economics and the London School of Oriental & African Studies. In Anthropology, he worked mainly in Highland Guatemala and Burma, eventually teaching for seven years at SOAS. Writing his first poem aged five, publishing his first poetry book *Old Savage/Young City* in 1964 with Cape and Random House, he began a long career, culminating this year with this book, the *Ins & Outs of the Forest Rivers* from New Directions in New York and another in California. He was an advisor at Jonathan Cape from 1964 to 1967, then directed the series Cape Editions & Cape Goliard for them from 1967–1969, bringing many titles and authors to the firm, living in London with his first wife Patricia and two children Andrea and Marc (now parents themselves), very active as a balletomane, indigent collector and student of the arts. As a translator, he gained respect for his work on Pablo Neruda, Victor Segalen and many younger poets. In 1970, he moved to the U.S. and taught on various occasions—as Professor of Romance Languages, English, Folklore, American Studies, Comparative Literature and Anthropology at Princeton, Pennsylvania, Rutgers, Colorado, New Mexico, Jilin (P.R.C.) and many other academic venues, retiring early in 1984 to concentrate on his own work. Since then, he has lived north west of Santa Fe, New Mexico with his second wife, poet and artist Janet Rodney, writing, flying, bird-watching, gardening and curating a very large library. He has continued reading his work all over the world and has worked as widely as possible in the U.S., Latin America, Europe, India, China, the Himalayas, Indonesia, the Philippines, Sarawak, New Guinea, Australia and, recently, the Antarctic. He plans to continue for a little while.

www.ingramcontent.com/pod-product-compliance
Lightning Source LLC
Chambersburg PA
CBHW022002160426
43197CB00007B/229